The Art of Transformation in Therapy and Coaching

The Art of Transformation in Therapy and Coaching brings Virginia Satir's pioneering work and timeless principles to life for today's therapists, coaches, and leaders seeking to foster authenticity, emotional resilience, and connection in individuals, families, and organizations.

Dr. Darya Haitoglou integrates contemporary insights from neuroscience, trauma theory, and systemic coaching to create a comprehensive roadmap for facilitating deep transformation. Building on Satir's Growth Model, this book combines foundational theory with over 20 years of applied experience, blending clarity of explanation with hands-on tools and case studies. Dr. Haitoglou's original framework (the Stasis-Kinesis Model) expands Satir's work into a multidimensional, trauma-informed, and embodied process of change, demonstrating how congruence, self-worth, and relational awareness can transform even the most complex systems. This book bridges theory and practice through vivid metaphors such as the Iceberg and Mobile, step-by-step exercises, and protocols for both individual and group work, offering readers an integrative approach to sustainable healing and growth.

Accessible yet rigorous and experiential, this book stands as both a reference and an inspiration for professionals dedicated to cultivating authentic, compassionate, and lasting change with their clients.

Darya Haitoglou, PsyD, CPsychol, MSc (Dist), is a family psychologist, researcher, and systemic coach. She is the Director of the Virginia Satir Institute UK and founder of Enrich Global. Darya's work integrates systemic therapy, embodied transformation, and evidence-based practice, and she is widely regarded for her depth, clarity, and integrative approach to healing and change.

"This is a wonderful new addition to the collection of seminal books on Satir's concepts and process... Especially needed in a post-pandemic world where heart connections are longed for."

Sharon Loeschen, *LCSW, Ex-President, Virginia Satir Global Network; creator of the Satir Coaching and Mentoring Certification Program*

"Dr. Haitoglou dispels the idea that Satir's work was simply charismatic... This book reveals her profound understanding of what it means to be fully human and strengthens our sacred work."

Jean McLendon, *LCSW, LMFT, Director of Training, Virginia Satir Center; Former President, Virginia Satir Global Network*

"*The Art of Transformation* is a beautiful example of the collective or family hero's journey. Darya brings Virginia Satir's legacy into the present moment, with tools and insights that illuminate human transformation and systemic healing. A mosaic of possibility."

Judith DeLozier, *Co-developer and trainer in Neuro-Linguistic Programming (NLP); Co-author of* The Encyclopedia of Systemic Neuro-Linguistic Programming and NLP New Coding

The Art of Transformation in Therapy and Coaching

Mastering Satir Tools in Practice

Darya Haitoglou

Routledge
Taylor & Francis Group
NEW YORK AND LONDON

Designed cover image: © Darya Haitoglou

First published 2027
by Routledge
605 Third Avenue, New York, NY 10158

and by Routledge
4 Park Square, Milton Park, Abingdon, Oxon, OX14 4RN

Routledge is an imprint of the Taylor & Francis Group, an informa business

ISBN: 978-1-041-20411-4 (hbk)
ISBN: 978-1-041-20040-6 (pbk)
ISBN: 978-1-003-71641-9 (ebk)

DOI: 10.4324/9781003716419

Typeset in Caslon
by SPi Technologies India Pvt Ltd (Straive)

To Virginia Satir,

Whose wisdom, compassion, and pioneering spirit continue to guide and inspire countless journeys of transformation.

Your work has touched the deepest parts of humanity and forever changed the way we heal and connect.

This book is a tribute to your legacy and an expression of gratitude for the profound impact you've had on my life and the lives of so many others.

In the sacred garden of healing hearts,
Grows Satir's wisdom, a tree where change starts.
Rooted in compassion, its branches reach high,
Leaves whispering truths that never die.
With a wand of wishes, dreams come to bloom,
Courage in hand, we step out of the gloom.
Her iceberg reveals the soul's hidden layers,
And five freedoms lift us like whispered prayers.
Her legacy lives, a forest of grace,
Where lost souls find light, and love finds a place.
In every rustling leaf, her spirit appears,
Softly reminding, "In you, I planted my cheer."

Contents

Foreword by Dr. John Banmen

Virginia Satir (1916–1988), one of the most influential figures in the history of family therapy, left a lasting legacy with her teachings. Her mantra, *Peace Within, Peace Between, Peace Among*, captures a universal message of harmony with oneself, others, and the world at large. The Satir Growth Model, grounded in biological, psychological, social, and spiritual dimensions, continues to offer a profound framework for personal transformation. In *Art of Transformation*, Dr. Darya Haitoglou expertly builds on this foundation, offering both fresh perspectives and practical applications that make Satir's work relevant to modern audiences.

What stands out in this book is Dr. Haitoglou's ability to extend the Satir Growth Model beyond its original therapeutic context. She masterfully demonstrates how its principles can be applied in coaching, consulting, and organizational work. The clarity with which she addresses the *how* of transformation, not just the *what*, is invaluable. Through clear examples and step-by-step guidance, readers will gain practical insights into how to apply key vehicles of change in their own practice or personal development.

Dr. Haitoglou highlights essential tools from Satir's work, such as the self-esteem maintenance toolkit, which helps individuals take responsibility for their experiences, and survival stances, which reveal how we respond to stress and how to achieve congruence. She also explores techniques like Temperature Reading to foster open communication, the Parts Party for resolving internal conflict, and family of origin mapping to uncover and shift limiting beliefs. These tools are not just described but illustrated with real-life examples, making them accessible and applicable for a wide audience.

What's particularly impressive about *Art of Transformation* is how it bridges the Satir Growth Model with other therapeutic approaches such as Cognitive Behavioral Therapy, Emotional Freedom Techniques (EFT), and Acceptance and Commitment Therapy (ACT). Dr. Haitoglou offers an integrative approach that enhances the effectiveness of both Satir's model and these contemporary methods. This synthesis opens new possibilities for therapists, coaches, and consultants seeking to deepen their practice and achieve lasting results.

The inclusion of numerous case studies and dialogues makes this book even more practical, offering readers the chance to see how these techniques work in real settings. Whether you are an experienced therapist, a coach, or someone exploring personal growth, Dr. Haitoglou's examples provide a solid and inspiring roadmap for transformational systemic change.

In *Art of Transformation*, Dr. Haitoglou has created a thoughtful and comprehensive guide to applying the Satir Growth Model in modern contexts. Her approach is both innovative and grounded in Satir's original teachings, making it a valuable resource for anyone looking to facilitate meaningful change in themselves or others. I highly recommend this book to anyone interested in deepening their understanding of human behavior and personal transformation.

The Satir Growth Model is widely taught around the world and online, and I encourage therapists, trainers, coaches, and consultants to study and incorporate its principles into their work. This book offers a clear and practical entry point to these techniques and strategies, making it a vital addition to the field.

Dr. John Banmen
Psychologist and Family Therapist
Co-author, *The Satir Model: Family Therapy and Beyond*
Director of Training Emeritus, Satir Institute of the Pacific
President, Banmen Satir China Management Center
Visiting Professor, Beijing Normal University (2014–2019)
Editor, *Satir Transformational Systemic Therapy*
Former Associate Professor, University of British Columbia (ret.)

ACKNOWLEDGEMENTS

This book is a culmination of years of dedication, inspiration, and support from many individuals who have played pivotal roles in my journey. First and foremost, I wish to express my deepest gratitude to my esteemed teachers and mentors. To the late Dr. Maria Gomori, your wisdom and guidance have profoundly shaped my understanding and practice of Satir's methods. Your mentorship has been invaluable, and your legacy lives on through your teachings. Dr. John Banmen, your teachings have provided a solid foundation and continuous inspiration for my journey. Sharon Loeschen, your insights and dedication to the Satir model have enriched my practice and understanding in immeasurable ways. Judy Delozier, your innovative approaches and support have expanded my horizons and deepened my appreciation for integrative therapeutic techniques.

To my partner, Alex, your unwavering support, love, and encouragement have been my bedrock. Your belief in me and this work has made this journey possible. To our wonderful children, Dimitris, Nikolai, and Athena, your presence in my life brings boundless joy and inspiration. You remind me daily of the importance of love, growth, and connection. To my parents, Olga and Yury, your unconditional love and support have been a constant source of strength throughout my life. Your teachings and values have laid the foundation for who I am today.

To my sister, Polina, thank you for your brilliant work in editing and for the invaluable suggestions you contributed to this manuscript. Your insights and attention to detail have strengthened this book, and your support has meant the world to me. To my assistant, Stefania, whose support, care, and amazing design work have helped make this book a reality.

To Virginia Satir herself: your groundbreaking work and compassionate spirit continue to inspire and guide therapists and coaches worldwide. Your legacy lives on through each of us who practice and teach your methods. To my colleagues and friends, your encouragement, collaboration, and shared passion for this work have been invaluable. You have all contributed to my growth and the realization of this book.

To the readers and Satir practitioners, without your interest, dedication, and practice, this work would not be. You are the ones who bring these tools to life, fostering transformation and healing in countless lives. Your commitment to personal and professional growth is what keeps Virginia Satir's legacy vibrant and impactful.

Thank you all for your support, inspiration, and belief in the power of transformation. This book is as much yours as it is mine.

Preface

In the world of psychotherapy, few names shine as brightly as that of Virginia Satir. Known as the "Mother of Family Therapy," her pioneering work in the mid-20th century revolutionized not only how therapists approached family dynamics but also how individuals within these families understood themselves and their relationships with others. Virginia Satir's humane, growth-oriented approach to therapy brought about a radical shift in treating mental and emotional health.

This book, *The Art of Transformation: Mastering Satir Tools in Therapy and Coaching*, aims to delve deep into the essence of Satir's work and its enduring impact on contemporary therapeutic practices. As we journey through the topics, we will explore the foundational principles of Satir's methods, her unique approach to healing and growth, and how her philosophies continue to resonate and evolve in the field of modern psychotherapy, coaching, and other fields of work.

Our exploration will not be a mere historical recounting. Instead, this book seeks to bridge the gap between the past and the present, illustrating how Satir's groundbreaking work continues to influence and inspire current methodologies in family therapy and beyond. Through comprehensive narrations, insights and real-world examples, we will discover how Satir's legacy lives on in the hearts and minds of therapists, coaches, and clients alike.

As you turn these pages, expect to embark on a journey that is both enlightening and transformative, one that pays homage to Virginia Satir's extraordinary contributions while illuminating the path for future explorations in the realm of psychotherapy.

With love and gratitude,
Darya

1

Foundations and Vision

The Birth of a Vision

Beneath the humble beginnings of a small-town upbringing emerged an iconoclast who would revolutionize the field of family therapy. Virginia Satir, born Virginia Mildred Pagenkopf on June 26, 1916, in Neillsville, Wisconsin, spent her childhood exploring the verdant fields around her family's isolated farmstead (Andreas, 1999). Despite the simplicity of midwestern life, complex family dynamics cultivated Satir's innate empathy and sensitivity from an early age (Banmen, 2009).

Virginia's birth came nine months after her parents' wedding. Earlier that year, on January 3rd, Carl Wilke, Virginia's maternal grandfather, had died. The 25-year-old Minnie Pagenkopf, Virginia's mother, must have been grieving acutely during her first year of marriage and pregnancy. Carl and Minnie had been very close, with Minnie being Carl's favorite field hand. He would often take her out to work with him in the fields. The loss was immense for this newlywed mother. Thus, little Virginia was born into a situation already burdened by the timing of her entry into the world (Suhd, as cited in Brothers, 2019).

At this point, Minnie and her husband Reinhold Pagenkopf lived on a family farm that belonged to Reinhold's father, Ferdinand, who lived there with his wife Wilhelmina. Reinhold's father, referred to as "old man Pagenkopf," had begun to slip into some kind of psychosis, and at some

DOI: 10.4324/9781003716419-1

point, the family put him into an institution. However, before being institutionalized, he engaged in a frightening scene that so terrified little Virginia that she dreamt about it for the next 40 years or so (Andreas, 1999). He died the year when Virginia was 2. By that time, Virginia already had a set of identical twin brothers, Russell and Roger, who were born when she was 18 months old. Virginia was the oldest of five children, taking on a nurturing role within her family from a young age (Suhd, as cited in Brothers, 2019).

Virginia learned to read at the early age of 3 and attended a one-room schoolhouse. This early education environment fostered her love for learning and exploration. Her curiosity and desire to understand the world around her were evident from a young age (Banmen, 2009). As the eldest child, Virginia often helped her parents with her younger siblings, further developing her sense of responsibility and care.

Virginia did not derive the renowned warmth and empathy she became famous for from observing her parents' relationship. Three weeks after her father's death on February 19, 1972, Virginia reflected on her family dynamics, saying, "My father was an alcoholic for a number of years. He always provided, but his beautiful self never really got manifested" (Suhd, as cited in Brothers, 2019, p. 18).

A poignant memory from seven years before her father's death highlighted the deep disconnect between her parents. On the day before her mother went into the hospital, she asked to be brought from her bed to where Virginia's father was sitting in the living room. In a moment of profound pain and honesty, she told him, "I'd rather die than go home and live with you." He did not react; he remained motionless. Virginia then took her mother back to bed, overwhelmed by the realization that the two people she had known all her life had never truly connected with each other (Suhd, as cited in Brothers, 2019, p. 19). This stark observation deepened her understanding of human relationships and further fueled her commitment to healing family dynamics.

A significant health scare marked Virginia's early childhood. When she was 5 years old, she developed a severe case of peritonitis after her appendix burst. Due to her mother's adherence to Christian Science beliefs, which discouraged medical intervention, Virginia's condition worsened over several weeks as her parents argued about whether to seek medical help (Andreas, 1999). Eventually, in desperation, her father, Reinhold, defied Minnie's wishes and took Virginia to a hospital in Marshfield. The doctors there managed to save her life, though she remained hospitalized for several months.

This traumatic experience left a lasting impression on Virginia. She later recounted how the severity of her illness and the delay in receiving medical care due to her mother's beliefs made her feel deeply vulnerable. She described how this period in her life influenced her early decisions and shaped her emotional responses to conflict and care. The impact of this life-threatening illness played a pivotal role in her childhood, affecting her decisions about how to relate to people and emphasizing the importance of emotional and physical health (Banmen, 2008). This event also contributed to the complex dynamics between Virginia and her mother, affecting their relationship for years to come.

This deep understanding kindled a lifelong calling to heal familial wounds similar to those she had endured. With tenacious curiosity and the courage to question, Virginia embarked on a pioneering professional journey that would transform the landscape of psychotherapy.

Educational Pathways and Professional Beginnings

From her humble midwestern roots, Virginia Satir accumulated numerous accolades in higher education. She attended Milwaukee State Teachers College, graduating in 1936 at just 20 years old. Satir then pursued a master's degree in social work from the University of Chicago, which she completed in 1948 (Banmen, 2009).

Virginia honed her natural counseling skills with compassionate clarity. As a young practicum student, she demonstrated insight beyond her years. Rather than discouraging her, conventional wisdom's limitations only fueled her innovative thinking and ambition to uncover what truly healed families from within (Andreas, 1999).

Virginia launched her career mentoring troubled youth and teaching family relations courses to military families on bases. Through counseling struggling spouses and children, she witnessed firsthand the healing power of communication therapy on wounds inflicted by the horrors of war. She later became Director of Chicago's Avondale Neighborhood House, a settlement home dedicated to alleviating the socioeconomic burdens of low-income families (Woods and Martin, 1984).

In 1959, Satir co-founded the Mental Research Institute (MRI) in Palo Alto, California. The MRI became a pivotal center for the development of family therapy techniques and theories. As the training director, Satir developed the first formal training program for family therapy, significantly shaping the field (Banmen, 2002). Her innovative approaches and dedication to teaching new therapists contributed greatly to the evolution of family therapy practices.

Satir also founded the International Human Learning Resources Network in 1970 and the Avanta Network in 1977, later renamed the Virginia Satir Global Network. These organizations were created to provide resources and support for mental health workers and to promote her methods of family therapy globally (Banmen, 2009).

The Emergence of a New Approach

At the time the young Virginia Satir entered the field in the early 1950s, prevailing therapeutic assumptions centered around identifying pathology in individuals rather than relationships between them. The possibility for healing emotional bonds themselves remained largely unexplored (Satir, 1983). Yet, having personally weathered the toll of her parents' strained marriage, Satir felt convinced relationship dynamics themselves caused mental anguish.

While volunteering at the Illinois Psychiatric Institute, a revelation struck when Satir witnessed a withdrawn psychiatric patient suddenly open up with friends. "His symptoms came from his relationships," Satir deduced. She began integrating family members into therapy sessions, finding their presence could rapidly shift stuck relational patterns (Andreas, 1999). During this period Satir also met influencers like Abraham Maslow and Carl Rogers whose humanistic approaches aligned with her client-centered, growth-oriented philosophy (Haber, 2002).

Satir's methods evoked both intrigue and skepticism from traditional circles. Undeterred, in 1955 she moved to Palo Alto's eminent Mental Research Institute (MRI) which studied interpersonal communication and human behavior. Though the MRI's medical model initially resisted framing mental illness relationally, Satir found support from likeminded luminaries like Gregory Bateson, Paul Watzlawick, and Donald D. Jackson who shared her systemic worldview (Jackson, Riskin, and Satir, 1961).

The MRI brought together bold and unconventional thinkers who were willing to question traditional psychological models. Instead of seeing problems as simple cause-and-effect chains, they explored the complexity of human relationships, paradoxes, and the invisible patterns shaping communication. This environment gave Satir the freedom to develop her experiential approach, which focused on helping clients move beyond surface defenses and reach the deeper emotional patterns beneath. Although her ideas were sometimes seen as controversial, the openness of this group allowed her work to grow. During these years, the team played an important role in shaping both the theory and practice of systemic family therapy.

Foundational Theories and Techniques

The experiential practices Satir pioneered at the MRI became enduring frameworks she termed her "Growth Model" and "The Process of Change." These embodied psychospiritual philosophies centered around how self-worth shapes behavior and life visions (Satir, Banmen, Gerber, and Gomori, 1991). By nurturing acceptance in the face of rigid "family rules," Satir sought to loosen these constraints to allow more authentic ways of relating.

Instead of dispensing expert techniques, Satir voraciously questioned assumptions in herself and others. She integrated metaphors, role-playing, and even comedy to help families "see their situation in a new way and accept themselves as adequate persons entitled to respect" (Satir and Baldwin, 1984). Satir operated as a meta-model rather than using rehearsed methods, ever leaning into immediacy by responding intuitively moment-to-moment (Andreas, 1999).

While Satir zoomed out to view clients' whole life contexts systemically, she simultaneously zoomed into granular micro-interactions revealing fractured communication flows. She might map family members spatially to demonstrate unlikely alliances, utilize parts parties to unblend polarized inner voices, externalize somatic burdens through sculpting, or dramatize scenes from the past for reinterpretation (Satir et al., 1991). This multi-layered framework encompassed cognitive, emotional, and bodily aspects of relating.

Such holism formed Satir into family therapy's heart; she taught that the purpose of therapy is to appreciate what family members can become, not just what they are. Guided by innate care beyond strategy, Satir initiated deep systemic shift through courageous compassion alone (Satir, 1983).

Challenges and Triumphs

While Satir was advancing family therapy radically for her era through the MRI, reception outside her siloed circle remained guarded. The patriarchal medical model considered her humanistic, phenomenological approach overly touchy-feely and lacking scientific rigor. Dismissed as a "basket-weaver" early on for employing interpretive methods, Satir remained determined (Andreas, 1999).

As a woman pioneering into the male dominated medical terrain alongside few female peers, her ideas provoked skepticism. Yet humiliations around having her offerings rejected by the American Psychiatric Association only strengthened her conviction (Freeman, 1999). She turned limitations into lessons, using discomfort surrounding emotional vulnerability as feedback revealing where inner old wounds and defensive patterns persisted.

Excluded from certain forums yet increasingly sought out by students, Satir garnered support from outsiders finding freedom in her courage to be unconventional. In 1967 she published *Conjoint Family Therapy* sharing techniques with an exponentially widening audience (Satir, 1983). Three more acclaimed books and an international teaching career ensued as family therapy itself opened around her visionary methods.

Four decades ahead of her time, an unassuming daughter of Wisconsin farm country followed her North Star faith in relational healing beyond existing paradigms. The creativity Satir brought into clinical spaces seeded solution-focused talk therapy, emotionally focused couples work, and inner systemic modalities still teaching therapists worldwide (Brubacher, 2006).

Above all Satir embodied unconditional presence. She did not merely see symptoms; through hours gazing into clients' eyes with somber, conspiratorial joy, Satir helped reveal the light of one's being. This quality of listening, of holding space she felt all deserved opened wide to flood family therapy with more gentle ways of seeing and lifting one other up (Cowley and Adams, 2000).

Theory and Methodology

Virginia Satir pioneered unprecedentedly compassionate lenses for viewing individuals and families. Unlike prevailing clinical models labeling patients' pathologies, Satir saw symptoms as survival mechanisms adopted for living under distorted perceptions, not inherent character flaws. Her humanistic orientation championed that beneath these constrained coping strategies lay miraculous reservoirs of courage and love in all people (Banmen and Maki-Banmen, 2014).

Such respect demanded Satir assume families' decency before judging difficulties. She understood predicaments as the inevitable fruit of conflicts between yearning for belonging versus struggling for autonomy across the human condition (Satir, 1983). With gentleness evoking inhabitants' wholeness, Satir cultivated contexts where people uncovered value in their own and others' longings. This philosophical foundation enabled the revelatory, nurturing family environments Satir facilitated.

The ultimate goal of the Satir Growth Model is to guide individuals toward a state of wholeness, where they live in alignment with their deepest essence and the universal life-force that connects all beings (Brothers, 2000). This model is not merely about achieving personal growth or transformation as isolated processes; it is about fostering a profound integration of the self with a greater, interconnected system (Cheung, 1997).

At its core, the Satir Growth Model seeks to awaken individuals to the fullness of their "I AM" – the core life-force within each person – and to cultivate an awareness that they are expressions of a larger divine system (Gabriel, 2014). By engaging in this process, individuals become empowered to embody congruence in their lives, aligning their thoughts, emotions, and actions with their inner truth and life-purpose (Lee, 2002).

The model encourages individuals to move through stages of growth that address various levels of their experience, from reducing suffering and achieving personal goals, to embracing relational harmony and eventually transcending ego-driven limitations (Leung, Lau, and Chung, 2018). As individuals advance, they become capable of contributing to the collective good, expressing their unique gifts, and fostering harmonious relationships within their families, communities, and beyond.

Ultimately, the Satir Growth Model leads individuals toward self-actualization and enlightenment, where they live not only as congruent selves but as contributors to a more compassionate, connected, and authentic world. This journey emphasizes the importance of both individual fulfillment and collective well-being, guiding people to experience their lives as interconnected expressions of the universal life-force.

Central to Satir's technique was skillfully unraveling family communication patterns both verbal and non-verbal. She firmly believed how people expressed themselves intimately shaped their realities. Mapping flow patterns of who spoke to whom, Satir displayed dysfunctional structures: coding members as placaters, blamers, super reasonable, or irrelevant (Satir, 1988). Through dramatizing the impacts of these dynamics somatically, she reorganized channels towards vulnerability and empathy.

By minding seemingly surface-level stylistic choices, Satir echoed core beliefs molding one's strategy for navigating belonging; how safe or dangerous it feels allowing authentic intimacy amidst loved ones' judgments defines one's inner security. Satir's fulcrum rested on transforming expression towards honesty, compassion and personal accountability as the bedrock of healthy relating (Satir, 1983).

The Satir Growth Model

Satir surmised that all beings inherently strive for meaning, connection, and realization of their highest selves. Yet traumas around exercising the five freedoms Satir outlined – seeing clearly, feeling fully, asking openly, risking authentically. and voicing your thoughts and feelings – often constrained individuals from manifesting this birthright (Satir, 1988). Therefore, Satir sought first to cultivate self-esteem resilience to stand confidently in these freedoms.

By creating playful, communal contexts for individuals embodying yearned-for ways of sharing themselves more fully, Satir organically dismantled internal objections. Her Growth Model mirrors scholar Peter Levine's assertion that the imagination helps nervous systems override overwhelm by demonstrating preferred realities are possible. Through impressing revised relational modes within families' muscle memories, Satir etched healthier systemic pathways towards fulfillment as their new normal (Satir et al., 1991).

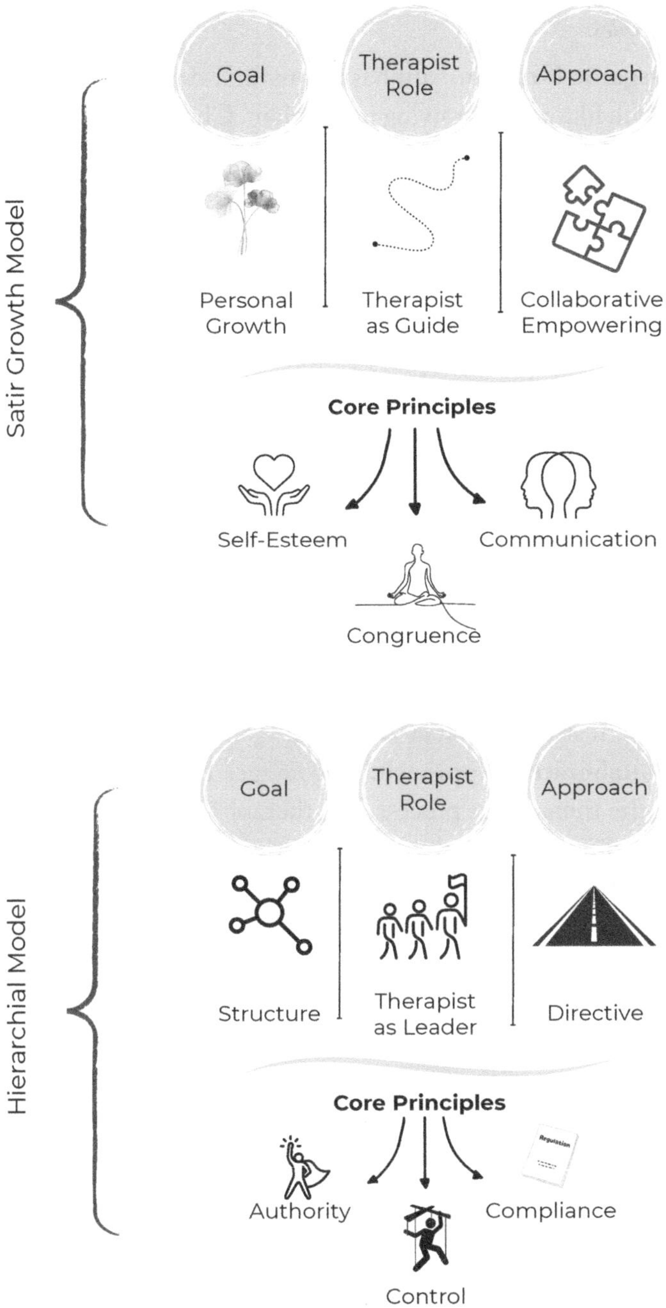

FIGURE 1.1 The Satir Growth Model

Key Principles

- **Organic Growth**: Emphasizes natural development and change, much like a seed growing into a plant. Change is seen as a dynamic, organic process rather than a mechanical fix (Leung, Lau, and Chung, 2018).
- **Systemic View**: Focuses on the family as a system where each member affects and is affected by others. It is a non-linear approach that aligns with social construction theories, positing that reality is co-created through relationship (Cheung, 1997).
- **Resourcefulness and Positivity**: Highlights the innate capabilities and strengths of individuals and families. Even in extreme crises, such as suicidality, the model posits that clients possess the internal resources necessary for survival and transformation (Smith, 2010; Lum, Smith, and Ferris, 2002).
- **Emotional and Relational Focus**: Prioritizes emotional experiences and relational dynamics as the key to understanding behavior and facilitating change. Recent studies confirm that this relational focus significantly bolsters mental health resilience during periods of high stress (Allen et al., 2022).
- **Collaborative Approach**: Encourages collaboration and equality in the therapeutic process. The therapist joins the family system as a facilitator rather than an authority, utilizing their own congruence to invite change (Lum, 2008).

Application

In therapy, the Growth Model is used to nurture growth and development, focusing on the potential and health within the family system. It views problems as opportunities for development and emphasizes nurturing conditions that allow for natural progression and healing (Banmen, 2002).

The Hierarchical Model

Key Principles

- **Top-Down Structure**: Based on a more traditional, often linear approach where roles and dynamics are viewed through a hierarchy.
- **Authority and Roles**: Emphasizes the importance of roles and authority figures within a system, such as a family or organization.

- **Problem-Focused**: Often more focused on identifying and fixing problems, sometimes through directive means (Satir et al., 1991).
- **Structure and Order**: Prioritizes maintaining structure, order, and stability within the system.
- **Expert-Directed**: The therapist or leader often assumes a position of authority or expertise, directing the process and solutions.

Application

In a therapeutic or organizational context, this model addresses issues through a more directive approach, focusing on restructuring or reorganizing roles and dynamics.

Comparison

- **Nature of Change**
  - Growth Model: Views change as a natural, organic process.
  - Hierarchical Model: Often sees change as something to be managed or directed.
- **Role of Therapist/Leader**
  - Growth Model: Facilitator who nurtures growth.
  - Hierarchical Model: Authority figure who directs change.
- **Focus of Therapy/Intervention**
  - Growth Model: Emotional and relational growth.
  - Hierarchical Model: Structural and behavioral adjustments.
- **Approach to Problem-Solving**
  - Growth Model: Problems are opportunities for growth (Satir, 1988).
  - Hierarchical Model: Problems require solutions and often restructuring.
- **Perception of Individuals/Family Members**
  - Growth Model: Each member is a resource with potential.
  - Hierarchical Model: Members have roles and positions within a hierarchy.

Satir's Growth Model offers a more fluid, organic approach to understanding and facilitating change, focusing on emotional and relational aspects and viewing each individual as inherently resourceful. In contrast, the Hierarchical Model takes a more structured, role-focused approach, often with a top-down methodology. The choice of model can significantly influence both the process and outcomes in therapy, family dynamics, and organizational management (Banmen, 2002).

Example: The Thompson Family – Struggling with Communication

Let's explore an example that contrasts the application of Satir's Growth Model with a Hierarchical Model in a therapy session context. This example will involve a family dealing with communication issues, and we'll see how each model approaches the situation differently.

The Family's Issue: The Thompson family, consisting of parents and two teenage children, are experiencing communication breakdowns, leading to frequent conflicts.

Satir's Growth Model Approach

Key Focus: Facilitating organic growth in communication and relationships.

Session Excerpt:

Therapist: Let's look at your family as a garden. Each of you is a unique plant with different needs to grow. How can you nurture each other?

Mother: I guess I've been like a gardener focusing only on the weeds. I need to appreciate the flowers, too.

Father I haven't been watering enough. I need to spend more time understanding what each of you needs.

Teenager: Sometimes, I feel like I'm in the shade. Maybe I need to step into the sunlight more – speak up about my feelings.

Therapist: It sounds like you're all finding ways to nurture growth in your family garden. How can you continue to cultivate this environment at home?

Hierarchical Model Approach

Key Focus: Structuring roles and communication in the family.

Session Excerpt:

Therapist: In a family, like in any team, there are roles and responsibilities. Let's define what each person's role is in ensuring effective communication.

Father: As the father, I suppose I should set rules for how we communicate during disagreements.

Mother: And I can ensure these rules are followed, especially during our family meetings.

Teenager: So, my role would be to express myself within these rules and respect the structure we have?

Therapist: Exactly. By defining and respecting these roles, you can create order and reduce conflicts. Let's plan how you will implement this at home.

In the Satir Growth Model, the focus is on understanding and nurturing each individual's emotional needs, fostering organic growth in relationships. The therapist facilitates exploration and self-discovery, encouraging the family to collaboratively find ways to nurture their relationships.

In contrast, the Hierarchical Model emphasizes defining roles and creating structured approaches to communication. The therapist directs the family in establishing rules and responsibilities, aiming to bring order and clarity to interactions.

Both models offer different pathways to improving communication and resolving conflicts, each with its unique approach to family dynamics and therapy.

Contemporary Evolution

As luminaries became disciples and Virginia Satir's once-marginalized message gained validation, her teachings spread beyond the MRI to encircle the planet. Satir's universal insights on family wellbeing attracted crowds internationally from the 1960s through the 80s (Banmen, 2009). This grassroots hunger for human understanding fertilized Satir's methods across diverse cultures.

From North America to Europe to Asia, "Virginia Satir Global Network" hubs convened to adapt her techniques for regional sensitivities yet maintain fidelity to Satir's core philosophical pillars around congruent communication, self-esteem, and systemic contextual dynamics (Banmen, 2006). As mental health shifted from pathologizing individuals towards interdependence and social ecology perspectives Satir had championed decades prior, her prescient wisdom offered maps to restore communal bonds.

Virginia Satir's groundbreaking work in family systems, communication, and self-esteem has laid the foundation for many modern therapeutic approaches. Therapies such as Neuro-Linguistic Programming (NLP), Internal Family Systems (IFS), Family Constellations, Emotion-Focused Therapy (EFT), Somatic Therapy, and others all build upon Satir's original insights, integrating them with new techniques to offer comprehensive pathways to healing.

Modern Adaptations of Satir's Work

Neuro-Linguistic Programming (NLP) – Use of Language and Meta–Model

NLP, co-developed by Richard Bandler and John Grinder, draws heavily on Satir's communication models. NLP's exploration of how language influences thought and behavior mirrors Satir's work on congruent communication and how internal belief systems shape our external actions (Bandler, Grinder, and Satir, 1976). Satir's intuitive understanding of how subtle shifts in language can transform perceptions laid the groundwork for NLP's methods in reprogramming cognitive and emotional responses.

Internal Family Systems (IFS) and Family Constellations – Parts Party and Systemic Work

IFS, developed by Richard Schwartz, shares foundational roots with Satir's Parts Party, and introduces a distinct approach – one centered on Self-leadership. Rather than externally negotiating harmony among parts, IFS encourages each part to be fully heard, understood, and welcomed with compassion (Schwartz, 2001). The goal is not just balance, but an inner relational shift where all parts trust the Self's presence.

Family Constellations, pioneered by Bert Hellinger, complements Satir's systemic approach by uncovering hidden family dynamics across generations. Like Satir's family sculpting technique, Constellations focuses on how unresolved issues in family systems influence present behaviors (Bitter, 1988). Both approaches help clients untangle familial entanglements to promote healing and understanding.

Emotion-Focused Therapy (EFT) – Congruent Communication

Sue Johnson, who developed Emotion-Focused Therapy (EFT), studied with John Banmen, a major figure in the Satir community. EFT focuses on repairing attachment bonds between partners by fostering emotionally attuned communication, directly paralleling Satir's work on congruent communication and her emphasis on fostering emotional safety in relationships (Brubacher, 2006). Both approaches emphasize the need for emotional expression, validation, and connection to heal and strengthen bonds.

Somatic Therapy (SE and SP) – Bodywork and Family Sculpting

Satir's focus on bodywork and non-verbal communication is further developed in Somatic Experiencing (SE) and Sensorimotor Psychotherapy (SP), both of which recognize the body's role in processing trauma. Satir's belief in the importance of bodily awareness and expression laid the groundwork for somatic therapies, where the body is viewed as a central component in emotional healing (van der Kolk, 2014).

Solution-Focused Therapy (SFT) – Validation and Positive Regard

Solution-Focused Therapy (SFT) builds on Satir's use of validation and positive regard by focusing on strengths and solutions rather than problems. Both approaches emphasize the client's inner resources, fostering hope and empowerment as essential elements for growth and transformation (Banmen, 2002).

Acceptance and Commitment Therapy (ACT) – The Satir Change Process

ACT emphasizes acceptance of difficult emotions and commitment to values-based action, aligning closely with Satir's Change Process, which describes the stages of personal transformation from chaos to integration. Both ACT and Satir's change process encourage clients to embrace discomfort as a catalyst for growth and change, promoting psychological flexibility and resilience (Satir et al., 1991).

Mindfulness-Based Stress Reduction (MBSR) – Centering Meditations

MBSR, developed by Jon Kabat-Zinn, shares Satir's focus on mindfulness and centering techniques. Satir's use of centering meditations helped clients become more present and grounded, principles that are key in mindfulness practices (Banmen and Banmen, 1991). Both approaches enhance emotional awareness and self-regulation.

Prolonged Exposure (PE) – Stances and Family Sculpting

Prolonged Exposure (PE) therapy, used primarily to treat trauma, integrates aspects of Satir's family sculpting and stances. Satir's work with family dynamics helps clients see how trauma impacts their relational roles, and PE helps process these experiences by directly confronting the trauma within the context of family relationships (Satir, Bitter, and Krestensen, 1988).

Psychodynamic Psychotherapy (PDP) – Triad Work

Satir's triad work, examining the dynamics between mother, father, and child, parallels psychodynamic psychotherapy's focus on early family relationships and their lasting impact. Both approaches help clients gain insight into how childhood experiences shape their current relational patterns (Satir, 1983).

Narrative Exposure Therapy (NET) – Family History

NET involves constructing a narrative of past trauma, which resonates with Satir's work on family history and transgenerational healing. By mapping out the family's past, clients can explore how ancestral traumas affect their present experiences, aligning with NET's goal of creating a coherent trauma narrative (Satir, 1988).

Intensive Short-Term Dynamic Psychotherapy (ISTDP) – Five Family Rules

Satir's Five Family Rules (e.g., don't talk, don't trust, don't feel) correspond with ISTDP's exploration of restrictive emotional environments. Both approaches aim to dismantle these internalized rules to foster emotional freedom and authentic expression (Satir et al., 1991).

Virginia Satir's work continues to evolve as her principles of congruence, emotional expression, and systemic healing are integrated into these diverse therapeutic frameworks. Whether through NLP's linguistic focus, IFS's exploration of internal parts, Family Constellations' generational healing, or EFT's work on attachment, Satir's legacy is unmistakable in the modern therapy landscape. Each of these models builds on her groundbreaking work, offering therapists and clients alike new pathways to healing and transformation.

While the digital age aggravates Attention Deficit Culture's epidemic by fracturing family time into 15-second bytes, Virginia Satir's hands-on healing arts foster richer engagement and presence. Yet, complementary tools – from virtual reality to biofeedback and eye movement therapies – build on somatic and systemic insights Satir introduced when few considered household relationships a serious science.

As immigration, blended families, and expanding definitions of kinship build a more pluralistic landscape, Satir's inclusive, tailored-to-each methods model cultural humility mental health systems still aspire towards. For sensitivity today demands not just tolerating different customs but affirming the equal value of multiple worlds people inhabit. Honoring Satir's spirit thus means perpetually broadening therapists' frames towards radical openness (Cheung and Chan, 2002).

Legacy and Empirical Evidence

The impact of Virginia Satir's systemic approach is substantial, reaching far beyond anecdotal success and gaining recognition across fields like education, law, and healthcare. Her pioneering work on emotional intelligence, family dynamics, and systemic healing is empirically supported, demonstrating the effectiveness of her methods in transforming lives, families, and communities. Rooted in a deep understanding of human relationships and the power of authentic communication, Virginia Satir's legacy extends well beyond individual therapy, offering transformative insights that have reshaped practices in multiple disciplines such as education, legal field, mental health, and healthcare.

Education

Satir's emphasis on congruence and self-worth has influenced modern educational practices, particularly those focused on emotional intelligence. Programs designed to foster emotional intelligence in students align with her vision of nurturing self-worth and authentic expression. Studies like Durlak et al. (2011) confirm the effectiveness of social and emotional learning (SEL) programs, which show an 11% increase in academic performance, alongside improvements in emotional regulation and social skills (Durlak et al., 2011). Satir's principles are also reflected in mindfulness initiatives such as MindUP, where a study by Schonert-Reichl et al. (2015) showed that students experienced a 24% improvement in empathy and a 15% decrease in aggressive behavior. These findings illustrate how emotional congruence and presence – key components of Satir's teachings – enhance both personal and academic growth.

Emotional Intelligence and Family Dynamics

Research on emotional intelligence (EI) aligns with Satir's emphasis on congruent communication, empathy, and self-awareness. According to Daniel Goleman's model, skills such as self-regulation and empathy are essential for both personal and relational well-being, echoing Satir's assertion that healthy communication underpins emotional healing (Boyatzis, Goleman, and Rhee, 2013). Studies like Francis et al. (2018) further support this, showing that emotional intelligence training can lead to a 16% improvement in outcomes related to emotional regulation and relationship satisfaction. Satir's iceberg metaphor, which explores underlying layers of thoughts, emotions, and unmet needs, is paralleled in cognitive-behavioral therapy, where examining core beliefs can reveal the roots of surface behaviors (Lum, 2008). Longitudinal studies from the American Psychological Association highlight that understanding family dynamics in this way fosters emotional insight and significantly improves therapeutic outcomes.

Legal

The legal field has increasingly adopted restorative justice principles that resonate with Satir's family sculpting and validation practices. Restorative justice prioritizes mending relationships over assigning blame, aligning with Satir's belief in addressing underlying emotional needs for sustainable solutions. A meta-analysis by Strang et al. (2013) revealed that restorative justice programs resulted in a 14% reduction in recidivism rates, with higher satisfaction levels reported among victims compared to traditional legal processes. This evidence supports Satir's view that fostering relational healing leads to more enduring positive outcomes. Interactive Justice, which uses family dynamics and group healing methods, incorporates family sculpting techniques to better understand how family structures influence behavior. Educational programs on Interactive Justice are increasingly offered in universities, underscoring Satir's impact on conflict resolution and relational justice.

Healthcare

In healthcare, Satir's systemic approach finds application in promoting empathy and emotional resilience, particularly among trauma recovery and caregiving contexts. Trauma recovery frameworks inspired by her model emphasize relational healing alongside clinical interventions, creating spaces for mutual support and emotional congruence. Research shows that emotionally attuned care models benefit both caregivers and patients, with studies like West et al. (2016) demonstrating a 29% reduction in burnout rates over two years among hospital staff engaged in empathy-based support programs. This mirrors Satir's emphasis on the importance of safe, supportive environments that prioritize congruent communication and emotional alignment. Additionally, somatic practices in trauma recovery, which acknowledge the body's role in storing and processing emotional pain, validate Satir's early insights into bodywork and non-verbal communication. Bessel van der Kolk's (2014) work in *The Body Keeps the Score* underscores the effectiveness of integrating cognitive and somatic approaches in trauma recovery, a view Satir championed long before its mainstream adoption (van der Kolk, 2014).

Virginia Satir's systemic methodology continues to evolve and inspire, providing practical solutions and a compassionate approach across diverse fields. Her work reaffirms a universal truth: by creating environments that honor emotional and relational well-being, we uplift humanity itself.

Business and Organizations

Satir's systemic principles have become a cornerstone in business and organizational development, shaping practices that foster congruence, effective communication, and collaborative growth. In team-building contexts, her emphasis on relational dynamics inspires methods like organizational sculpting, which draws from her family sculpting technique to identify hidden power dynamics and improve workplace interactions (Strider, 2013). Emotional intelligence training programs, rooted in Satir's philosophies, have shown to improve leadership effectiveness by 33% and team collaboration by 23% (Boyatzis, Goleman, and Rhee, 2013). These insights align with her belief in the importance of understanding both visible behaviors and underlying emotional needs within relational systems.

Transformational Leadership and Change Management

Satir's Change Process has been widely adopted in leadership and change management, providing a framework for navigating organizational transitions with empathy and systemic insight. Her model emphasizes addressing both surface-level disruptions and deeper emotional resistances, equipping leaders to guide their teams through phases of resistance, chaos, and alignment. Research from Burke and Litwin (1992) affirms that addressing relational and emotional dimensions leads to more sustainable change outcomes, reflecting Satir's foundational principles (Burke and Litwin, 1992). Additionally, strengths-based leadership approaches inspired by her work focus on leveraging existing organizational assets, mirroring her vision of growth through resilience and adaptability.

A Collection of Case Narratives

Beyond empirical research, Satir's work is illuminated through the transformative personal stories of her clients. One couple, married for over

50 years, shared that they "never knew what love could feel like" until experiencing Satir's full presence. An adolescent girl, struggling with self-worth, discovered her inner value after Satir mirrored back her inherent goodness. These deeply personal breakthroughs showcase the emotional power of unconditional positive regard, a core tenet of Satir's approach, and demonstrate how empathy alone can lead to profound transformation (Banmen, 2008).

As Satir's work expanded, so did its reach, from grassroots organizations to prisons and social work communities. Her methods inspired burned-out therapists and social workers to adopt a more hopeful, human-centered approach to care. Satir's ability to connect with the inherent worth of each person continues to resonate, particularly in sectors where burnout and compassion fatigue are prevalent.

Virginia Satir's techniques continue to transform families by dissolving rigid survival roles that unconsciously constrain family members. Through her unique tools such as Family Mapping, Family Sculpting, and Parts Work, Satir revealed the hidden emotional dynamics beneath family conflicts, offering pathways for healing and authentic communication. Let's explore a few case narratives that highlight the profound impact of her work.

The Wilson Family: Healing through Family Mapping and Parts Work

The Wilsons, married for over 25 years, sought help when their teenagers' rebellious behavior culminated in vandalism arrests. Satir's Family Mapping technique revealed a hidden alliance between the parents, who unconsciously blamed their children, resulting in the children feeling scapegoated (Satir, 1983). By identifying these dynamics, Satir allowed the family to address the root causes of their conflicts.

Research Insight

Studies on family systems therapy suggest that parental alliances and scapegoating behaviors can lead to maladaptive coping mechanisms in children, such as rebellion or withdrawal (Goldenberg and Goldenberg, 2013). Satir's approach aligns with findings that highlight the importance of restructuring family dynamics to create a more supportive environment for all members.

Through a reenactment of a botched birthday ritual, Satir uncovered the weakening bond between siblings who were once close but had become estranged. Mrs. Wilson, during Parts Work, confronted the inner critic that had distanced her from her children. This self-awareness allowed her to recognize how her unresolved family history with her own sisters contributed to the dysfunction. The catharsis of seeing each other's coping strategies as expressions of pain opened new channels for communication. The Wilson family continues to communicate authentically, building stronger relationships.

The Castellanos Family: Bridging Cultural and Generational Divides

The Castellanos, an immigrant household, struggled with tensions across cultural and generational divides. Teenage daughter Carla rejected her cultural roots, while her parents demanded obedience to tradition. Using Family Sculpting, Satir illuminated how both generations were frozen in fear – Carla fearing the loss of her identity and parents fearing the erosion of tradition (Satir et al., 1991).

Cultural Relevance

Research on immigrant families often emphasizes the intergenerational tension between maintaining cultural heritage and assimilating into a new culture. Satir's work in role reversal allowed both generations to see the emotional needs behind their actions, humanizing both sides and creating mutual understanding.

By engaging in role reversal exercises, each family member was able to step into the shoes of the other. Through this process, the family bridged the impasse by recognizing the shared human need for connection and understanding, regardless of cultural differences.

Individual Growth and Healing: Raj and Hannah

While Satir's work is renowned for transforming families, she also profoundly impacted individual journeys. One example is Raj, whose academic failures and relational dysfunctions stemmed from childhood emotional neglect. Through Parts Work, Satir externalized Raj's inner critic, embodied as a fire-breathing dragon – a manifestation of his father's shaming influence. By nurturing this "dragon" with unconditional care, Satir helped Raj transform it into a protective force, symbolized by a guardian lion. This allowed Raj to find self-acceptance and open himself to intimacy (Banmen, 2008).

Psychological Insight

Research in Internal Family Systems (IFS), which directly builds on Satir's Parts Party, has shown that externalizing internal parts can reduce internal conflict and foster self-compassion (Schwartz, 2001). Raj's transformation illustrates how recognizing and nurturing different parts of the self can lead to personal growth.

Similarly, Hannah struggled with anxiety and traumatic amnesia linked to a painful medical procedure in her youth. Satir used Family Reconstruction to reenact her vague memories, allowing Hannah to grieve freely for the loss she experienced when the surgery left her separated from her mother. This process helped her reframe her trauma and process her residual panic reactions constructively, restoring her self-trust (Satir, Bitter, and Krestensen, 1988).

Trauma Research

Trauma recovery literature, including the work of Bessel van der Kolk in *The Body Keeps the Score*, supports the idea that revisiting past events in a safe therapeutic setting can help clients reprocess unresolved grief and fear. Satir's Family Reconstruction method aligns with modern trauma-informed approaches, emphasizing the importance of safe emotional expression (van der Kolk, 2014).

Satir's Timeless Wisdom and Its Modern Relevance

Throughout her career, Virginia Satir crystallized revolutionary insights that honored both our shared humanity and the unique circumstances of each family. Her methods emphasized the critical role empathy plays in bridging divides – whether in families, communities, or broader societal contexts. By promoting open, authentic communication, Satir believed we could walk in each other's shoes and foster deeper mutual understanding.

Satir's parallel process model revealed how internal conflicts mirrored interpersonal dynamics, which, in turn, reflected larger systemic issues. Just as conflicting internal "parts" within an individual can lead to emotional fragmentation, dysfunctional family communication creates pain that often passes down through generations. Modern research, such as Yehuda's studies on epigenetics and transgenerational trauma, supports Satir's early recognition of how unresolved emotional wounds affect future generations (Yehuda, 2015).

In today's world, with rising levels of depression and anxiety – often worsened by digital alienation – Satir's hands-on, humanizing methods hold revolutionary potential for rebuilding connection. As technology displaces face-to-face interaction, leading to diminished intimacy, her techniques offer practical solutions for reconnecting fragmented families and communities. Satir's emphasis on authentic, in-person communication remains highly relevant in counteracting these effects and fostering emotional resilience (Allen et al., 2022).

Whether it's helping families divided by political polarization or nurturing student well-being in under-resourced schools, Satir's holistic frameworks – integrating empathy, somatic work, and systemic dynamics – provide invaluable guidance for addressing today's challenges. Her philosophy of nurturing self-worth from the inside out remains a powerful tool for restoring personal and relational health in our increasingly disconnected society.

More than 50 years after declaring that "Peace will come through family transformation," Satir's vision continues to resonate as global mental health crises surge. With modern trauma treatments increasingly embracing somatic and systemic approaches, Satir's work offers a timeless blueprint for healing. As family definitions expand and non-biological kinships gain recognition, her model of inclusive, empathetic healing reminds us that emotional safety and belonging are crucial, regardless of how "family" is defined.

Virginia Satir's legacy remains a guiding force in navigating the complexities of today's world. Her principles of systemic healing, congruent communication, and emotional wholeness are visionary models for transforming not only individuals but the relational fabric of communities – and, ultimately, the world.

References

Allen, E.E., Anaya, I.M., Dearing, T.A., D'Aniello, C., Roberts, F.E., Smith, M. (2022). Satir family therapy and adolescent mental health implications of COVID-19. *The American Journal of Family Therapy, 51*(5), 659–672. https://doi.org/10.1080/01926187.2022.2031342

Andreas, S. (1999). *Virginia Satir: Patterns of Her Magic.* Moab, UT: Real People Press.

Bandler, R., Grinder, J., Satir, V. (1976). *Changing with Families: A Book About Future Education for Being Human* (Vol. 1). Palo Alto, CA: Science and Behaviour Books, Inc.

Banmen, A., Banmen, J. (1991). *Meditations of Virginia Satir: Peace within, Peace between, Peace among.* Palo Alto, CA: Science and Behaviour Books, Inc.

Banmen, J. (2002). The Satir model: Yesterday and today. *Contemporary Family Therapy: An International Journal, 24*(1), 7–22.

Banmen, J. (Ed). (2006). *Applications of the Satir Growth Model.* Seattle, WA: Avanta, the Virginia Satir Network.

Banmen, J. (Ed.). (2008). *In Her Own Words: Virginia Satir Selected Papers 1963–1983.* Phoenix, AZ: Zeig, Tucker and Theisen, Incorporated.

Banmen, J. (2009). Virginia Satir: A short story. *The Satir Journal, 3*(1), 62–68.

Banmen, J., Maki-Banmen, K. (2014). What has become of Virginia Satir's Therapy Model since she left us in 1988? *Journal of Family Psychotherapy, 25*, 117–131.

Bitter, J. R. (1988). Family mapping and family constellation: Satir in Adlerian context. *Individual Psychology: Journal of Adlerian Theory, Research and Practice, 44*, 106–111.

Boyatzis, R. E., Goleman, D., Rhee, K. (2013). Emotional and social intelligence competencies: Cross-cultural implications. *Cross Cultural Management: An International Journal, 20*(1), 20–30.

Brothers, B.J. (2000). Virginia Satir and wholeness. *Journal of Couples Therapy, 9*(1/2), 1–4.

Brothers, B.J. (2019). *Well-Being Writ Large: The Essential Work of Virginia Satir.* Hillsborough, OR: Beyond Words.

Brubacher, L. (2006). Integrating emotion-focused therapy with the Satir model. *Journal of Marital and Family Therapy, 32*(2), 141–153.

Burke, W.W., Litwin, G.H. (1992). A causal model of organizational performance and change. *Journal of Management, 18*(3), 523–545.

Cheung, G.Y.K., Chan, C. (2002). The Satir model and cultural sensitivity: A Hong Kong reflection. *Contemporary Family Therapy: An International Journal, 24*(1), 199–215.

Cheung, M. (1997). Social construction theory and the Satir model: toward a synthesis. *The American Journal of Family Therapy, 25*(4), 331–343.

Cowley, A.S., Adams, R.S. (2000). On Satir's use of self. *Journal of Couples Therapy, 9*(3/4), 51–68.

Durlak, J.A., Weissberg, R.P., Dymnicki, A.B., Taylor, R.D., Schellinger, K.B. (2011). The impact of enhancing students' social and emotional learning: A meta-analysis of school-based universal interventions. *Child Development, 82*(1), 405–432.

Francis, L.J., Payne, V.J., Emslie, N.J. (2018). The construct validity of the Schutte Emotional Intelligence Scale in light of psychological type theory: A study among Anglican clergy. *Mental Health, Religion and Culture, 21*(9–10), 945–959.

Freeman, M. (1999). Gender matters in the Satir growth model. *American Journal of Family Therapy, 27*(4), 345–363.

Gabriel, C. (2014). I am. *Satir International Journal, 2*, 29–31.

Goldenberg, I., and Goldenberg, H. (2013). *Family Therapy: An Overview.* Cengage Learning.

Haber, R. (2002). Virginia Satir: An integrated humanist approach. *Contemporary Family Therapy: An International Journal, 24*(1), 23–37.

Jackson, D., Riskin, J., Satir, V. (1961). A method of analysis of a family interview. *Archives of General Psychiatry*, *5*, 321–339.
Lee, B.K. (2002). Congruence in Satir's model: Its spiritual and religious significance. *Contemporary Family Therapy: An International Journal*, *24*(1), 57–81.
Leung, P., Lau, W., Chung, C. (2018). Development and Validation of Perceived Self Transformation Scale for the Satir Model. *Contemporary Family Therapy: An International Journal*. https://doi.org/10.1007/s10591-018-9477-7
Lum, W. (2008). Therapists' experience using Satir's personal iceberg metaphor. *The Satir Journal*, *2*(2), 45–88.
Lum, W., Smith, J., Ferris, J. (2002). Youth suicide intervention using the Satir model. *Contemporary Family Therapy: An International Journal*, *24*(1), 139–159.
Satir, V. (1983). *Conjoint Family Therapy*. Palo Alto, CA: Science and Behavior Books, Inc.
Satir, V. (1988). *The New Peoplemaking*. Palo Alto, CA: Science and Behavior Books, Inc.
Satir, V., Baldwin, M. (1984). *Satir Step-by-Step: A Guide to Creating Change in Families*. Palo Alto, CA: Science and Behavior Books, Inc.
Satir, V., Banmen, J., Gerber, J., Gomori, M. (1991). *The Satir Model: Family Therapy and Beyond*. Palo Alto, CA: Science and Behavior Books, Inc.
Satir, V., Bitter, J.R., Krestensen, K.K. (1988). Family Reconstruction: The family within – a group experience. *Journal for Specialists in Group Work*, *13*(4), 200–208.
Schonert-Reichl, K.A., Oberle, E., Lawlor, M.S., Abbott, D., Thomson, K., Oberlander, T.F., Diamond, A. (2015). "Enhancing cognitive and social–emotional development through a simple-to-administer mindfulness-based school program for elementary school children: A randomized controlled trial." *Developmental Psychology*, *51*(1), 52.
Schwartz, R.C. (2001). *Introduction to Internal Family Systems*. New York: Guilford Press.
Smith, J.W. (2010). Dead kids talking: Youth suicide prevention using the Satir Transformational Systemic Therapy. *The Satir Journal*, *4*(1), 84–108.
Strang, H., Sherman, L.W., Mayo-Wilson, E., Woods, D.J., Ariel, B. (2013). "Restorative justice conferencing (RJC) using face-to-face meetings of offenders and victims: Effects on offender recidivism and victim satisfaction." *Journal of Experimental Criminology*, *9*(4), 325–334.
Strider, E. (2013). Re-sculpting an organization: A different kind of family. *Satir International Journal*, *1*, 96–102.
van der Kolk, B.A. (2014). *The Body Keeps the Score: Brain, Mind, and Body in the Healing of Trauma*. New York: Viking.
West, C.P., Dyrbye, L.N., Erwin, P.J., Shanafelt, T.D. (2016). "Interventions to prevent and reduce physician burnout: A systematic review and meta-analysis." *The Lancet*, *388*(10057), 2272–2281.
Woods, M., Martin, D. (1984). The work of Virginia Satir: Understanding her theory and technique. *The American Journal of Family Therapy*, *12*(4), 3–11.
Yehuda, R. (2015). Transgenerational transmission of trauma effects: Putative biological mechanisms. *Progress in Brain Research*, *221*, 51–66.

2

The Satir Growth Model in Depth

Introduction

Virginia Satir's Growth Model offers a comprehensive way to understand family dynamics, communication, and individual self-worth. The model is based on the idea that how family members communicate can either nurture or undermine a person's self-esteem. The process emphasizes validation and healthy interactions, which are essential for emotional well-being.

This model not only helps resolve immediate family conflicts but also supports deeper personal growth by encouraging individuals to strengthen their self-esteem, make better choices, take responsibility for their emotions, and align their internal experiences with their external behaviors.

Key Components

Self-Worth and Self-Esteem

At the heart of Satir's model is the belief that an individual's sense of self-worth is greatly influenced by how they are treated within their family. Validation plays a critical role here. When family members acknowledge each other's emotions, perspectives, and experiences, it reinforces a person's inherent value. This nurtures higher self-esteem, giving each individual a sense of worth independent of external achievements or roles.

DOI: 10.4324/9781003716419-2

Conversely, when family members invalidate each other – whether through criticism, neglect, or dismissiveness – self-worth can be damaged. Over time, this can lead to feelings of inadequacy and low self-esteem, as individuals internalize these negative interactions.

Therapy focused on validation helps rebuild self-worth by encouraging more supportive and affirming interactions within the family. Through these experiences, individuals begin to recognize their own value and develop a more positive relationship with themselves.

Communication Patterns

Effective communication is central to the validation process. Satir emphasized the importance of congruence, clarity, and empathy in interactions. Congruence refers to when a person's internal experiences – what they feel and think – are aligned with their external expressions – what they say and do. Clarity ensures that messages are direct and easily understood, while empathy allows family members to connect emotionally, fostering deeper understanding and trust.

Dysfunctional communication patterns, such as incongruence or mixed messages, often lead to misunderstandings, emotional hurt, and distancing within families. By improving communication patterns, family members are able to share their needs, feelings, and perspectives more authentically, which leads to healthier, more supportive relationships.

When family members communicate with congruence and clarity, it becomes easier to make choices that are grounded in understanding rather than reacting to assumptions or defensiveness. With clearer communication, individuals feel more empowered to explore multiple perspectives, enabling them to make better, more thoughtful decisions.

Family Roles and Rules

Within families, individuals often fall into specific roles, such as caretaker, peacemaker, or scapegoat, and these roles shape how they communicate and relate to others. In addition to roles, unspoken family rules dictate what behaviors or emotions are acceptable within the family system.

Over time, these roles and rules may become restrictive, limiting personal growth and emotional expression. For instance, someone in a caretaker role may feel unable to express their own needs, while someone in a peacemaker role might avoid addressing conflict altogether.

Satir encouraged families to become aware of these roles and rules and to challenge them when they no longer serve the family's well-being. By doing so, family members can redefine their roles and create more flexible, supportive relationships.

Recognizing these roles and rules also helps individuals take responsibility for their own thoughts, feelings, and actions. Instead of unconsciously following old patterns, they become more aware of their choices and can act with greater intention.

Coping Mechanisms

Satir identified four primary coping mechanisms that individuals use when faced with stress or dysfunction in family dynamics: placating, blaming, being super-reasonable, and becoming irrelevant. These are defensive strategies developed early in life to protect against emotional pain or discomfort. While these mechanisms might provide temporary relief, they often prevent genuine connection and hinder emotional growth.

Placating, for example, involves denying one's own needs to keep the peace, while blaming shifts responsibility onto others. Being super-reasonable involves hiding behind logic to avoid emotions, and becoming irrelevant might involve distracting oneself or others from the issue at hand.

Therapy helps individuals become aware of their default coping mechanisms and explore healthier, more congruent ways of expressing their emotions and needs. As they become more attuned to their internal states, they can move away from defensive reactions and toward more authentic communication.

Growth and Change

The ultimate goal of Satir's model is to foster growth and transformation within the family system. By improving communication, increasing self-awareness, and challenging outdated roles and rules, families can create more nurturing and validating environments for all members.

This process involves breaking free from rigid, dysfunctional patterns and embracing new, healthier ways of relating. Growth and change are not limited to resolving conflicts but extend to creating a family dynamic that promotes ongoing personal and relational development.

As family members take responsibility for their own emotional experiences and behaviors, they become more empowered to make conscious, thoughtful choices. This shift not only enhances personal growth but also strengthens the family as a whole.

Application and Benefits

Therapy and Counseling

In therapy, the *Satir Systemic Transformational Model* is used to assess family dynamics and improve communication. Therapists guide family members to explore how their interactions influence each other's self-worth and help them identify unhealthy patterns that may need to change. The focus on validation, congruence, and empathy fosters stronger, more supportive relationships within the family.

Through exercises and guided conversations, families practice new ways of communicating that emphasize understanding, respect, and validation. Over time, these new patterns become ingrained, transforming the way family members relate to one another.

Personal Development

Beyond family therapy, individuals can apply the insights from this model for personal growth. By reflecting on their communication patterns, family roles, and coping mechanisms, they can gain a deeper understanding of how their early family experiences continue to influence their current relationships and behaviors. This awareness enables individuals to consciously develop healthier, more authentic ways of interacting with others.

Recognizing one's own coping mechanisms and family patterns is the first step in moving toward more congruent and empowering choices in communication. As individuals practice expressing themselves more honestly and with greater empathy, their self-esteem improves, and they begin to make decisions that reflect their true needs and desires.

Conflict Resolution

The *Satir Systemic Transformational Model* provides valuable tools for resolving conflicts within families. By encouraging clear, congruent communication and focusing on mutual validation, the model helps de-escalate conflicts and create space for understanding. When family members feel heard and validated, they are more likely to approach conflicts with empathy rather than defensiveness.

This approach to conflict resolution not only addresses the immediate issue but also strengthens the family's ability to handle future challenges. By learning to communicate more effectively, families build resilience and create a foundation for ongoing emotional growth and connection.

The *Satir Systemic Transformational Model* offers a powerful framework for understanding and improving family dynamics. By focusing on validation, self-worth, and effective communication, the model helps families move beyond dysfunction and embrace healthier, more supportive ways of relating. As individuals grow in self-esteem, take responsibility for their emotions, and develop congruence in their communication, they are better equipped to make empowered choices that enhance both their personal growth and their relationships.

Case Study: The Smith Family

The Smith family, consisting of John (father), Sue (mother), and two teenage children, Emily and Mark, are in a therapy session. The family has been struggling with communication issues and a lack of mutual understanding.

Therapist's: Introduction

Therapist: Today, let's focus on how each of you feels heard and understood within the family. We'll explore communication patterns and see how we can improve the sense of validation for everyone. John, let's start with you. Can you recall a time when you felt really understood by the family?

John's Perspective

John (Father): Well, I can't remember many times. It seems like whenever I speak, everyone assumes I'm just being critical.

Therapist: It sounds like you feel your intentions are often misunderstood. How does that affect your sense of being part of the family?

John: It's frustrating. I feel like I'm just seen as the bad guy. I'm trying to help, but it's like my words are always taken the wrong way.

Exploring Sue's Perception

Therapist: Sue, how do you perceive John's communication? Do you feel there's room for improvement in how his messages are received?

Sue (Mother): I think we sometimes dismiss what John says because we're used to him being stern. But he has good points. Maybe we need to listen more openly and try to understand where he's coming from.

Involving the Children

Therapist: Emily, Mark, how do you feel about what your parents have shared? Is there a time when you felt particularly validated or understood by them?

Emily: I feel heard when Mom asks about my day and really listens. But with Dad, I'm always on edge, like I'm being judged.

Mark: Yeah, Dad seems to always find fault. It's hard to share things with him.

Therapist's Guidance

Therapist: This is valuable feedback. It seems like there's a need for more open and empathetic communication. John, hearing this, how do you think you can adjust your approach to make your children feel more understood and less judged?

John: I guess I need to work on how I phrase things and maybe try to listen more before I respond.

Developing New Patterns

Therapist: Great. Let's work on developing new communication patterns. We can start by practicing active listening and validation in our conversations. This means listening to understand, not to respond, and acknowledging each other's feelings and perspectives.

Conclusion

Therapist: Today's session has been insightful in highlighting the importance of how we communicate and perceive each other. By focusing on validation and empathetic listening, we can start to shift these dynamics. For our next session, let's each think of ways we can contribute to a more understanding and validating family environment.

This example demonstrates the application of the *Satir Systemic Transformational Model* in a family therapy setting. The model is used to uncover and address the underlying issues in family communication, emphasizing the need for validation, empathy, and active listening to foster a healthier and more supportive family dynamic.

The *Satir Systemic Transformational Model* is a comprehensive approach that helps families and individuals understand and improve their communication patterns. By focusing on validation and healthy interaction, it aids in building stronger, more empathetic family relationships, enhancing each member's sense of self-worth and emotional well-being.

Stages of Therapy

Virginia Satir's therapeutic approach is a profound journey toward self-discovery, connection with the life-force, and the achievement of wholeness. Her Growth Model evolves beyond enhancing communication to embrace deeper goals: reaching higher states of consciousness, embodying the essence of "I am," and connecting to the universal Source energy. Let's explore these stages, reflecting this enriched framework:

Stage 1: Making Contact

- **Description**: This stage is about building trust, not only between the therapist and the client but also within the client themselves. The therapist creates a safe, sacred space, encouraging clients to connect with their inner life-force and express their true essence. Satir emphasized addressing individuals as whole beings, recognizing their unique identity beyond roles.
- **Key Focus**: Establishing a connection to the self and others, creating a sacred therapeutic space, and fostering safety. Recognizing the universal energy within each individual (e.g., calling them George, not Dad).

Stage 2: Validating Individual Essence

- **Description**: Beyond acknowledging feelings, this stage focuses on validating the unique essence and inherent value of each individual. The therapist recognizes the sacredness of each person's journey, affirming their worth and life-force energy. This validation extends beyond emotional expression to the acknowledgment of their core self.
- **Key Focus**: Affirming the individual's life-force, encouraging authenticity, and recognizing their divine connection to Source.

Stage 3: Awakening Congruence

- **Description**: This stage involves helping clients align their inner truth with their external expression, fostering congruence. Satir's focus shifts from merely improving communication to empowering individuals to embody their true selves in their interactions. The therapist gently guides clients to recognize and release blocks that inhibit the flow of their life-force energy.
- **Key Focus**: Facilitating alignment between the authentic self and outward behavior, fostering congruence, and embracing vulnerability as a path to wholeness.

Stage 4: Transforming Patterns

- **Description**: Transformation involves identifying and dissolving limiting patterns, beliefs, and roles that no longer serve the individual or system. This stage embraces the metaphorical shedding of old skins to reveal the deeper potential within. Clients learn to co-create their reality by tapping into higher states of awareness and Source energy.
- **Key Focus**: Releasing limiting beliefs and roles, accessing creativity and divine potential, and reimagining new possibilities for being and relating.

Stage 5: Integrating Wholeness

- **Description**: The final stage centers on integration – anchoring new insights, behaviors, and higher states of consciousness into everyday life. The goal is not just functional change but an embodied sense of divinity, bliss, and harmony with the universal life-force. Clients step into their full "I am" presence, co-creating their lives with intention and connection to Source.
- **Key Focus**: Anchoring higher consciousness, embodying the "I am" essence, achieving congruence with the universal life-force, and living a harmonious, transcendent life.

This updated framework emphasizes that Satir's Growth Model transcends the surface-level goals of communication and interaction, embracing the profound potential for transformation, self-actualization, and connection to the Source energy. Therapy becomes not just a journey of healing but a pathway to enlightenment and ultimate wholeness.

Case Study: The Wilson Family

Stage 1: Making Contact (Establishing Connection with the Self and Others)

Therapist: Welcome, Wilson family. I'm here to provide a sacred space where everyone can feel safe to express their truth. Let's begin by sharing what brings you here, in your own words.

Mr. Wilson: We've been having trouble understanding our son, Jake. There's a lot of tension at home.

Therapist: It sounds like you're searching for a deeper connection and understanding. Jake, what is your experience of this tension? How do you feel within yourself?

Stage 2: Validating Individual Essence

Jake (Son): *I feel like they're always on my case. They don't get me.*

Therapist: Jake, I hear that you're feeling misunderstood and pressured. That must feel heavy. It's important to honor your feelings and your unique perspective. Mr. and Mrs. Wilson, how does it feel to hear Jake express his experience?

Mrs. Wilson: It's hard to hear, but I can see how he might feel that way.

Therapist: This recognition is the beginning of seeing one another not just as family members, but as individuals with your own life-force and journeys.

Stage 3: Awakening Congruence (Aligning the Inner and Outer Self)

Mrs. Wilson: We didn't realize you felt that way, Jake. We're just worried about some of your choices.

Therapist: Let's focus on aligning what each of you feels inside with how you communicate it. Congruence means speaking your truth with openness and compassion. Jake, how might you express your feelings in a way that reflects your true self?

Jake: Maybe I could tell them when I feel overwhelmed instead of shutting down.

Therapist: That's a great step toward congruence. Mr. and Mrs. Wilson, how might you respond to Jake in a way that invites connection?

Stage 4: Transforming Patterns (Releasing Blocks to Growth)

Therapist: I've observed that conversations often escalate into frustration because underlying emotions aren't fully expressed. Let's practice a new approach – recognizing and releasing these blocks. Jake, when you feel criticized, what's the first thought or emotion that arises?

Jake: I feel like I'm failing.

Therapist: Thank you for sharing that. Let's explore how this belief might block your life-force and connection to your family. Together, let's reframe this into something empowering.

Stage 5: Integrating Wholeness (Co-creating a New Reality)

Therapist: Over the past few weeks, I've seen each of you step into greater alignment with your true selves. You've begun expressing feelings openly and connecting deeply. How can you continue building on this at home?

Jake: Maybe we can have a family meeting once a week to check in with each other.

Therapist: That's a beautiful idea. It's not just about maintaining changes but co-creating a reality that reflects your shared growth and wholeness. Let's plan how these meetings can become a practice of staying connected to your life-force and each other.

In this example, the therapist guides the Wilson family through the evolved Satir Growth Model, emphasizing alignment with the self's life-force, transformation of patterns, and integration of higher consciousness. The process goes beyond communication to foster authentic connection, individual wholeness, and harmonious family dynamics rooted in love and awareness.

Making Contact

"Making Contact" is an essential concept in Virginia Satir's therapeutic approach, emphasizing the importance of genuine connection and presence in interactions. This concept is not only crucial in therapy but also valuable in everyday relationships, whether in families, among friends, or in professional settings.

Definition and Elements

Making Contact refers to the process of establishing a real, authentic connection with another person. It involves being fully present, both physically and emotionally, in the interaction.

- **Eye Contact**: Engaging in direct eye contact, which conveys attention and respect.
- **Active Listening**: Truly hearing what the other person is saying, without planning a response or judgment.
- **Empathy**: Understanding and sharing the feelings of another, creating a space of emotional safety.
- **Authenticity**: Being genuine in one's expressions and responses, not hiding behind masks or roles.
- **Physical Presence**: Being aware of one's body language and using it to convey openness and engagement.

Benefits of Making Contact

1. **Builds Trust**: People feel more comfortable opening up when they sense genuine interest and understanding.
2. **Enhances Communication**: It breaks down barriers, leading to clearer and more honest conversations.
3. **Facilitates Emotional Healing**: In therapeutic settings, it helps clients process and express emotions more effectively.
4. **Strengthens Relationships**: Leads to stronger connections and mutual respect in all types of relationships.
5. **Encourages Empathy**: Fosters a deeper understanding of others' experiences and perspectives.

Application in Therapy and Relationships

In a therapy session, Making Contact is fundamental for building trust and rapport. Therapists model this behavior to help clients feel seen, heard, and understood. In personal relationships, Making Contact fosters deeper connections and more meaningful interactions.

In Therapy

Therapist: (*Making eye contact*) I hear the pain in your words. It sounds like you're feeling really overwhelmed.

Client: Yes, it's been hard. I feel like you truly understand.

EXTENDED EXAMPLE

Context: A client, Laura, is discussing her feelings of isolation in her relationship.

Therapist: (*Maintaining eye contact, voice gentle and empathetic*) Laura, as you share about feeling isolated, I sense a deep loneliness. It seems like you're carrying this weight for quite some time. Can you tell me more about what that's been like for you?

Laura: (*Hesitant at first, then gradually opening up*) Yes, it's like… no matter how much I'm with people, there's this wall. I smile, I engage, but inside, it feels so hollow. Like I'm there, but not really there.

Therapist: (*Nodding, reflecting her words*) So, even when you're with others, there's a part of you that remains hidden, disconnected. That must be quite exhausting, feeling present but not truly being seen or understood.

Laura: (*Tears forming*) Exactly. It's like I'm screaming inside, but on the outside, I just keep on pretending everything is fine.

Therapist: (*Leaning forward slightly, a gesture of engagement*) That sounds incredibly tough, Laura. Pretending everything is fine when inside it's anything but. Let's explore this wall you mentioned. What do you think it's made of? What keeps it there?

In Family Setting

Parent: (*Actively listening*) So, you're saying you're upset because your curfew is earlier than your friends'. I can understand why that's frustrating for you.

Teen: Exactly, it just feels so unfair.

EXTENDED EXAMPLE

Context: A conversation between a father, Mark, and his teenage son, Alex, about Alex's academic performance.

Mark: (*Turning off the TV, giving Alex full attention*) Alex, I want to talk about your recent grades. I'm not here to lecture you, but I genuinely want to understand what's going on. Can we talk about it?

Alex: (*Defensive at first*) It's just… school's been tough. I don't know, I guess I just don't get it.

Mark: (*Maintaining a calm tone, showing concern*) I hear you saying it's tough. Are there specific subjects you're finding more challenging? Or is it something else about school?

Alex: (*Opening up a little*) Well, math's been a nightmare. And I guess… I dunno, I just feel out of place there. Like I don't really fit in.

Mark: (*Nodding, empathetically*) It sounds like it's not just about the subjects, but also about how you feel in that environment. Feeling out of place can be really hard. Do you want to talk about what makes you feel that way?

In the Professional Context

Manager: (*With empathy*) I know this project has been challenging. Your hard work and dedication really stand out.

Employee: Thank you, I appreciate that you recognize the effort we've put in.

EXTENDED EXAMPLE

Manager: (*With empathy*) I know this project has been particularly challenging, and I want to take a moment to express my appreciation. Your hard work and dedication really stand out. I want you to know that I'm here to support you, and I value the effort you've been putting in.

Employee: Thank you, I appreciate that you recognize the effort we've put in. It's been a demanding project, and your words mean a lot.

Manager: I understand that it hasn't been easy, and I'm here to listen and support you. It's important to me that you feel heard and valued in our team.

Employee: That means a great deal to me. It's reassuring to know that my efforts are acknowledged, and I can openly discuss the challenges we're facing.

Manager: Absolutely, open communication is key. I'm here to collaborate with you and address any concerns or obstacles you encounter. Your perspective is essential in helping us move forward together.

Employee: I'm grateful for your willingness to work together to overcome challenges. It's important to feel that we're a cohesive team, and your approach definitely fosters that sense of unity.

Manager: I'm committed to fostering a positive and supportive work environment where every team member feels valued and comfortable sharing their thoughts. Your feedback and dedication are integral to our success.

In this example, the manager emphasizes their commitment to supporting the employee, creating an atmosphere of openness, and valuing the employee's contributions. This approach focuses on making contact and building rapport by ensuring the employee feels heard, valued, and supported.

"Making Contact" is a powerful tool in the realm of interpersonal interactions. By consciously practicing the elements of this concept, individuals can enhance their communication skills, deepen their relationships, and create a more empathetic and connected community. In a world often dominated by digital communication and superficial interactions, Making Contact reminds us of the value and impact of genuine human connection.

Self, Other, and Context

Virginia Satir's profound insights into the nature of Self, Other, and Context have opened a pathway toward understanding the sacred interconnectedness that we all share. Her approach transcends the boundaries of individual identity and invites us to explore the greater system of life as a unified whole, where each of us is a unique yet inseparable expression of the divine essence. This perspective has profoundly shaped my own practice, guiding me to see each person not merely as an individual but as a living manifestation of the universal life force, eternally connected to all others and to the broader tapestry of existence.

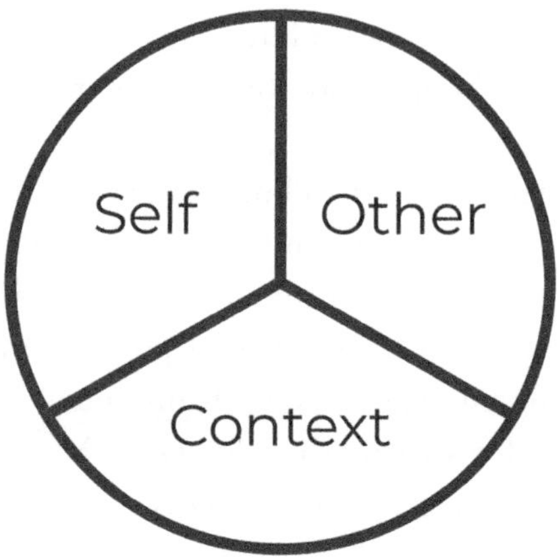

FIGURE 2.1 Self, Other, and Context

In my work with individuals and families, I have come to view these essential elements – Self, Other, and Context – not as separate realms but as facets of a single, divine network that binds us all. The Self is a reflection of the divine within; Others serve as mirrors through which we encounter different aspects of our own essence; and Context is the vast, interconnected field in which all life unfolds. Together, these elements form a sacred system of interconnectedness, one in which every interaction, every relationship, and every moment holds the potential for awakening to the unity that underlies all existence.

This exploration delves into the transformative power of recognizing this unity and the profound shifts that occur when we align our awareness with the divine connectivity at the heart of life. It is an invitation to step beyond the surface and into the depths, to journey from the personal into the universal, and to embrace the Self, Other, and Context as gateways to a deeper understanding of the sacred life force that flows through all.

The Self: A Journey into the Divine Essence

To embark on the journey of understanding the Self is to step into an encounter with the core of existence itself. The Self, in this expanded view, is not simply a collection of personal attributes, memories, or beliefs; it is the individualized pulse of a divine life force, an infinite presence manifesting through each of us. This Self is not bound by personality or ego, nor confined within the limits of personal history or societal identity. Rather, it is the eternal "I AM," the essence that connects all beings within a sacred, interconnected whole.

In our exploration of the Self, we are not merely uncovering aspects of who we think we are. We are peeling away layers of conditioned identity to reveal a deeper truth: that each of us is an expression of a divine source, one that transcends the personal and reflects the universal. This journey requires us to let go of old paradigms, moving beyond the familiar constructs of "me" and "mine," and opening to an awareness of the Self as both deeply individual and part of an all-encompassing unity. The Self is not an isolated entity but an eternal presence, rooted in the same life force that connects all beings, all moments, and all realms.

As clients begin to perceive the Self in this light, they come to realize that their sense of "I AM" is a direct connection to the divine. This Self is the still, constant essence beneath the waves of experience, the abiding presence that persists regardless of circumstance. To encounter the Self is to stand in awe of the spark of life within and to feel the profound connectivity to others and to the whole of existence. This understanding moves beyond the practical or the psychological; it is a spiritual awakening, an acknowledgment that to know oneself is, ultimately, to glimpse the infinite.

In this space, self-discovery transforms into a sacred exploration, a voyage to reclaim the wholeness that we may have forgotten but never truly lost. Each step into the Self is a step into deeper communion with the divine, a remembrance of our place in the vast, interconnected system of life. This journey is not about self-improvement in the traditional sense; it is about self-realization. It is a path of returning to the essence we have always been – the life force that animates each of us, the shared heartbeat of all existence.

The Unfolding of the Divine Self

As we journey deeper into the understanding of the Self, we begin to witness a process of unfolding, a gradual revealing of the layers that have obscured our true essence. Each layer we release – whether it be a belief, a fear, or a past experience – is like a veil lifting, allowing us to perceive the radiance within. This inner light, often concealed beneath layers of conditioning, is the very core of our being, the spark of divinity that each of us embodies. In this unfolding, we do not discover something new; rather, we return to the timeless truth of who we have always been.

In this journey, the Self reveals itself not as a fixed identity but as a living presence, a divine essence that is continuously evolving and expanding. Each person's unique experience, far from isolating them, contributes to the richness of this shared existence. The Self, therefore, is not a static entity to be defined or confined; it is a dynamic force, a flow of life that reflects the wholeness of the universe in each individual expression. We are both singular and collective, individual and universal, embodying the paradox of being distinct while also part of an inseparable unity.

In this way, self-awareness becomes more than an understanding of one's own thoughts, feelings, or personal history. It becomes a deep remembrance of our interconnectedness, an awakening to the shared life force that courses through each of us. This awareness shifts our perspective, allowing us to see ourselves not as separate entities but as essential components of a divine system, each of us reflecting and enriching the whole. As we reconnect with this essence, we move from seeking fulfillment externally to realizing that the source of all peace, love, and wisdom resides within, anchored in the "I AM" that is both personal and universal.

Living as the Divine Self in Connection with All

To embody this understanding of the Self as a divine essence is to live with a sense of profound responsibility and reverence. This Self is not ours to possess or control; it is a gift, a sacred trust, a life force that flows through us and connects us to all beings. As we come to realize that the Self is an expression of the whole, our lives take on a greater sense of purpose. We see ourselves as stewards of this divine presence, carrying the light of awareness into our relationships, our communities, and our world.

In this state of alignment, relationships are no longer mere interactions; they become sacred exchanges, opportunities to recognize and honor the divine in each other. Each encounter is a mirror, reflecting back the shared essence that unites us. When we relate to others from this place of inner wholeness, we are able to see beyond differences, beyond the surface-level identities that often divide us, and into the heart of our shared existence. We begin to experience love not as a fleeting emotion but as a steady, abiding force that flows from our recognition of unity.

This realization also transforms how we engage with life's challenges. Knowing ourselves as part of a divine system gives us resilience and strength, a trust that whatever we face, we are supported by a vast network of connection. We no longer see obstacles as threats to our identity but as opportunities to deepen our understanding of the Self, to shed further layers and grow in wisdom. Challenges become teachers, guiding us back to the core, to the unwavering presence within, reminding us that we are never separate from the life force that sustains us.

The Path of Self-Realization as a Sacred Journey

This journey of self-realization is, at its core, a sacred journey – a path that invites us to transcend the personal and touch the divine. Each step we take is a movement toward greater harmony, both within ourselves and with the world around us. As we awaken to the truth of our essence, we come to understand that our purpose is not to accumulate achievements or accolades but to embody the fullness of who we are. In this, we become vessels of the divine, channels through which love, wisdom, and compassion flow naturally.

The more we align with this essence, the more we are able to live in congruence with the greater system of life. We no longer act from a place of ego or separation but from an awareness of our role within the collective. Our thoughts, words, and actions become expressions of the interconnected whole, each one contributing to the harmony of the system. In this state, life itself becomes a meditation, a continuous unfolding of the divine Self, as we move through the world with grace, presence, and reverence.

Ultimately, the journey to know the Self is a journey to know the divine. It is a path of remembering that each of us is a unique yet inseparable part of the ultimate connectivity, the sacred life force that binds all beings. In this awareness, we find not only inner peace but a profound sense of belonging, a knowing that we are part of something vast, eternal, and beautiful. This is the essence of the Self – the "I AM" that is both personal and universal, an ever-present reminder that we are, and have always been, one with all that is.

Awakening to the Divine Flow: The Ripple of Self-Realization

As we awaken to the reality of the Self as an expression of the divine, the journey becomes not merely an individual transformation but a shift that extends far beyond ourselves, resonating throughout the world around us. This realization is like a stone dropped into a still pond, creating ripples that touch every aspect of life – our relationships, our communities, and the greater system of existence. This awakened state of Self moves us to live with an expanded awareness, seeing our role in life as one of alignment and co-creation with the whole.

The essence of the Self, when truly realized, cannot remain contained; it radiates outward, impacting how we connect with others, how we serve, and how we bring our unique gifts to the world. This state of self-realization carries a natural impulse toward harmony and balance, a movement that arises from our awareness of being interconnected parts of a divine system. No longer driven by personal ambition alone, we are guided by a desire to uplift, to contribute, and to act in ways that honor the collective well-being. This ripple effect creates a field of influence that not only transforms our own lives but inspires those around us to awaken to their own divine essence.

Living in Harmony with the Greater System

As we align with this awareness of the Self, we begin to feel a natural sense of responsibility to the greater system of life. We come to understand that every thought, word, and action is part of the interconnected web of existence, a system in which each of us plays a vital role. This knowledge encourages us to live mindfully, to choose consciously, and to act with compassion and integrity. Life becomes a dance of reciprocity, a continuous exchange in which we give to the whole and receive from it, recognizing that our true purpose is to serve and support the harmony of the system.

This sense of interconnectedness shapes our relationship with nature, with humanity, and with the planet itself. We see that we are not separate from the natural world but are intimately woven into its rhythms and cycles. Our actions toward the environment, for example, shift from a mindset of control or exploitation to one of stewardship and care. We begin to live in alignment with the natural order, respecting the earth as a living being, just as we respect the divine essence within ourselves. This reverence extends to all beings, seeing each one as a unique expression of the same life force, deserving of love, dignity, and respect.

Relationships as Reflections of the Divine Self

As our understanding of the Self deepens, so too does our experience of relationships. No longer do we view others as separate or external; we see them as mirrors, reflecting back aspects of our own essence, reminding us of our shared connection within the divine system. Relationships become sacred encounters, opportunities to recognize the divine in each other, to honor the "I AM" that we all share. In this way, love is not something we seek or possess but an expression of our mutual recognition, a natural extension of our awareness of unity.

This realization allows us to approach relationships from a place of wholeness rather than need. We no longer look to others to complete or fulfill us; instead, we engage from a sense of fullness, bringing our authentic selves and inviting others to do the same. Conflicts and misunderstandings, rather than sources of division, become invitations to deepen our awareness, to recognize where we may be disconnected from the life force within ourselves or the other. By approaching each relationship as a sacred opportunity for growth, we create spaces where love, compassion, and understanding can flourish, fostering connections that are rooted in mutual respect and reverence for the divine.

Embracing Life's Challenges as Divine Guidance

With this deeper understanding of the Self, we come to see life's challenges not as obstacles but as essential parts of our journey. Each experience, whether joyful or painful, serves as a teacher, guiding us back to our core essence and inviting us to shed the layers that keep us from fully embodying our divine nature. This perspective transforms how we face adversity. Rather than resisting or fearing challenges, we embrace them with trust, knowing that they are opportunities for growth and alignment with the life force within us.

In this view, suffering is no longer something to be avoided; it is a path to deeper understanding, a chance to release attachments and illusions that cloud our true essence. We learn to meet pain with compassion, both for ourselves and others, recognizing that suffering is part of the human experience and a doorway to empathy, connection, and transformation. This approach to challenges allows us to live with a sense of resilience and faith, knowing that every experience, no matter how difficult, serves a purpose within the divine system and brings us closer to the realization of our true Self.

Manifesting the Divine Self in the World

As we continue this journey, the realization of the Self as a divine essence becomes a guiding light, illuminating the path of purpose and contribution. This awareness calls us to bring our unique gifts into the world, to serve not from a desire for recognition but from a place of genuine love and reverence for the interconnected whole. Our actions become extensions of our essence, expressions of the divine within us, and contributions to the harmony of the greater system.

In this state, work, creativity, and service are not separate from our spiritual path; they are the path. Each act, no matter how small, becomes an opportunity to embody the divine, to infuse the world with love, wisdom, and compassion. We move through life as channels of the life force, allowing it to flow through us and touch others, inspiring them to connect with their own divine essence. This is the ultimate fulfillment of self-realization: to live as an expression of the whole, to become a vessel through which the divine can manifest in the world.

In embracing this journey, we find that the true purpose of life is not to achieve or accumulate but to align, to awaken, and to serve. This is the path of the Self as a divine presence, a journey that leads us back to our own essence and unites us with all that is. In this way, we fulfill our highest potential, not as isolated beings but as integral parts of the divine life force, honoring the sacred connection that binds us all.

Congruence

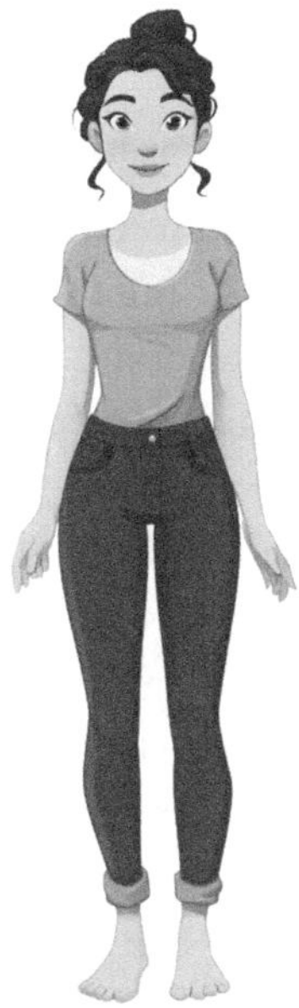

FIGURE 2.2 Congruence

Virginia Satir's insights into congruence extend far beyond communication techniques; they are a profound invitation to live in alignment with our life-force, embodying the truth of our inner essence. Congruence, as Satir taught, is not just about honest communication – it is about embodying a unity of thoughts, emotions, and actions, creating a deep resonance between our inner and outer worlds. When we are congruent, we don't just communicate clearly; we manifest our life-force, living in connection with the universal life-force that animates us all.

Understanding Congruence as an Embodied State

Congruence begins with a commitment to embody our life-force fully, not merely to express thoughts or feelings, but to align with the essence of our being. In Satir's framework, congruence is a way of existing in the world – it is the integration of self-awareness, self-acceptance, and authentic self-expression. This understanding elevates congruence from a practical skill to a path of self-realization, a journey to become fully present in each moment, to connect with the universal life-force within us, and to express it genuinely.

The journey toward congruence is, therefore, an invitation to live one's truth, to embody one's values, and to create harmony between one's inner essence and outward actions. It is a call to engage in a relationship with the self that is honest, compassionate, and deeply accepting. In my practice, I encourage clients to embrace this journey, not just as a means to improve communication, but as a path to reclaim their inner power, to stand fully present, and to live in alignment with the divine life-force within.

Manifesting the Life-Force through Congruence

Congruence requires that we attune to the universal life-force, allowing it to guide our actions and inform our expressions. This connection enables us to manifest our essence – not merely by sharing thoughts or feelings accurately but by embodying our deepest truths in every interaction, decision, and relationship. When individuals become congruent, they are no longer fragmented by external expectations or internal conflicts; they become integrated beings, expressing a unified, coherent self that resonates with the world around them.

This form of congruence invites us to experience life as a fluid exchange with the universe. It is not a static state; it is a dynamic, evolving process that deepens as we grow in self-awareness and acceptance. Satir's approach encourages us to understand congruence as a lifelong journey, one that requires continuous mindfulness and a willingness to honor our life-force, even when it challenges societal norms or confronts deeply held fears.

Congruence as a Path to Authentic Presence

To live congruently is to embody authenticity, to bring our whole self into every moment without holding back or fragmenting our essence. This form of presence transforms relationships, as it invites others to encounter us as we truly are, rather than as we think we should be.

In therapeutic practice, I guide clients in discovering and embracing this congruent self, helping them to peel back layers of conditioning, release limiting beliefs, and access the core of their being. Living in congruence means that our internal life and external expressions are aligned, and that we engage with others from a place of genuine connection. This alignment fosters an authentic presence that is powerful, peaceful, and deeply fulfilling. It allows individuals to engage in relationships and communities with a sense of wholeness, contributing to a world where each person's life-force is honored and expressed.

Congruence as an Embodied Practice

Congruence is a practice, an ongoing commitment to live in alignment with our life-force. This practice is about nurturing a state of being where thoughts, emotions, and actions are harmonized, where we feel at peace within ourselves and in connection with the universal life-force. Congruence calls us to continually revisit our intentions, to reconnect with our essence, and to express ourselves from a place of unity and coherence.

In therapeutic settings, congruence becomes a powerful tool for transformation. By fostering a safe, accepting environment, I encourage clients to explore their inner world, to identify incongruences, and to take steps toward aligning their life with their inner truth. This journey toward congruence requires self-awareness, patience, and a willingness to confront and release that which no longer serves their authentic self.

This version expands congruence into a practice of living one's life-force and connecting to the universal essence within and beyond communication.

The Embodiment of Congruence

The journey to congruence is one of discovering and embodying the life-force that animates each of us. For Virginia Satir, congruence was far more than a technique for communication; it was the very act of aligning one's entire being with an inner, universal truth. Congruence involves an unwavering commitment to live fully, where our thoughts, emotions, and actions flow from a place of authenticity, in harmony with our deepest values and purpose.

This alignment means that congruence is not just about expressing oneself clearly; it is about manifesting the essence of who we are. It requires that we attune to our life-force and allow it to guide every interaction, decision, and expression. Through this connection to our core, we become vessels through which the universal life-force flows, expressing a self that is both deeply individual and universally connected.

Congruence as a Dynamic, Evolving Process

Congruence is not a destination but a continuous process, a dynamic state of balance that evolves as we grow. It is a practice of revisiting our inner world, of reconnecting with our essence, and of realigning ourselves when life pulls us off course. This journey invites us to embrace flexibility and mindfulness, to see congruence as something we cultivate moment by moment rather than as a fixed attribute.

In therapeutic practice, I work with clients to help them recognize and realign with this life-force. We explore the places where they feel disjointed or misaligned, and we work to release the blocks that prevent them from expressing their authentic selves. The process is one of continuous self-discovery and integration, where individuals learn to embrace all aspects of themselves – including parts that may have been suppressed or disregarded – and bring them into harmony.

The Courage to Live Congruently

To live congruently requires courage, for it means presenting ourselves as we truly are, beyond societal expectations or fear of judgment. Satir's teachings emphasize that congruence is about claiming our full authenticity, stepping into the world with a sense of wholeness and integrity. This authenticity is not simply about saying what we feel or think; it is about embodying our truth, letting our words, actions, and presence reflect our inner reality without reservation.

In my work with clients, I encourage them to see congruence as a way of being that involves both vulnerability and strength. It asks us to drop the masks and defenses that keep us disconnected from ourselves and others, allowing us to bring forth a self that is open, genuine, and aligned with our inner life-force. This journey requires a willingness to face our fears and to let go of the parts of ourselves that are not in service to our true nature.

Congruence in Therapeutic Practice

In the therapeutic space, congruence forms the foundation of all healing interactions. Satir's model of congruence emphasizes the importance of creating a setting where clients feel safe to express themselves fully and honestly. By modeling congruence in my interactions with clients, I aim to create an environment that fosters trust and authenticity. This approach encourages clients to mirror this congruence, to move from guarded self-expression to a place where their true thoughts, feelings, and intentions are in harmony.

Therapeutic congruence also involves guiding clients to recognize and release patterns of incongruence. We work to identify the ways in which they may withhold or distort their expressions due to fear, conditioning, or unresolved experiences. By bringing these patterns into awareness, clients are empowered to step into a more authentic way of being, aligning their words and actions with their true inner experience. This alignment not only deepens self-understanding but fosters healthier, more fulfilling relationships.

Congruence in Self-Discovery and Growth

The path to congruence is intimately tied to the journey of self-discovery. In order to live congruently, individuals must first know themselves, explore their values, understand their emotions, and confront their fears. Satir's approach emphasizes that true congruence arises from a profound connection to one's inner self, a process that requires introspection and acceptance of all aspects of our being.

In guiding clients through this journey, I encourage them to delve into their inner world, to explore the motivations and beliefs that drive their actions. Through reflective exercises, open dialogue, and other therapeutic tools, clients are invited to connect with their core, to embrace both their strengths and vulnerabilities, and to find a sense of harmony between their internal and external expressions. This process of self-discovery is not about creating a new self but about revealing the essence of who they have always been, allowing that essence to shine through their words, actions, and interactions.

The Transformative Power of Congruence

When individuals align with their inner truth, they experience a profound shift in how they relate to the world. Congruence creates a sense of inner peace and clarity, a feeling of being "at home" within oneself. This inner alignment fosters resilience, as individuals become grounded in their own values and life-force, allowing them to navigate challenges with confidence and authenticity.

In my practice, I witness the transformative power of congruence as clients begin to live in alignment with their true selves. This alignment extends into their relationships, enhancing communication, deepening empathy, and fostering a sense of connection that transcends superficial interactions. Congruence allows individuals to create lives that reflect their true desires and purpose, cultivating a sense of fulfillment and joy that is rooted in authenticity.

Congruence as an Embodiment of Universal Connection

Ultimately, congruence is about more than self-alignment; it is about aligning with the universal life-force that connects all beings. To live congruently is to honor this interconnectedness, to see oneself as part of a larger system, and to act in ways that reflect this unity. Satir's teachings guide us toward a deeper understanding of congruence as a pathway to living in harmony with the whole, recognizing that our individual lives are expressions of a greater divine essence.

By embodying congruence, we become conduits of this universal life-force, channels through which love, compassion, and wisdom flow freely. This alignment with the universal essence is the ultimate expression of congruence, one that transforms not only the individual but also the world around them. Through this awareness, we find that to live congruently is to live in service to the whole, contributing to the harmony and well-being of the collective.

Self-Esteem Maintenance Toolkit

In a world where hearts often hide,
I walk gently, with empathy as my guide.
With each step, I seek to understand,

To nurture growth, to lend a hand.
In families where silence loudly speaks,
I search for the love that each heart seeks.
With a wand, a hat, a medallion in tow,
I light the path where understanding can grow.
I wear a detective's hat to see,
The hidden truths that yearn to be free.
A wishing wand in my outstretched hand,
Granting courage to firmly stand.
The medallion swings, yes and no,
Boundaries set, allowing respect to grow.
With a courage stick, we face our fears,
Embracing change as it nears.
My wisdom box, filled with tales of old,
Stories of warmth, stories bold.
The golden key unlocks the door,
To inner worlds unexplored before.
The heart I hold, beats with compassion's tune,
Reminding us that love is our greatest boon.
In this dance of life, complex and vast,
We find our true selves, free at last.
So hear my words, let them ring true,
The power for change resides in you.
In each of us lies a seed, waiting for light,
In the garden of life, let's grow to new heights.
For I am Satir, with a vision to impart,
A journey of healing, a work of heart.
In each word, a drop of my soul's rain,
Nurturing love, where once was pain.

Virginia Satir's therapeutic approach is renowned for its focus on building and maintaining self-esteem. The Self-Esteem Maintenance Toolkit is a collection of metaphorical tools designed to help individuals explore and strengthen their self-worth. Each tool represents a key aspect of the self-discovery and personal growth process. Let's explore these tools in detail.

Detective Hat: Unearthing Hidden Truths

The journey to self-understanding often begins with curiosity and a willingness to explore the deeper aspects of one's psyche. The **Detective Hat** symbolizes this journey of introspection and self-examination. It encourages individuals to become investigators of their own lives, delving into past experiences, current thought patterns, and emotional responses.

When introduced in therapy sessions, the Detective Hat invites clients to question the "why" behind their actions and beliefs. By fostering a non-judgmental and inquisitive stance, clients can uncover hidden truths about themselves, which in turn deepens their understanding of how these factors influence their self-esteem.

Medallion of Yes and No: Empowering Choices

The **Medallion of Yes and No** is a powerful emblem of autonomy and self-determination. It represents the critical role of boundary-setting and the freedom to make choices that align with one's true self. In therapy, this tool is used to empower clients to assert their needs and desires confidently.

Discussions around the Medallion often focus on moments where clients have felt powerless or struggled to make decisions. By exploring scenarios where saying "no" might be challenging, clients practice expressing their boundaries assertively. This process empowers them to make choices that enhance their well-being and self-esteem.

Courage Stick: Manifesting Aspirations

Chasing dreams and facing fears requires bravery, and the **Courage Stick** is a symbol of that necessary courage. It represents the boldness needed to pursue one's aspirations, no matter how daunting they may seem. The Courage Stick encourages clients to acknowledge their dreams and take the steps required to make them a reality.

In therapy, clients are encouraged to verbalize their goals, using the Courage Stick as a reminder of their inner strength. By focusing on the resources and actions needed to overcome obstacles, clients reinforce the belief that they possess the courage to achieve their aspirations.

Wishing Wand: Visualizing Possibilities

The **Wishing Wand** complements the Courage Stick by emphasizing the power of visualization and intention. It symbolizes hope and the ability to manifest one's desires through focused thought and action. The Wishing Wand encourages clients to dream big and to see their goals as attainable.

During sessions, the Wishing Wand is used as a symbolic gesture of commitment to one's dreams. Clients are guided to visualize their wishes and explore the pathways to making them come true. This practice fosters a positive mindset and strengthens the belief that anything is possible with the right focus and determination.

Golden Key: Unlocking Potential

The **Golden Key** is a powerful symbol of unlocking one's inner potential and strengths. It represents the realization that within each person lies a wealth of resources and capabilities waiting to be discovered and utilized. The Golden Key encourages clients to identify and celebrate their unique talents and abilities.

Through guided conversations and reflective exercises, clients are invited to explore their strengths. The Golden Key metaphor helps them unlock these attributes, leading to enhanced self-esteem as they recognize and embrace their inherent capabilities.

Wisdom Box: Integrating Life's Lessons

Life is full of lessons, and the **Wisdom Box** serves as a metaphorical repository for these invaluable insights. It symbolizes the accumulation and integration of personal wisdom gained from life's experiences. The Wisdom Box encourages clients to reflect on their past, identify key learnings, and use them as a guide for future challenges.

In therapy, clients are guided to metaphorically "place" their life lessons into the Wisdom Box, creating a personal reservoir of knowledge. This practice not only bolsters self-esteem but also builds resilience, as clients learn to draw upon their inner wisdom in times of need.

Heart: Embracing Self-Compassion

At the core of self-esteem lies self-compassion, and the **Heart** symbolizes this essential quality. It represents the acceptance and kindness one must show oneself to foster true emotional well-being. The Heart encourages clients to practice self-love, especially during difficult times.

In therapy, the Heart is introduced to help clients cultivate a compassionate relationship with themselves. Clients explore ways to be gentler and more accepting of their imperfections. By embracing self-compassion, they strengthen their self-esteem and resilience, leading to a more positive and balanced sense of self.

The Self-Esteem Maintenance Toolkit is a collection of powerful metaphors that guide individuals on their journey toward self-discovery, empowerment, and growth. Each tool in the kit serves a specific purpose, from unearthing hidden truths to embracing self-compassion. Together, they provide a holistic approach to maintaining and enhancing self-esteem, empowering individuals to live more fulfilling and authentic lives.

Satir's Self-Esteem Maintenance Toolkit is more than a set of tools; it's a journey towards deep self-awareness and empowerment. In my practice, these tools have been instrumental in guiding clients towards a more robust sense of self-worth and confidence. They serve not only as instruments of change but also as constant reminders of the journey towards self-realization and growth.

FIGURE 2.3 Self-Esteem Maintenance Toolkit

Self-Esteem and Self-Worth

Virginia Satir emphasized that at the heart of human development and relationships lie *Self-Esteem* and *Self-Worth*. In her book *The New Peoplemaking*, she explores these concepts, particularly in the context of family interactions, communication, and personal growth. Satir believed that understanding and nurturing these elements is key to fostering a strong, empowered self and healthier relationships.

Self-Worth vs. Self-Esteem

Satir made a clear distinction between *Self-Worth* and *Self-Esteem*, two closely related but distinct concepts.

1. **Self-Worth** refers to an individual's intrinsic sense of value. It is the deep belief that "I am enough" simply because of who I am, not because of what I do or how others perceive me. Self-worth is unconditional and exists regardless of external achievements or failures. It is the foundation of one's identity, a constant belief in one's inherent value, irrespective of circumstances. In therapy, helping clients reconnect with their innate self-worth is crucial for healing. When self-worth is strong, it provides resilience against the ups and downs of life, allowing individuals to feel secure and valuable even in the face of criticism or setbacks.
2. **Self-Esteem**, on the other hand, is how much we appreciate and like ourselves based on our self-assessments, behaviors, and achievements. It fluctuates depending on how we perceive our success or failures, how we think others view us, or how well we perform in various aspects of life. Unlike self-worth, which is stable and unconditional, self-esteem is more fragile and conditional, easily influenced by external circumstances.
3. For example, a person with strong self-worth will still feel valuable after a failure, but their self-esteem might dip temporarily as they process feelings of disappointment. Therapy can help clients develop a more resilient self-esteem by reinforcing the idea that their worth is not contingent on perfection or success.

Self-Worth: The Core of Identity

In Satir's view, *Self-Worth* is shaped early in life, largely through family interactions. Parents and caregivers have a profound impact on a child's sense of self-worth. When children experience love, validation, and acceptance, they internalize the belief that they are worthy just as they are. However, if a child is exposed to criticism, neglect, or emotional invalidation, they may grow up with a diminished sense of self-worth, often feeling inadequate or unworthy of love.

In *The New Peoplemaking*, Satir describes the family as a "peoplemaking machine," with the ability to either nurture or erode this fundamental sense of worth. Therapy aims to help individuals recognize how early family dynamics shaped their sense of self and to rebuild or strengthen a healthy sense of worth where it may have been damaged.

Building Self-Worth in Therapy

Therapists work to create a safe, supportive space where clients can explore their internal beliefs and reconnect with their inherent value. By offering consistent validation and unconditional positive regard, therapists model the acceptance that may have been missing in a client's upbringing. Over time, this helps clients internalize a more positive sense of self-worth.

1. **Challenging Negative Beliefs**: Clients often come into therapy with deeply ingrained beliefs like "I'm not good enough" or "I don't deserve happiness." These beliefs are challenged as part of the therapeutic process, encouraging clients to replace them with affirmations of their intrinsic value.
2. **Moving Beyond External Validation**: A key goal in therapy is helping clients realize that their self-worth does not depend on their achievements, roles, or external validation. This allows them to live with greater self-acceptance and authenticity.

Self-Esteem: Reflecting Self-Worth in Action

While *Self-Worth* represents a person's deep, internal sense of value, *Self-Esteem* is how this value is reflected outwardly in their actions and interactions with others. It is shaped by how a person evaluates their abilities, accomplishments, and relationships. Healthy self-esteem allows individuals to approach life with confidence, take risks, and maintain a positive self-image, even when facing challenges.

However, because self-esteem can fluctuate based on external factors, it is important to ground it in a strong foundation of self-worth. In therapy, individuals learn to balance their self-esteem with a more stable understanding of their intrinsic worth. When self-esteem falters, a strong sense of self-worth can act as an anchor, reminding individuals that they are valuable regardless of their successes or failures.

Practical Application in Therapy

In Satir's model, strengthening self-esteem and self-worth is a central goal of therapy:

- **Nurturing Self-Worth**: The therapist helps clients reconnect with their inherent sense of worth by creating an environment of acceptance and validation. This process helps clients see themselves as worthy of love, care, and respect, independent of their achievements.
- **Building Resilient Self-Esteem**: Clients learn to evaluate themselves more positively and realistically. Instead of basing their self-esteem on external validation or perfectionism, they learn to appreciate their efforts, progress, and inherent strengths.
- **Empowering through Self-Validation**: A core aspect of Satir's work is teaching clients to validate themselves. As they internalize their self-worth, clients become less dependent on external validation and better equipped to handle life's challenges with self-compassion and confidence.

By helping clients differentiate between *Self-Worth* and *Self-Esteem*, therapists guide them toward a more stable, resilient sense of identity. In doing so, clients can experience deeper growth, greater congruence, and more meaningful relationships – key outcomes in Satir's model of therapy.

Virginia wrote this beautiful poem about self-esteem that encompasses all elements:

I am me.
In all the world, there is no one exactly like me.
There are persons who have some parts like me,
but no one acts exactly like me.
Therefore, everything that comes out of me is automatically mine
Because I alone chose it.
I own everything about me –
my body, including everything it does,
my mind, including all its thoughts and ideas,
my eyes, including the images of all they behold,
my feelings, whatever they may be –
anger, joy, frustration, love, disappointment, excitement –
my mouth, and all the words that come out of it,
polite, sweet or rough, correct or incorrect,
my voice, loud or soft,
and all my actions, whether they be to others or myself.
I own my own fantasies,
my dreams, my hopes, my fears.
I own all my triumphs and successes,
all my failures and mistakes.
Because I own all of me,
I can become intimately acquainted with me.
By so doing I can love me and be friendly with me in all my parts
I can then make it possible for all of me
to work in my best interests.
I know there are aspects about myself that puzzle me,
and other aspects that I do not know.
But as long as I am friendly and loving to myself,
I can courageously and hopefully look
for the solutions to the puzzles,
and for ways to find out more about myself.
However I look and sound

whatever I say and do, and
whatever I think and feel at a given moment in time
is authentically me.
Later, if some parts of how I looked, sounded, thought,
and felt turn out
to be unfitting, I can discard that which is unfitting,
keep the rest,
and invent something new for that which I discarded.
I can see, hear, feel, think, say, and do.
I have the tools to survive,
to be close to others,
to be productive,
and to make sense and order out of the world of people
and things outside of me.
I own me, and therefore I can engineer me.
I am me and I am okay.

Surviving Stances and Stasis–Kinesis

One of the most illuminating aspects of Virginia Satir's work is her identification of the Surviving Stances—distinct patterns of behavior that individuals adopt when they experience internal stress, emotional threat, or relational disconnection. These stances offer deep insight into how people protect themselves when they feel overwhelmed or unsafe. Each stance represents a way of coping that may temporarily reduce internal discomfort but often constrains authentic communication and impedes meaningful connection.

In my practice, I integrate Satir's Surviving Stances with a broader developmental framework that I refer to as Stasis–Kinesis-Flow. This model expands Satir's original insights by considering how individuals move from rigid, reactive survival patterns (Stasis), toward greater internal awareness and reorganization (Kinesis), and ultimately toward congruent, integrated ways of relating (Flow).

This part examines each surviving stance in detail – its defining characteristics, psychological underpinnings, systemic meaning, and impact in both therapeutic and everyday relational contexts. The analysis draws on Satir's original concepts, contemporary systemic understanding, and my own applied work with clients across diverse cultural and relational environments. Each stance is also paired with its corresponding Flow stance, representing the balanced, congruent expression of the same underlying energy once freed from the constraints of fear and survival.

The Blaming Stance

FIGURE 2.4 The Blamer

The Blaming stance is one of Satir's primary survival patterns and reflects a reactive way of coping with internal distress or emotional threat. Although it may appear outwardly forceful, accusatory, or controlling, the Blaming stance is typically driven by deeper insecurity, unresolved fear, or a felt sense of powerlessness. The person attempts to restore internal equilibrium by externalizing responsibility and directing tension outward. The internal message becomes: "If I can control, correct, or dominate you, I will feel safer inside."

The Self–Other–Context Model

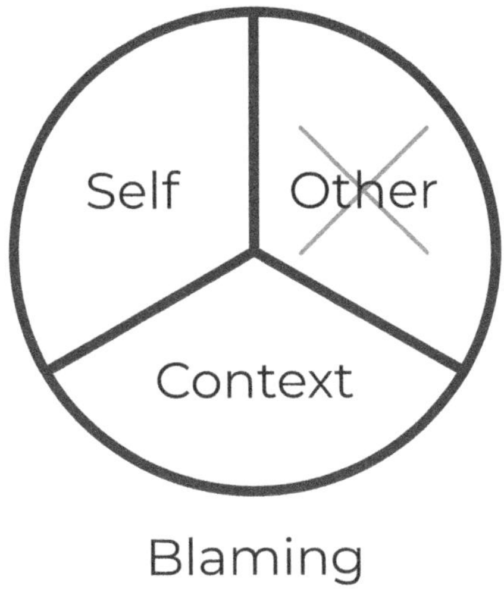

FIGURE 2.5 The Blamer Circle

Satir conceptualized human interaction through three interdependent internal reference points: Self, Other, and Context. These dimensions form a systemic triad through which people make meaning and respond to relational experiences.

- Self refers to one's inner world: feelings, needs, beliefs, values, yearnings, identity, and internal sense of worth.
- Other refers to one's perception of another person's emotional reality, intentions, needs, and impact.
- Context refers to the environment, situation, culture, history, and broader conditions surrounding the interaction.

Under stress, this triad becomes imbalanced. Each surviving stance "discounts" one part of the system.

In the Blaming stance, the Other is discounted. The person's field of awareness narrows, often leaving little space to understand or acknowledge the other's perspective.

CIRCLE REPRESENTATION

To visually illustrate this imbalance, the Self–Other–Context circle marks the Other segment with an "X," indicating that the person has lost access to, or is actively suppressing, awareness of the other's experience. The Self and Context remain partially available, but perception is rigid and dominated by internal threat.

Characteristics of the Blaming Stance

Individuals in a Blaming stance often exhibit behaviors that deflect responsibility away from themselves while asserting dominance or correctness. Common characteristics include:

- Accusatory or critical language.
- A forceful or raised tone of voice.
- Rigid body posture and a forward-leaning stance.
- Focus on others' mistakes, faults, or shortcomings.
- Minimization of their own contribution to the problem.

The stance is not malicious in origin. It is an attempt to manage an internal sense of instability or vulnerability.

Psychological Underpinnings

Blaming often stems from environments where expressing vulnerability felt unsafe or where perceived strength was rewarded. Individuals who adopt this stance may have internalized the belief that control, criticism, or dominance protects them from emotional exposure, shame, or rejection. The stance provides a temporary sense of certainty or authority, but at the cost of relational connection. Internally, individuals in this stance are often frightened, overwhelmed, or hurting beneath the surface intensity.

Application in Therapy

In therapeutic work, clients who tend toward Blaming benefit from learning to recognize the underlying emotions driving the stance. Our focus includes:

- Helping the client identify the vulnerable feelings beneath the blaming behavior.

- Teaching skills to pause before reacting.
- Expanding awareness of the Other's internal world.
- Developing language that expresses needs and fears directly rather than through accusation.

Therapy often includes somatic awareness, emotion naming, and relational attunement, which help reintroduce the discounted dimension of the triad.

Blaming in Professional Settings

EXAMPLE

A team leader, John, frequently blames his team for project delays, publicly pointing out errors and asserting that others are not meeting expectations. While this may appear as strong leadership, internally John may be experiencing fear about performance metrics, pressure from upper management, or anxiety about losing authority.

IMPACT

Blaming creates defensiveness, reduces psychological safety, and discourages initiative. Team members become hesitant to share concerns or ideas, leading to decreased innovation and hidden errors. Productivity suffers because the relational climate becomes tense and punitive.

APPLICATION

Helping such individuals shift out of Blaming involves developing awareness of their internal experience, learning to express concerns constructively, and broadening perspective to include the experiences of others. Leadership coaching may include emotional regulation techniques, communication modelling, and exploration of contextual pressures.

Blaming in Personal Relationships

EXAMPLE

Sarah frequently blames her partner, saying, "You never listen to me," or "You always ignore my needs." Although she appears angry, the deeper emotion may be loneliness, fear of disconnection, or longing for understanding.

IMPACT

This stance activates defensiveness in the partner, leading to escalating conflict, mutual distrust, and repeated cycles of rupture. The relational field becomes dominated by accusation and counter-accusation.

APPLICATION

Therapeutic work includes restoring awareness of the partner's internal world, slowing down reactive patterns, and helping the client articulate authentic needs – such as "I feel unheard and I need reassurance" – instead of attacking. Couples therapy often focuses on emotional attunement and creating space for vulnerability.

Moving Toward Healthier Communication

Transitioning away from the Blaming stance involves expanding capacity for self-reflection and relational presence.

Key strategies include:

1. Recognizing activation: Becoming aware of rising tension, narrowed attention, or bodily signs (tight chest, clenched jaw).
2. Naming underlying emotions: Identifying fear, shame, or insecurity beneath the reactive behavior.
3. Reattuning to the Other: Expanding perception to include the other person's emotions, needs, and intent.
4. Using direct, non-accusatory expressions: Replacing blame ("You always...") with grounded communication ("I feel overwhelmed and need support").
5. Acknowledging contextual factors: Considering situational pressures, histories, and external stressors influencing the interaction.

These steps support the shift from Stasis – a rigid survival response – into Kinesis, where internal and relational reorganization become possible.

Biological Modulators: Testosterone and the Blaming Stance

Although the Blaming stance is primarily shaped by psychological and relational factors, certain hormonal influences – particularly testosterone – may modulate how strongly a person reacts to perceived threat or status challenge. Research has associated testosterone with dominance motivation and increased reactivity to social threat, which can amplify the urgency behind blaming behaviors in moments of stress (Mazur and Booth, 1998; Eisenegger et al., 2011). This is not a causal explanation, but rather one element of the internal context that may influence how quickly an individual shifts into a Blaming stance.

Stasis–Kinesis–Flow

Reframing the Blaming stance within the Stasis–Kinesis–Flow continuum provides a map for transformation:

- Stasis: The person becomes rigid, defensive, and closed, discounting the Other to stabilize the Self.
- Kinesis: Awareness expands, vulnerability becomes accessible, and the Other is reintroduced into perception.
- Flow: The person engages from a centered, grounded state, integrating Self, Other, and Context.

Flow Stance: The Peaceful Warrior

FIGURE 2.6 The Peaceful Warrior

The balanced, congruent expression of the energy underlying the Blaming stance is the Peaceful Warrior.

This Flow stance embodies strength without aggression, clarity without domination, and integrity without rigidity.

Characteristics include:

- Firm boundaries expressed respectfully.
- Strength grounded in self-awareness rather than fear.
- Attunement to the other person's experience.
- Ability to maintain presence during conflict without escalation.

In the Self–Other–Context circle, the Peaceful Warrior contains all three segments open and in balance, reflecting full internal congruence.

FIGURE 2.7 The Peaceful Warrior Circle

The Placating Stance

FIGURE 2.8 The Placater

The Placating stance is a survival pattern in which individuals suppress their own needs, preferences, or emotions to avoid conflict, maintain relational harmony, or preserve a sense of belonging. Although it often appears cooperative, attentive, or caring, Placating emerges from internal fear – fear of rejection, fear of disapproval, or a belief that one's worth is conditional upon meeting others' expectations. The internal message becomes: "If I make you happy, I will be safe."

Within the Self–Other–Context triad introduced earlier, Placating reflects a discounting of the Self. The individual relinquishes their internal authority in favor of accommodating the perceived needs or emotions of the Other. In the Self–Other–Context circle, the Self segment is marked, indicating a temporary collapse of self-expression and internal legitimacy.

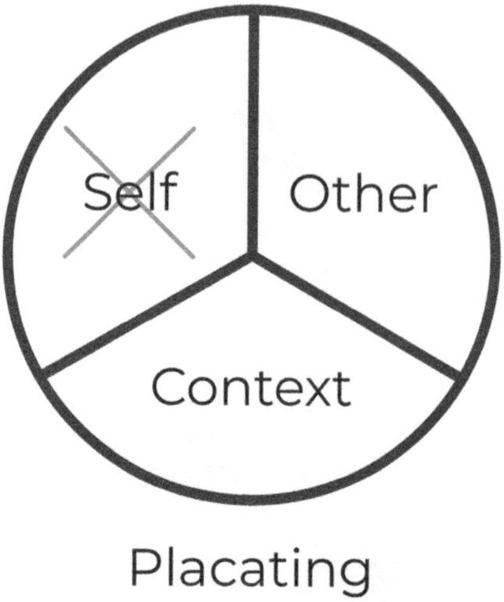

FIGURE 2.9 The Placater Circle

Characteristics of the Placating Stance

Placating often manifests in behaviors shaped by fear of conflict or a desire to maintain relationships at any personal cost. Typical expressions include:

- Apologizing excessively.
- Agreeing outwardly while disagreeing internally.
- Minimizing one's own needs or opinions.
- Soft, hesitant, or deferential speech patterns.
- Submissive or non-threatening body language.

Psychological Underpinnings

Individuals who adopt a Placating stance often grew up in environments where:

- Disagreement was punished or unsafe.
- Needs were dismissed or invalidated.
- Approval was conditional.

As adults, they may experience a diminished sense of self-worth or a learned belief that safety depends on being agreeable or accommodating.

Application in Therapy

With clients who tend toward the Placating stance, therapeutic work focuses on:

- Rebuilding internal legitimacy.
- Increasing self-connection.
- Developing assertiveness.
- Strengthening boundaries.
- Expanding emotional tolerance for relational tension.

Role-playing exercises help individuals practice expressing needs and limits in a safe environment. Internal resourcing, identity work, and esteem-building are central elements of this process.

Placating in Professional Settings

EXAMPLE

A team member, Anna, routinely agrees with her manager's ideas – even when she has concerns or alternative perspectives. She avoids offering her own opinions for fear of negative evaluation or interpersonal conflict.

IMPACT

While this may create temporary harmony, it leads to reduced innovation, hidden resentment, diminished job satisfaction, and unbalanced workloads. The absence of the Self in communication deprives the team of critical insights and prevents genuine collaboration.

APPLICATION

Professional interventions include assertiveness training, boundary-setting, and communication practices that validate the legitimacy of the individual's perspective. Encouraging Anna to voice concerns supports more balanced organizational functioning.

Placating in Personal Relationships

EXAMPLE

In relationships, placating may take the form of deferring to a partner in all decisions, avoiding disagreements, over-apologizing, or assuming responsibility for tensions that are not one's fault.

IMPACT

Over time, this pattern erodes mutuality and authenticity. The placating partner becomes unseen, and the other partner may feel burdened by carrying the emotional and decision-making load.

APPLICATION

Therapeutic work includes helping individuals express preferences, tolerate disagreement, and explore early relational learning about conflict, worth, and safety. Couples work may involve increasing differentiation while strengthening emotional connection.

Strategies for Overcoming the Placating Stance

1. Self-Reflection: Exploring the origins of the stance – fear of conflict, low self-worth, or early relational dynamics.
2. Assertiveness Training: Practicing direct communication and self-expression without apology.
3. Setting Boundaries: Learning to say "no," identifying limits, and reframing boundaries as relationally protective rather than threatening.
4. Role-Playing: Simulating challenging conversations to build confidence and internal permission to speak.
5. Self-Esteem Building: Reinforcing intrinsic self-worth in ways not dependent on external validation.

Biological Modulator: Estrogen and the Placating Stance

While the Placating stance arises primarily from learned patterns of self-protection and relational conditioning, certain hormonal factors may subtly influence its expression. Estrogen, for example, has been linked to affiliative behavior, empathy, and social bonding, which may heighten sensitivity to relational harmony and discomfort with conflict (McCarthy, 1995; Eisenegger et al., 2011). This influence should be understood as one aspect of the person's internal physiological context, not as a determinant of behavior.

Stasis–Kinesis–Flow: Reframing the Placating Stance

Using the Stasis–Kinesis–Flow model:

- Stasis reflects the collapse of the Self – the individual retreats into compliance to avoid perceived danger.
- Kinesis begins when the person reintroduces their own feelings and needs into relational interactions.
- Flow reflects integrated self-expression aligned with relational awareness and authenticity.

Flow Stance: The Power Tree

FIGURE 2.10 The Power Tree Stance

The Flow counterpart to Placating is the Power Tree.

Where Placating suppresses the Self, the Power Tree embodies grounded authenticity, inner stability, and relational presence.

Characteristics include:

- Expressing needs without apology.
- Maintaining flexible yet firm boundaries.
- Remaining present during tension without collapsing or withdrawing.
- Engaging relationally from a centered, rooted sense of Self.

In the Self–Other–Context circle, the Power Tree stance is depicted with all three segments open and balanced, illustrating full congruence.

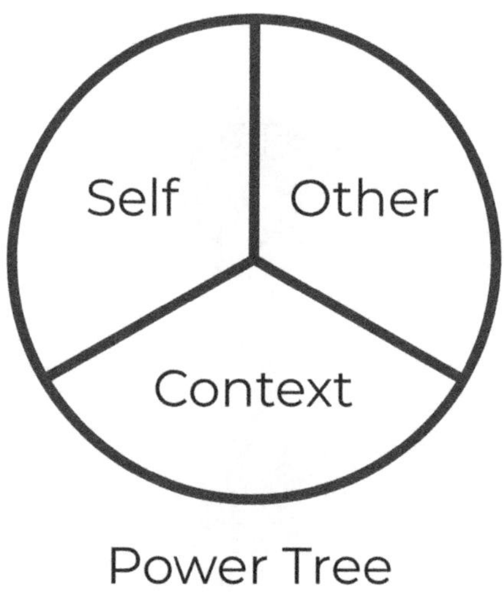

FIGURE 2.11 The Power Tree Circle

The Super-Reasonable Stance

FIGURE 2.12 The Super-Reasonable Stance

The Super-Reasonable stance is a survival pattern characterized by an overreliance on logic, structure, and intellectual reasoning, often at the expense of emotional presence and relational attunement. Individuals adopting this stance seek safety in rationality and distance themselves from emotions – both their own and others'. The internal message becomes: "If I stay rational and controlled, I cannot be hurt."

Within the Self–Other–Context triad introduced earlier, the Super-Reasonable stance reflects a discounting of the emotional dimension of Context. Emotional cues, relational signals, and the affective atmosphere are minimized or disregarded. In the Self–Other–Context circle, the Context segment is marked, indicating withdrawal from emotional information in favor of cognitive certainty.

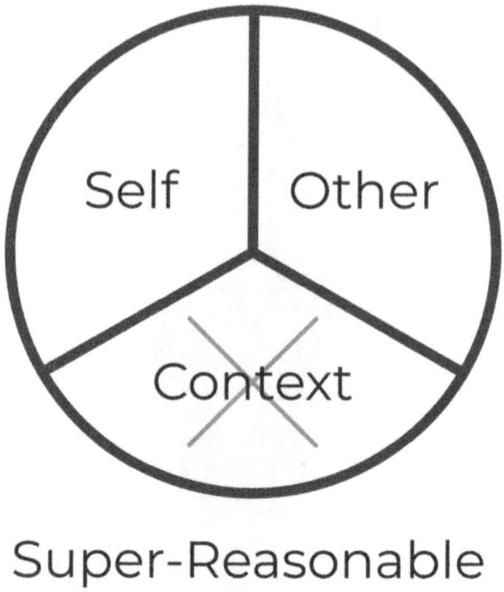

FIGURE 2.13 The Super-Reasonable Circle

Characteristics of the Super-Reasonable Stance

Individuals in this stance prioritize facts, logic, and rationality above emotional connection. Common traits include:

- An emphasis on data, principles, and objective reasoning.
- Detachment from emotional expression or discomfort with emotional intensity.
- A steady, controlled tone even in emotionally charged situations.
- Communication that may be perceived as impersonal or lacking empathy.
- Avoidance of vulnerability or emotional disclosure.

Psychological Underpinnings

This stance often develops in environments where emotions were discouraged, invalidated, or considered disruptive. Over time, individuals may come to believe that emotions are irrational, unreliable, or unsafe. Intellectualization becomes a protective strategy, shielding the person from vulnerability or relational unpredictability.

Application in Therapy

Therapeutic work involves helping clients re-engage with emotional experience and reconnect with their bodies. Useful interventions include:

- Emotional awareness exercises.
- Mindfulness and breathwork.
- Somatic tracking.
- Naming and validating internal states.
- Exploring fears associated with emotional exposure.

The aim is not to diminish the value of logic, but to support an integrated experience in which thoughts and feelings coexist.

The Super-Reasonable in Professional Settings

EXAMPLE

Robert, a manager, addresses workplace challenges exclusively through logical analysis. When team members express emotional concerns, he responds with procedural explanations rather than empathy.

IMPACT

His team may feel unseen or unsupported, leading to reduced morale, increased tension, and a lack of authentic communication. Emotional issues remain unaddressed, even when they significantly influence performance.

APPLICATION

Professional development may involve emotional intelligence training, reflective listening, and relational skills that help leaders like Robert integrate emotional awareness into decision-making and team dynamics.

The Super-Reasonable in Personal Life

EXAMPLE

In intimate relationships, a Super-Reasonable individual may approach conflict by presenting facts, solutions, or logical arguments while neglecting emotional needs. They may remain externally calm while their partner feels invalidated or dismissed.

IMPACT

This may create emotional distance and frustration. Partners can become caught in a cycle where one becomes more analytical and the other more emotional, escalating disconnection.

APPLICATION

Cultivating emotional presence – through active listening, empathy exercises, and mindfulness – helps individuals balance rational clarity with relational connection.

Strategies for Addressing the Super-Reasonable Stance

1. Emotional Awareness: Developing the ability to identify and name emotions in oneself and others.
2. Balancing Logic with Emotion: Valuing emotional information as a valid part of communication and decision-making.
3. Practicing Emotional Expression: Using role-play and structured exercises to gradually increase comfort with emotional disclosure.
4. Understanding the Role of Emotions: Recognizing that emotions inform needs, values, and relational connection—not weaknesses to be eliminated.

These practices help counteract emotional suppression and support movement toward more integrated communication.

Biological Note: Serotonin and Emotional Regulation

While the Super-Reasonable stance primarily reflects psychological and relational learning, certain neurobiological factors may contribute to its expression. Serotonin, a neurotransmitter involved in mood regulation and behavioral inhibition, has been associated with emotional modulation and cognitive control. Variations in serotonin activity may influence a person's tendency to rely on logical processing while dampening access to emotional cues (Young, 2007). This perspective does not reduce behavior to biology; rather, it offers a supplementary lens within the broader internal context influencing coping patterns.

Stasis–Kinesis–Flow: Reframing the Super-Reasonable Stance

Through the Stasis–Kinesis–Flow framework:

- Stasis appears as emotional detachment, rigidity, and over-intellectualization.
- Kinesis begins when the individual reconnects with emotional experience and allows feelings to enter conscious awareness.
- Flow emerges when cognition and emotion become integrated, allowing for grounded, relationally responsive communication.

Flow Stance: The Humble Monk

FIGURE 2.14 The Humble Monk Stance

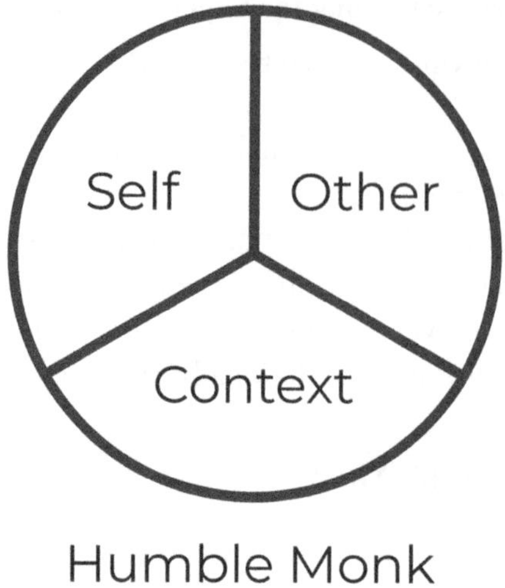

FIGURE 2.15 The Humble Monk Circle

The Flow counterpart to the Super-Reasonable stance is the Humble Monk. This stance retains the clarity, insight, and steadiness of the Super-Reasonable energy but integrates emotional softness, humility, and presence.

The Humble Monk reflects:

- Calm rooted in authenticity rather than suppression.
- Wisdom balanced with empathy.
- Openness to relational nuance.
- Reflective communication that honors both thought and feeling.

In the Self–Other–Context circle, the Humble Monk is represented by all three segments open and balanced, signalling integrated awareness.

The Distracted / Irrelevant Stance

FIGURE 2.16 The Distracted/Irrelevant Stance

The Irrelevant (also called the Distracted) stance is a survival pattern in which individuals divert attention away from uncomfortable emotions, relational tension, or difficult conversations. The person often changes the subject, uses humor, becomes scattered, or shifts into unrelated topics to reduce internal stress. The internal message becomes: "If I distract you and myself, I don't have to feel what is happening."

Within the Self–Other–Context triad, the Irrelevant stance reflects a discounting of Context – specifically the emotional or relational relevance of the moment. The person disconnects from what is actually happening in order to escape discomfort. In the Self–Other–Context circle, the Context segment is marked, indicating a break in the individual's ability to stay present with the emotional or situational reality.

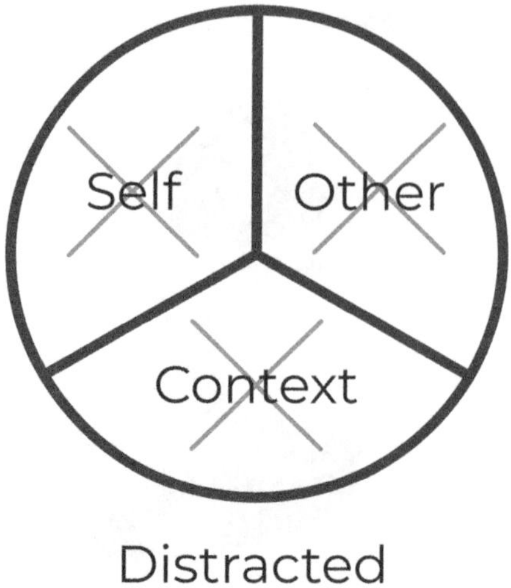

FIGURE 2.17 The Distracted/Irrelevant Circle

Characteristics of the Irrelevant Stance

The Irrelevant stance is characterized by avoidance of direct communication through distraction, humor, or sudden shifts in topic. Common traits include:

- Changing the subject to avoid staying with emotionally charged material.
- Using humor or silliness to deflect seriousness.
- Appearing disconnected or aloof.
- Body language that signals disengagement, restlessness, or fidgeting.
- Difficulty maintaining focus during uncomfortable conversations.

Psychological Underpinnings

This stance often arises from environments where emotional expression was unsafe, where conflict was overwhelming, or where "not being noticed" was a protective strategy. By disrupting the flow of communication, the individual avoids painful feelings or feared consequences of emotional engagement. The stance protects against vulnerability by creating distance from the emotional present.

Application in Therapy

Therapy focuses on bringing gentle awareness to avoidance patterns and building the individual's capacity to tolerate emotional presence. Interventions may include:

- Identifying triggers that lead to distraction.
- Slowing down the moment to notice internal cues.
- Practicing staying with feelings instead of shifting away.
- Developing emotional vocabulary.
- Exploring fears associated with being seen, serious, or emotionally available.

The aim is to help clients experience that staying present is safe and possible.

Irrelevant Stance in Professional Settings

EXAMPLE

Dave, a team member, consistently uses humor whenever discussions become serious or tension arises. While his humor initially lightens the mood, it repeatedly disrupts important conversations.

IMPACT

Dave's avoidance limits the team's capacity to address key concerns, dilutes accountability, and can create frustration or confusion. The emotional tone of the meeting becomes fragmented, preventing cohesive problem-solving.

APPLICATION

Support may include setting clearer expectations for communication, providing space for emotional expression, and training in active listening. Helping Dave recognize when he is avoiding discomfort is a key step toward more grounded and effective participation.

Irrelevant Stance in Personal Relationships

EXAMPLE

In intimate relationships, an individual may steer conversations away from emotional topics with jokes, tangents, or by suddenly shifting to unrelated tasks.

IMPACT

This leads to emotional shallowness, a sense of disconnection, and unresolved issues. Partners may feel dismissed or unimportant, even when the irrelevance is not intentional.

APPLICATION

Creating emotional safety and helping the individual express feelings directly allows deeper connection. Mindfulness, presence exercises, and role-playing difficult conversations support this transition.

Strategies for Addressing the Irrelevant Stance

1. Self-Reflection and Awareness: Recognizing the moments when one diverts or deflects is the first step.
2. Staying Present: Mindfulness practices help individuals remain grounded during discomfort.
3. Expressing Emotions Safely: Practicing emotional sharing in contained, supportive environments increases tolerance for vulnerability.
4. Professional Support: Therapy or coaching can help identify the deeper fears and unmet needs driving the avoidance.
5. Relevance Training: Building the capacity to stay with the actual topic – especially emotional material – strengthens relational depth.

These steps foster greater presence and reduce the need for distraction.

Biological Note: Dopamine and Avoidance–Reward Cycles

Although the Irrelevant stance is grounded primarily in psychological avoidance, dopamine may play a subtle role in reinforcing distraction behaviors. Dopamine is associated with reward, novelty-seeking, and momentary relief from discomfort. Redirecting attention, using humor, or shifting topics can create a quick internal "reward" that temporarily reduces emotional tension, reinforcing the behavior pattern (Schultz, 2007). This influence forms part of the internal context, not a determinant of the stance, and helps explain why distraction can feel momentarily soothing.

Stasis–Kinesis–Flow: Reframing the Irrelevant Stance

- Stasis occurs when the individual habitually escapes emotional presence through distraction.
- Kinesis begins when they notice the impulse to divert and choose to stay engaged.
- Flow appears when the individual can remain present, responsive, and attuned to emotional reality without fleeing into irrelevance.

Flow Stance: The Core Harmonizer

FIGURE 2.18 The Core Harmonizer Stance

The Flow expression of the Irrelevant stance is the Core Harmonizer.

Where irrelevance scatters attention away from the present moment, the Core Harmonizer remains centered, attuned, and grounded in both self and relational reality.

Characteristics include:

- Presence that softens but does not avoid.
- Humor used consciously rather than defensively.
- Capacity to stay with emotional truth.
- Balancing lightness with depth.
- Integrating spontaneity with grounded awareness.

In the Self–Other–Context circle, all three segments are open, reflecting full engagement with the present moment without fleeing or fragmenting.

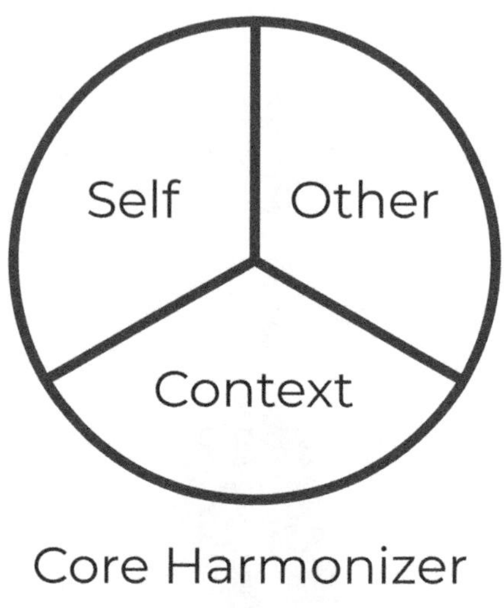

FIGURE 2.19 The Core Harmonizer Cirlce

The Withdrawing Stance

FIGURE 2.20 The Withdrawing Stance

The Withdrawing stance is a survival pattern in which individuals retreat – emotionally, verbally, or physically – from interactions that feel overwhelming or threatening. What may appear as aloofness or disinterest is often a protective response to internal discomfort. The internal message becomes: *"If I pull back, I cannot be hurt..."*

Within the Self–Other–Context triad, the Withdrawing stance reflects a **constriction of Self in relation to Context**. Emotional or relational intensity feels unmanageable, so the individual removes themselves from engagement. In the Self–Other–Context circle, the **Self segment collapses inward**, representing reduced internal presence.

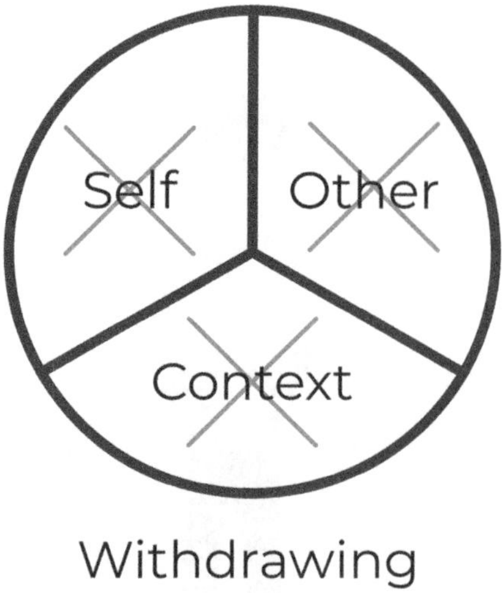

FIGURE 2.21 The Withdrawing Circle

Characteristics of the Withdrawing Stance

Individuals who adopt this stance often:

- Avoid eye contact.
- Offer minimal verbal responses.
- Use closed or protective body language.
- Physically remove themselves from interactions.
- Appear disconnected, numb, or shut down.

Psychological Underpinnings

This stance frequently develops when emotional expression was unsafe or when withdrawal was the only available means of protection. It may reflect early experiences of overwhelm, rejection, or relational unpredictability.

Application in Therapy

Work with withdrawing clients focuses on:

- Creating emotional safety.
- Building tolerance for presence.
- Reconnecting with internal sensation before overwhelm peaks.
- Reintroducing relational engagement slowly and gently.

Therapy emphasizes expanding internal capacity, not forcing expression.

Withdrawing in Professional Settings

EXAMPLE

Emily consistently avoids speaking during team meetings despite having insights to contribute.

IMPACT

Her withdrawal can result in under-recognition of her skills, missed opportunities for contribution, and feelings of isolation.

APPLICATION

A supportive environment, gentle invitation to participate, and reassurance of psychological safety can help her gradually re-engage.

Withdrawing in Personal Relationships

EXAMPLE

During conflict, a partner may become silent, emotionally absent, or physically leave the room.

IMPACT

As emotions remain unspoken, connection erodes. Partners often feel abandoned, while the withdrawing person feels overwhelmed.

APPLICATION

Non-judgmental dialogue, slow pacing, and emotional safety allow for gradual reconnection.

Strategies for Transforming the Withdrawing Stance

1. Self-Reflection: Understanding triggers and the origins of withdrawal.
2. Window of Tolerance Expansion: Using grounding, breathwork, and pacing to stay present longer.
3. Safe Expression: Practicing small steps of communication in low-pressure settings.
4. Supportive Environments: Encouraging relational spaces where the person feels respected and not overwhelmed.
5. Professional Guidance: Addressing deeper fears of inadequacy or emotional overload.

Biological Note: Cortisol and Stress Withdrawal

The Withdrawing stance is primarily psychological, but elevated **cortisol** – the body's primary stress hormone – can intensify feelings of overwhelm and emotional flooding. High or prolonged cortisol activation can increase the urge to retreat or disengage during stressful interactions, reinforcing withdrawal as a coping response (Sapolsky, 2004). This serves as part of the individual's **internal physiological context**, not a determinant of behavior.

Stasis–Kinesis–Flow: Reframing the Withdrawing Stance

- **Stasis**: Protective retreat, emotional shutdown, inward contraction.
- **Kinesis**: Awareness of withdrawal cues; tentative steps toward presence.
- **Flow**: The ability to stay open, connected, and grounded even when emotions intensify.

Flow Stance: The World Hugger

FIGURE 2.22 The World Hugger Stance

The Flow counterpart to the Withdrawing stance is the **World Hugger** – a stance of gentle openness, grounded presence, and relational warmth. Rather than retreating, the individual softens outward, reconnecting internally and externally with safety.

Characteristics include:

- Openness without overwhelm.
- Grounded presence in the body.
- Ability to stay connected during emotional intensity.
- Warmth, empathy, and steady relational engagement.
- Integration of Self, Other, and Context without collapse.

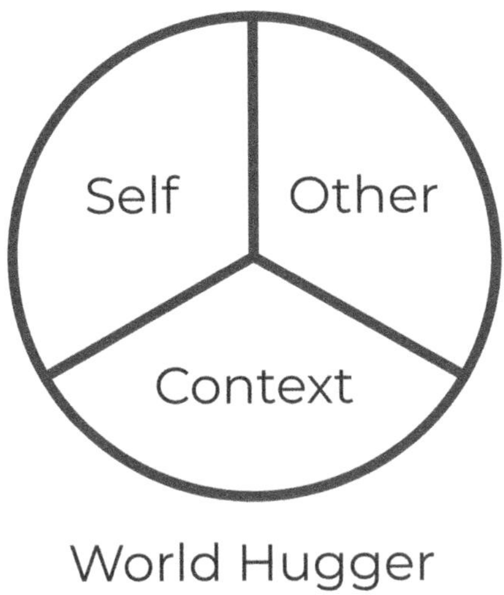

FIGURE 2.23 The World Hugger Circle

Biological Note: Oxytocin and Reconnection

The World Hugger stance aligns with the biological role of **oxytocin,** a neuropeptide associated with bonding, trust, and relational approach. Oxytocin promotes feelings of safety and connection, supporting the shift from guarded withdrawal into open, engaged presence. Its influence can be understood as part of the **internal support** that makes relational reconnection possible – not as a cause, but as a facilitator of the Flow state.

Transition: From Survival to Congruence

Having explored the Surviving Stances and their protective purpose, we now stand at the threshold of a deeper transformation. Satir taught that beneath every defensive pattern lies an unexpressed truth, a yearning for connection, and an innate impulse toward growth. When individuals learn to recognize their stances with compassion and awareness, they begin the essential movement from reacting to responding, from defending to revealing, and from survival to authentic presence. This unfolding marks the beginning of congruence.

The journey from Stasis to Kinesis and ultimately to Flow prepares the ground for what Satir considered the core of therapeutic change: the ability to live, speak, and relate from the Congruent State. It is here that the internal world aligns with external expression, where the Self is fully welcomed, and where transformation becomes not only possible but natural.

With this foundation, we now turn to the Congruent State – the heart of transformation in Satir's model.

Congruent State: The Heart of Transformation

Virginia Satir's vision of transformation goes far beyond improving communication or resolving familial conflicts. At the core of her Growth Model lies the **Congruent State** – a state of being that transcends survival and thriving to reach a harmonious alignment with one's **authentic essence, life-force, and higher Self**. This chapter explores the Congruent State as the cornerstone of transformation, offering a pathway to wholeness, spiritual alignment, and ultimately, transcendence.

Understanding the Congruent State

The **Congruent State** is a dynamic expression of authenticity and harmony. It is the integration of thoughts, emotions, and behaviors into a unified whole, deeply connected to the **"I am" presence**. Congruence is not just about saying what you feel or acting in alignment with your thoughts – it is about living from the essence of your true self. This state reflects a profound connection to the **Source energy**, allowing individuals to embody their highest potential.

In the Congruent State, individuals move beyond the reactive patterns of survival and step into a realm of co-creation. They align with the flow of life's universal principles, experiencing a sense of oneness with the world around them. Congruence fosters **inner peace, clarity, and empowerment**, enabling individuals to navigate life with grace, intention, and purpose.

Characteristics of the Congruent State

- **Authentic Alignment**: Words, thoughts, emotions, and actions resonate in harmony, reflecting the individual's inner truth.
- **Integration of the Self**: The Congruent State brings together all parts of the self, including vulnerabilities, strengths, and past experiences, into a unified whole.
- **Connection to Source**: Individuals experience a deep connection to their life-force and the universal energy that flows through all existence.
- **Empowered Co-creation**: From this state, individuals co-create their reality with intention and clarity, aligned with their higher purpose.
- **Inner Peace and Bliss**: Congruence brings a sense of contentment, fulfillment, and even states of joy and transcendence.

The Congruent State in Therapy

Therapy grounded in the Satir Growth Model sees the promotion of the Congruent State as its ultimate goal. The therapeutic process is a journey of helping clients rediscover their authentic essence, align with their higher Self, and embrace their divine potential. It is about creating the conditions for clients to transition from disconnection and fragmentation to wholeness and harmony.

1. Fostering Inner Awareness

The journey toward congruence begins with **self-awareness**. Clients are guided to recognize their internal world – their thoughts, emotions, sensations, and beliefs. They learn to observe these elements without judgment, uncovering patterns and blockages that inhibit their flow of life-force.

2. **Awakening Emotional and Spiritual Intelligence**

Beyond understanding emotions, clients are encouraged to connect with their deeper essence and the universal energy that sustains them. This step includes practices like centering meditations, mindfulness, and visualization to awaken their **inner life-force** and **higher consciousness**.

3. **Encouraging Authentic Expression**

In therapy, congruence is modeled and practiced. Clients are encouraged to align their internal truth with their outward expression. This involves learning to express their emotions, needs, and desires openly and constructively, without fear or defensiveness. Authentic expression becomes a bridge to deeper connection – with themselves and others.

4. **Releasing Blocks to Growth**

Congruence requires the identification and release of limiting patterns, beliefs, and roles. Therapy helps clients shed these "skins" that no longer serve them, allowing their deeper essence to emerge. This stage focuses on transforming fears, shame, or guilt into acceptance, compassion, and courage.

5. **Integrating Wholeness**

Integration is the culmination of the therapeutic journey. Clients anchor their new insights, practices, and states of consciousness into their daily lives. They embody their "I am"presence, co-creating their reality with intention, harmony, and connection to their Source energy.

Living the Congruent State

The Congruent State is not a destination but a way of being. It is a dynamic process of aligning with one's essence in the face of life's ever-changing circumstances. From this state, individuals experience a profound sense of freedom, empowerment, and joy. They are no longer confined by survival patterns but are free to explore and create their highest possibilities.

Living congruently means embracing the **sacredness of the present moment**, being fully alive to oneself and others, and living in alignment with the universal flow of life. It is the heart of transformation – the path to wholeness, self-actualization, and bliss.

Practical Applications for Transformation

1. **Daily Centering Practices**
   Start each day with a practice that connects you to your life-force, such as a centering meditation, breathing exercises, or journaling.
2. **Authenticity Check-ins**
   Throughout the day, pause and ask: "Am I speaking and acting from my truth? Does this align with my essence?"
3. **Reframing Challenges**
   View obstacles as opportunities to explore deeper layers of your authentic self and connect with Source energy.
4. **Embracing Vulnerability**
   Practice being open and vulnerable with those you trust. Congruence grows when you allow yourself to be fully seen and heard.
5. **Reflection and Integration**
   At the end of each day, reflect on moments of congruence and incongruence. Integrate lessons by reaffirming your commitment to alignment with your true Self.

The Congruent State is the essence of transformation in the Satir Growth Model. It is a gateway to living fully and authentically, connected to the flow of universal energy and one's divine potential. By fostering congruence, we not only heal ourselves but also radiate wholeness and harmony to the world around us. This journey of alignment with the "I am" presence offers a pathway to peace, joy, and the highest states of being.

The Change Process

In the realm of life, where change softly calls,
A journey begins, affecting us all.
From the quiet status quo, where comfort resides,
To the brewing of storms, where growth abides.
A foreign element disrupts the flow,
Challenging the patterns we've come to know.
Resistance arises, clinging to the past,
Fearing the unknown, holding tight, steadfast.
Yet chaos unfolds, a tempest within,
Breaking old patterns, letting growth begin.

Amid the disorder, new visions appear,
A chance for transformation, both profound and clear.
Integration follows, a delicate art,
Weaving the new into every heart.
And soon, a new balance gently takes hold,
A fresh status quo, more vibrant, more bold.
In this cycle of change, Satir's truth remains:
Through life's constant tides, growth always sustains.

Overview of the Satir Change Process

The Satir Change Process is not just a roadmap for navigating life's disruptions but a journey through the profound stages of human and systemic evolution. By integrating the concept of the "fourth birth," this framework transcends traditional change processes, guiding individuals and systems toward self-actualization and higher states of consciousness.

The Four Births

To fully understand the depth of the Satir Change Process, it is essential to contextualize it within the framework of human development as defined by the Four Births:

1. **First Birth: Sperm-Egg Conception**
   This is the physical beginning, the union of cells that marks the inception of life. It represents potentiality – the raw, undifferentiated possibility of what can be.
2. **Second Birth: Physical Birth**
   This marks the emergence of the individual into the world, a transition from being nurtured within the mother's body to existing as a separate entity. It symbolizes the first step into independence and interaction with the external environment.
3. **Third Birth: Taking Responsibility for One's Actions**
   This birth occurs when an individual moves beyond reactive living and begins to take conscious responsibility for their thoughts, behaviors, and choices. It signifies the maturation of self-awareness and the ability to navigate life with intentionality.

4. **Fourth Birth: Awakening to Higher Consciousness**
   The Satir Change Process aligns with this birth, which represents a profound awakening to one's connection with the universal life-force. This stage transcends ego-driven actions and focuses on living in harmony with one's essence and the interconnected whole. It is the realization of self-actualization and congruence.

Late Status Quo

The late status quo represents a stable but often unfulfilling state. Patterns, behaviors, and roles are predictable, providing comfort but also stagnation. While it may feel safe, this stage often masks underlying tensions, unmet needs, and unfulfilled potential.

Description

- **Individuals**: Living on autopilot, stuck in routines that do not challenge personal growth or bring deeper fulfillment.
  Example: A person staying in a job they dislike because it feels secure, even though it limits their creativity and potential.
- **Families**: Families maintaining rigid roles to avoid conflict.
  Example: A family where one parent takes all decision-making responsibility, while others feel unheard but fear rocking the boat.
- **Organizations**: Workplaces relying on outdated processes to maintain a sense of stability.
  Example: A company resisting innovation because the existing system feels reliable, even if it's inefficient.

Foreign Element

The foreign element disrupts the status quo, introducing a challenge or opportunity that forces individuals or systems to confront their current limitations. It can come from external events (e.g., a job loss, illness) or internal realizations (e.g., dissatisfaction with life).

Description

- **Individuals**: An unexpected event or realization compels reflection and adaptation.
  Example: A health scare forces someone to reevaluate their lifestyle choices.

- **Families**: A major life event disrupts established dynamics.
  Example: A teenager challenges traditional parental authority, leading to a need for a new family dynamic.
- **Organizations**: External pressures such as market competition or internal pressures like employee dissatisfaction push the organization to act.
  Example: A new competitor enters the market, threatening the company's dominance.

Resistance

Resistance arises as a natural reaction to the unknown. It reflects fear of losing control, attachment to familiar patterns, or a reluctance to confront deeper truths. This stage is characterized by denial, avoidance, or active pushback against the need for change.

Description

- **Individuals**: Rationalizing or minimizing the need for change to avoid discomfort.
  Example: A person denies the seriousness of a health issue, continuing unhealthy habits.
- **Families**: Avoiding difficult conversations or clinging to outdated roles.
  Example: A family avoids discussing finances after a job loss, maintaining routines as if nothing has changed.
- **Organizations**: Employees resist new processes or leadership due to fear of losing their roles or security.
  Example: Staff push back against a new technology implementation, citing inconvenience.

Chaos

Chaos is the most critical and transformative stage. It is the period where old patterns collapse, and new ones have not yet formed. This stage is often marked by confusion, emotional intensity, and a sense of instability.

Description

- **Individuals**: Struggling with the loss of familiar structures and grappling with uncertainty.

Example: A person feels disoriented after leaving a long-term relationship, unsure of their identity without it.

- **Families**: Communication breakdowns and heightened emotions as old roles are questioned.
  Example: A family experiences conflict as members adjust to a new caregiving role after a parent's illness.
- **Organizations**: Productivity dips as old workflows no longer function, and new ones are not yet established.
  Example: A company undergoing restructuring faces staff confusion and decreased morale.

Transformation

Transformation occurs when individuals or systems begin to access inner resources, reframe their perspectives, and imagine new possibilities. This stage marks the turning point, where creativity and insight replace fear and confusion.

Description

- **Individuals**: Experiencing breakthroughs in understanding and alignment with core values.
  Example: A person realizes they can thrive independently after years of dependence on others for validation.
- **Families**: Finding new ways to connect and support each other authentically.
  Example: A family opens up emotionally after a heartfelt conversation during therapy.
- **Organizations**: Leaders and teams identify innovative solutions and rally around a shared vision.
  Example: A company reinvents itself with a new business model after market disruption.

Integration

Integration involves the gradual adoption of new patterns that align with the lessons of transformation. It is a time of experimentation, adaptation, and refining new behaviors or processes.

Description

- **Individuals**: Practicing habits that align with newfound clarity and purpose.
  Example: A person commits to daily meditation and healthier lifestyle choices.
- **Families**: Developing new traditions and communication styles that reflect the family's growth.
  Example: A family begins holding weekly meetings to check in on each member's needs and feelings.
- **Organizations**: Embedding new systems and processes into the company culture.
  Example: A business adopts flexible work policies to increase employee satisfaction.

New Status Quo

The new status quo reflects a transformed state where individuals, families, or organizations operate with greater alignment, resilience, and connection to their higher purpose. It is not a static endpoint but a foundation for continued growth.

Description

- **Individuals**: Living authentically, with a sense of fulfillment and alignment with core values.
  Example: A person feels empowered in their career and relationships, actively contributing to their community.
- **Families**: Functioning as a cohesive, supportive unit with open communication and mutual respect.
  Example: A family navigates future challenges with confidence and unity after developing healthier dynamics.
- **Organizations**: Thriving with innovation, collaboration, and a clear sense of purpose.
  Example: A company leads its industry with a culture of adaptability and employee engagement.

Application in Various Industries and Fields

Business and Organizational Development

- **Managing Organizational Change**: The model aids businesses in navigating the chaos of mergers, acquisitions, or market shifts, helping leaders and employees adapt to new structures and strategies.
- **Team Dynamics**: Understanding the model helps teams adapt to new leadership, shifts in team composition, or new project requirements.

Healthcare

- **Patient Care and Rehabilitation**: In healthcare settings, the model can guide patients and caregivers through the emotional journey of diagnosis, treatment, and recovery.
- **Healthcare Management**: Administrators can use the model to manage transitions such as policy changes, technological advancements, or shifts in healthcare practices.

Education

- **Curriculum Changes**: Educators can use the model to smoothly integrate new teaching methods or curricular reforms.
- **Student Counseling**: The model can help students navigate personal changes, such as transitioning to higher education or coping with academic pressures.

Personal Development and Coaching

- **Career Transitions**: Individuals can use the model to adapt to new career paths or job roles.
- **Personal Growth**: It aids individuals in personal transformation journeys, helping them embrace and integrate changes in their personal lives.

Technology and Innovation

- **Adapting to Technological Advances**: Helps teams and organizations adapt to rapid technological changes and integrate new systems or processes.
- **Product Development**: Useful in managing the lifecycle of product development from conception through launch and adaptation.

Counseling and Social Work

- **Family Therapy**: Originally developed for this field, it helps families navigate through changes like divorce, loss, or behavioral issues.
- **Community Development**: Useful in managing social changes, community programs, or interventions.

Environmental and Social Change

- **Adapting to Environmental Shifts**: Helps communities and organizations adapt to changes due to environmental factors or policies.
- **Social Movements**: Can guide the progression and adaptation strategies of social movements and advocacy campaigns.

Government and Public Policy

- **Policy Implementation**: Assists in managing the public and institutional response to new policies or reforms.
- **Crisis Management**: Useful in navigating the phases of crisis response and recovery at a communal or governmental level.

The universality of the Satir Change Process lies in its ability to articulate the emotional and psychological journey through change. By understanding and applying its stages, individuals and organizations across various fields can navigate the uncertainties of change more effectively, leading to growth, innovation, and improved resilience. This model offers a lens through which the challenges of change can be understood and managed constructively.

The Johnson Family Example

Stage 1: Old Status Quo

Background: The Johnson family, like many others, found themselves in a routine pattern of interaction. Each member played their role, maintaining a delicate balance.

Mr. Johnson: We've always done things this way. It's not perfect, but it's our normal.

Me: It sounds like you've established a familiar pattern. What feelings lie beneath this "normal?"

Stage 2: Introduction of a Foreign (Enriching) Element

The Shift: A significant event occurred – Mrs. Johnson lost her job. This unexpected change disrupted their established patterns.

Mrs. Johnson: I feel like I've let everyone down. Everything's changed.

Me: This change, as difficult as it is, can also be an opportunity. Let's explore what this means for each of you.

Stage 3: Resistance to the Foreign Element

Initial Reactions: The family resisted this new reality, clinging to their old patterns in an attempt to regain a sense of normalcy. This resistance created tension as each member struggled to accept the changes.

Mr. Johnson: I don't see why we have to change everything. We've always managed just fine.

Teenage Daughter: Why does everything have to be different? I just want things to go back to how they were.

Me: Resistance is a natural response to change. It's the mind's way of holding onto what feels familiar and safe, but it can also keep us stuck.

Stage 4: Chaos

As the family grappled with this new reality, their interactions became more erratic. The once stable family dynamics were now in a state of flux.

Teenage Daughter: Nothing's the same anymore. Mom's always stressed, and Dad's trying too hard to keep things normal.

Me: It's natural to feel unsettled when familiar patterns are disrupted. Let's navigate this chaos together, finding new ways to connect and support each other.

Stage 5: Transformation

The Turning Point: In this pivotal stage, the family began to shift their perspective. Emotional breakthroughs occurred as they embraced vulnerability and explored their inner resources. This was the moment they began to see the potential for growth amid the disruption.

Mrs. Johnson: I've been so focused on what I lost that I didn't see the opportunity to try something new.

Teenage Daughter: Maybe we could do things differently and make it better.

Me: This is the moment where transformation begins. By releasing old patterns and opening up to new possibilities, you're discovering your capacity to grow as a family.

Stage 6: Integration of the Foreign Element

Through therapy, the Johnsons began to integrate this change into their lives, finding new ways to relate to one another.

Mr. Johnson: Maybe this is a chance for us to rethink how we do things as a family.

Me: Exactly. This integration is about creating a new understanding and a new normal that includes this change.

Stage 7: New Status Quo

Gradually, a new pattern emerged, one that acknowledged and embraced the changes they had experienced.

Mrs. Johnson: Losing my job was hard, but it's also brought us closer. We communicate more openly now.

Me: You've navigated through the chaos and transformation and have arrived at a new status quo, one that reflects your growth and resilience as a family.

The Johnsons' journey through the Satir Change Process is a testament to the power of embracing change. It highlights how disruptions, while challenging, can lead to a deeper understanding of ourselves and our relationships. This model not only maps the process of change but also offers hope and a pathway to navigate through life's inevitable upheavals.

The Anderson Family Example

Stage 1: Late Status Quo

Background: The Andersons were a close-knit family, content with their familiar routines. Each member had a well-defined role, and there was a sense of predictability in their daily lives.

Tom: Our life wasn't perfect, but it was ours. We had our rhythm, and it worked for us.

Me: It sounds like you found comfort in that stability. How did that routine make you feel safe?

Stage 2: Introduction of a Foreign Element

Tom's sudden diagnosis of a chronic illness brought an unanticipated disruption. This news shook the foundation of the Anderson family's well-established structure, making the future feel uncertain.

Mrs. Anderson: I've always been the one who managed everything, but now I don't know what to do. I feel lost.

Me: Change often brings feelings of loss and uncertainty. Let's explore what this shift means for each of you, and how it impacts your family's dynamic.

Stage 3: Resistance to the Foreign Element

At first, the Andersons resisted acknowledging the impact of Tom's diagnosis. Each family member tried to hold onto their old patterns, refusing to fully face the new reality.

Tom: I don't want to depend on anyone. I'm used to being the strong one. I'm not ready for this.

Teenage Son: Why does this have to change everything? Can't we just keep things the way they were?

Me: It's normal to want to hold onto what feels familiar. But resisting change can create even more tension. How might it feel to start opening up to what's really happening?

Stage 4: Chaos

As the family struggled to reconcile with the changes, their usual ways of interacting no longer seemed effective. Tension mounted as everyone tried to maintain control while the old structure crumbled.

Teenage Daughter: Mom's stressed all the time, Dad's pretending nothing's wrong, and it feels like nobody knows what to do anymore.

Me: When the old ways of functioning stop working, it can feel chaotic. Let's explore new ways to communicate and support one another in this uncertain time.

Stage 5: Transformation

The Turning Point: In this pivotal stage, the Andersons began to shift their perspective. Breakthroughs occurred as they embraced vulnerability and tapped into their inner resources.

Tom: I've been hiding how scared I am because I didn't want to worry anyone, but I realize that's only made things harder.

Me: By sharing your fears, you're allowing your family to be there for you. You're also modeling vulnerability, which can create space for deeper connection. How does that feel for you?

Teenage Son: Hearing Dad talk about being scared makes me feel like we're all in this together.

Stage 6: Integration of the Foreign Element

Gradually, the Andersons began to integrate the reality of Tom's condition into their lives. They started to express their fears, frustrations, and needs more openly, creating new patterns of relating to one another.

Tom: I've been hiding how scared I am because I didn't want to worry anyone, but I realize that's only made things harder.

Me: By sharing your fears, you're allowing your family to be there for you. You're also modeling vulnerability, which can create space for deeper connection. How does that feel for you?

Teenage Son: Hearing Dad talk about being scared makes me feel like we're all in this together.

Stage 7: New Status Quo

Eventually, the Anderson family found a new rhythm. Though their life had changed, they discovered a renewed sense of connection by embracing vulnerability and supporting one another through the challenge.

Mrs. Anderson: We've learned to lean on each other in a way we never did before. This has brought us closer, even though it was hard.

Me: You've navigated through the chaos and found a new way of being together. This new normal is a reflection of your family's resilience and strength.

The Andersons' experience highlights how challenging disruptions can ultimately deepen relationships. By embracing the process, they moved from resistance and chaos to a place of greater openness and connection. The Satir Change Process provided a roadmap for them to navigate the complexities of change, transforming not only their family dynamic but their understanding of one another.

Integration of the Change Process and Iceberg Metaphor

Virginia Satir's Iceberg Metaphor provides a profound understanding of human behavior by revealing how deeper, often hidden layers of emotions, perceptions, and beliefs influence our visible actions. When combined with the Satir Change Process, these two frameworks offer a comprehensive approach to understanding and navigating change.

- **Late Status Quo (Iceberg's Surface and Depths Unexplored)**: In the Late Status Quo, observable behaviors – the tip of the iceberg – reflect the stability and routines individuals or families have established. Below the surface, deeper layers of feelings, perceptions, beliefs, values, and yearnings remain unexamined but actively support the existing patterns. These hidden aspects contribute to the maintenance of the status quo, even if it's dysfunctional.

- **Behavior**: What we see on the surface – how people act in predictable, familiar ways.
- **Feelings and Feelings About Feelings**: Emotions and judgments about those emotions remain unspoken, buried below the surface.
- **Perceptions, Beliefs, Values, Yearnings**: The deeper reasons behind behaviors – beliefs, perceptions, and unmet yearnings – keep individuals and families locked in habitual patterns.
- *Example*: A family might avoid difficult conversations, driven by unacknowledged feelings of fear or the belief that conflict should be avoided at all costs.

- **Introduction of a Foreign Element (Disruption of the Iceberg's Balance)**: When a foreign element (such as a sudden change or new realization) disrupts the status quo, the surface behaviors begin to break down, and the deeper layers of the iceberg are forced to rise to awareness. This disruption reveals underlying emotions, beliefs, and values that were previously hidden.
  - **Behavior**: Behaviors start to change or falter as the foreign element disrupts routines.
  - **Feelings**: The hidden emotions beneath the surface, such as fear or insecurity, begin to surface.
  - **Feelings About Feelings**: Individuals may experience discomfort or resistance to their own feelings, leading to internal conflict.
  - **Perceptions, Beliefs, Values, Yearnings**: The foreign element challenges existing beliefs or perceptions, creating a conflict between old ways of thinking and new realities.
  - *Example*: A job loss disrupts the family's financial stability, surfacing underlying fears of inadequacy or failure.
- **Resistance to the Foreign Element (Struggling to Maintain the Iceberg's Old Shape)**: As the foreign element continues to challenge the old ways of functioning, individuals resist the change.

Resistance manifests as attempts to hold onto familiar behaviors and avoid confronting the deeper emotional and perceptual shifts happening beneath the surface.

- o **Behavior**: Attempts to cling to old routines or ways of coping, even though they no longer work.
- o **Feelings**: Anxiety, frustration, and fear arise as individuals resist confronting uncomfortable emotions.
- o **Feelings About Feelings**: Individuals may feel guilty or ashamed about their emotions, reinforcing resistance.
- o **Perceptions, Beliefs, Values, Yearnings**: Long-held perceptions and beliefs (e.g., "I need to be strong" or "change is bad") clash with the reality of the situation, making it harder to accept the foreign element.
- o *Example*: A family resists accepting a loved one's illness, clinging to routines that are no longer sustainable.

- **Chaos (the Iceberg's Hidden Layers Erupt)**: As resistance becomes unsustainable, the system descends into chaos. Old behaviors no longer work, and individuals are forced to confront the deeper layers of their iceberg. Emotions become turbulent, and previously hidden beliefs, values, and yearnings surface in unexpected ways.

  - o **Behavior**: Confusion and erratic behaviors emerge as the old system unravels.
  - o **Feelings**: Raw emotions – fear, anger, sadness – bubble to the surface.
  - o **Feelings About Feelings**: People may feel overwhelmed, unsure how to manage their emotions, and may express frustration with themselves or others.
  - o **Perceptions, Beliefs, Values, Yearnings**: As old perceptions and beliefs crumble, individuals question their core values and yearnings, trying to make sense of the disruption.
  - o *Example*: Family members may react unpredictably, arguing or withdrawing as deep-seated fears and unmet needs surface, creating emotional chaos.

- **Integration of the Foreign Element (Rebuilding the Iceberg's Structure)**: In the integration phase, individuals begin to consciously align their behaviors with the deeper changes that are happening within them. They experiment with new ways of relating to their feelings, perceptions, and beliefs, reshaping their inner iceberg. This alignment allows for healthier, more adaptive behaviors to emerge.
    - **Behavior**: New behaviors that reflect a greater awareness of underlying feelings and beliefs begin to take shape.
    - **Feelings**: Emotions are acknowledged and expressed more openly, reducing the emotional turbulence of the chaos stage.
    - **Feelings About Feelings**: Individuals start to accept their feelings without judgment, creating space for healing.
    - **Perceptions, Beliefs, Values, Yearnings**: As beliefs and perceptions realign with the new reality, individuals find clarity about their core values and begin to act in ways that honor their yearnings.
    - *Example*: A family begins to communicate more openly about their fears and needs, finding new ways to support each other in the face of a difficult diagnosis.
- **New Status Quo (a Reformed Iceberg)**: At this final stage, the iceberg has been restructured to support new behaviors and interactions. The family or individual has created a new equilibrium, one that reflects the growth, insights, and emotional shifts that occurred during the change process. This new status quo is more adaptable, resilient, and reflective of the deeper layers of feelings, beliefs, and values.
    - **Behavior**: Healthier, more congruent behaviors emerge, supported by a deeper understanding of oneself and others.
    - **Feelings**: Emotions are expressed more freely, and there is greater emotional safety within the family or system.
    - **Feelings About Feelings**: Individuals feel more accepting of their own and others' emotional experiences, reducing internal conflict.

- **Perceptions, Beliefs, Values, Yearnings**: The new beliefs and perceptions that have emerged align with core values and yearnings, leading to a more fulfilling and harmonious state of being.
- *Example*: The family creates a new way of living that supports open communication, emotional expression, and mutual support, adapting to the challenges they've faced together.

Application in Various Contexts

- **Individual Therapy**: Therapists can use this combined model to help clients understand how their visible behaviors (reactions to change) are deeply connected to their inner world (feelings, perceptions). It aids in processing and integrating changes such as life transitions, personal crises, or behavioral modifications.
- **Organizational Change**: In businesses or organizations, this model helps in mapping the journey through organizational changes like mergers, policy shifts, or leadership changes. It underscores how surface-level changes in processes or structures are underpinned by the collective emotions, perceptions, and attitudes of the workforce.
- **Personal Development**: For individuals seeking personal growth, this integrated model offers a roadmap for understanding how their responses to life changes are rooted in deeper emotional and cognitive layers. It guides them through the process of aligning their internal beliefs and feelings with their external actions and behaviors.

The fusion of the Change Process with the Iceberg Metaphor creates a powerful tool for understanding the complexity of change. It highlights the importance of addressing both the visible and invisible aspects of change, providing a holistic approach to managing transitions, growth, and transformation in various areas of life. This combined framework offers invaluable insights into the dynamic interplay between our inner experiences and outer expressions, especially during times of change.

Ingredients of Interaction

In every relationship, communication is the foundation that either fosters connection or creates distance. Virginia Satir's work emphasizes that how we interact with others shapes the quality of our relationships, our self-esteem, and our personal growth. The Ingredients of Interaction framework, outlined in The Satir Growth Model and *The New Peoplemaking*, helps us break down the processes that underlie communication, allowing for greater awareness and improvement in how we relate to one another.

This chapter delves into the key ingredients that shape interactions and provides practical guidance on how to apply these concepts in therapeutic settings and everyday life.

Satir identified seven key ingredients that form the basis of all interactions:

1. **The Message**: What you see and hear, the factual observation.
2. **The Meaning**: The interpretation or meaning you assign to what you observed.
3. **Feelings About the Meaning**: The emotional response triggered by the meaning.
4. **Feelings About Your Feelings**: Secondary emotions triggered by your primary feelings, often tied to self-judgment or family rules.
5. **Defenses**: The coping mechanisms that surface to protect your vulnerability.
6. **Rules for Commenting**: The internal guidelines that determine how and whether you express your thoughts and feelings.
7. **Response**: The final behavior or verbal expression seen and heard by others.

Let's explore each of these ingredients in greater depth, considering their role in shaping interactions and the dynamics of communication in therapeutic settings.

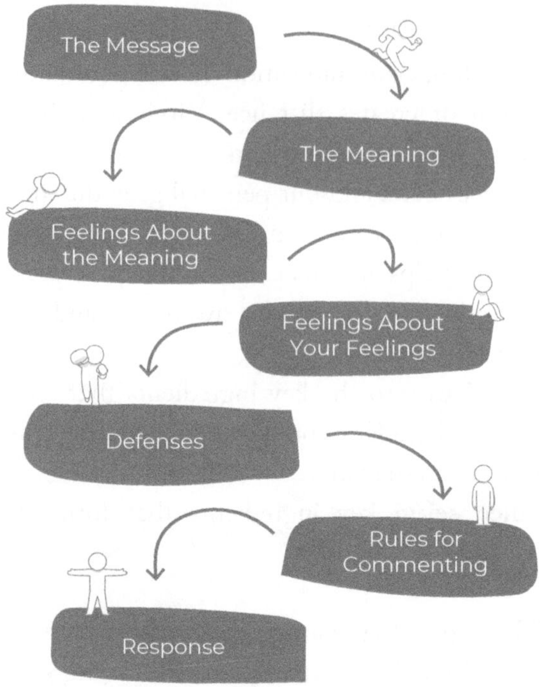

FIGURE 2.24 Ingredients of Interaction

1. The Message: What You See and Hear

Every interaction begins with the messages we receive through our senses – what we see, hear, and sometimes even taste, touch, or smell. However, these messages are often filtered by internal and external barriers, such as personal biases, emotions, and past experiences.

In *The New Peoplemaking*, Satir emphasizes the importance of separating objective observation from interpretation. This distinction is crucial in avoiding premature judgments or assumptions. Before assigning meaning to an interaction, we must ask ourselves: *What do I actually see and hear, without adding my own interpretation?*

Clinical Application

In therapy, this step encourages clients to first describe their experiences objectively. For example, rather than stating "My partner never listens to me," a client might be guided to say, "When I spoke to my partner yesterday, they looked at their phone instead of making eye contact." This helps to clarify the message and lays a factual foundation before emotional layers are added.

2. *The Meaning: What Interpretation Do You Make?*

Once we receive a message, we instantly assign meaning to it. However, the meaning we give to an interaction is often shaped by our past experiences, family-of-origin patterns, and self-esteem. These underlying influences can distort the meaning, leading to misunderstandings or conflict.

Satir often pointed out that our family background plays a major role in how we interpret interactions. A person who grew up in an environment where they were constantly criticized may interpret neutral feedback as an attack. It is crucial in therapy to help clients differentiate between the actual message and the meaning they have constructed.

Clinical Application

Therapists can guide clients through exercises that explore how past experiences shape present interpretations. By bringing awareness to these patterns, clients can begin to separate old beliefs from current reality, leading to more accurate meanings.

3. *Feelings About the Meaning*

Feelings naturally follow from the meaning we make of an interaction. It is important to note that feelings are not a direct result of what we saw or heard; they are a response to the meaning we assigned to the message.

For example, if a client interprets a partner's silence as indifference, feelings of hurt or anger may arise. However, if they assign the meaning that their partner is simply tired, their emotional response might be more compassionate. The challenge lies in becoming aware of the emotions triggered by our interpretations, not by the objective message.

Clinical Application

Encouraging clients to explore their feelings in response to the meanings they have constructed is key. The therapist can ask, "*What feelings are coming up for you based on the meaning you've made of this situation?*" This helps clients connect their emotional responses with the interpretations they hold.

4. *Feelings About Your Feelings*

Our feelings are often followed by a secondary emotional layer – how we feel about the feelings we are experiencing. These "feelings about feelings" are frequently tied to family rules or personal judgments about which emotions are acceptable.

For instance, someone may feel angry, but then immediately feel guilty for feeling that way, especially if they were taught that anger is unacceptable. Satir called attention to this secondary emotional layer, noting that it often exacerbates emotional distress. Recognizing and accepting feelings without judgment is a crucial step in congruent communication.

Clinical Application

Therapists can guide clients to explore whether they are judging themselves for their emotions. By asking, "*How do you feel about feeling angry (or sad, or afraid)?*" clients become more aware of their emotional layers and can begin to release unnecessary judgments.

5. *Defenses*

When our feelings or our feelings about feelings are uncomfortable, we often activate defenses to protect ourselves. Satir identified four main defense mechanisms: blaming, placating, being super-reasonable, or becoming irrelevant. These coping stances are survival strategies developed in childhood to manage difficult emotions or situations.

These defenses, however, often block authentic connection and congruent communication. When clients become aware of their defenses, they can begin to explore healthier ways to express themselves without needing to shield their vulnerability.

Clinical Application

Therapists can help clients recognize their default defense mechanisms and explore when these defenses are triggered. Through this awareness, clients can learn to pause, acknowledge their emotional reactions, and choose a more authentic, congruent response.

6. *Rules for Commenting*

The rules we follow when expressing ourselves are often learned in our families of origin. These rules – whether explicit or implicit – govern how open we are in communication, how assertive we feel we can be, and how much we are willing to reveal to others.

In therapy, uncovering these internalized rules is important for creating new, more flexible patterns of communication. Satir emphasized that understanding and transforming these rules allows individuals to make more conscious choices about how they express themselves.

Clinical Application

A therapist might ask, "*What rules did you grow up with about expressing emotions or needs?*" By identifying these family rules, clients can start to examine whether they still serve them, and whether they can adapt or release these rules to foster healthier communication.

7. *External Response: Congruent or Incongruent?*

The final ingredient in interaction is the external response – what others see and hear from you. If the previous steps are processed mindfully, the response is likely to be *congruent*, meaning it accurately reflects the person's true thoughts and feelings. If defenses are at play or emotions are suppressed, the response may be *incongruent*, leading to miscommunication and frustration.

Congruent communication allows for authentic connection and resolution of conflict. It invites clarity and openness, rather than defensiveness and misinterpretation.

Clinical Application

In therapy, clients can practice congruent responses by slowing down and processing each step of the interaction. Through role-play, reflection, or guided dialogue, they can learn to express themselves in ways that align with their true emotions and intentions.

Mastering the Ingredients of Interaction

By breaking down the complex process of interaction into these seven ingredients, we gain a clearer understanding of how communication succeeds or breaks down. Satir's framework provides therapists and clients alike with a powerful tool for improving interactions, fostering self-awareness, and building stronger relationships.

In your work with clients, encourage them to practice this process in their daily interactions. As they become more mindful of the ingredients of interaction, they will be better equipped to communicate with clarity, empathy, and congruence – ultimately transforming their relationships and their sense of self.

Case Study: Ingredients of Interaction in Practice

Therapist:	Sarah, today I'd like to introduce you to a tool developed by Virginia Satir called the Ingredients of Interaction. This model will help us break down an interaction into its various components, such as the context, the meaning you made from the event, and the feelings that arose. By dissecting these elements, we can gain deeper insight into how and why certain interactions unfold the way they do. Would you like to apply this to the recent disagreement you had at work?
Sarah:	Sure, that sounds interesting. Let's give it a try.
Therapist (exploring Context):	Let's begin with the Context. Can you describe the setting and circumstances of the disagreement?
Sarah:	It happened during a team meeting about a project I'm leading. We were discussing the current progress and some potential changes to the plan.

Therapist's Note: The context sets the stage for understanding how external factors like environment, roles, or power dynamics may have influenced Sarah's experience. In this case, the professional setting and Sarah's leadership role likely contributed to the emotional weight of the interaction.

Therapist (exploring Message):	Now, let's focus on the Message – what was actually said or done, without any interpretation or judgment. Can you recount the factual details?
Sarah:	One of my colleagues suggested we change a few aspects of the project. They pointed out some potential issues with the current plan.

Therapist's Note: Separating the objective facts from interpretations helps Sarah examine the interaction without the emotional charge attached to it. This distinction is key to creating a clear foundation for deeper exploration.

Therapist (exploring Feelings):	What Feelings came up for you in response to your colleague's suggestion?
Sarah:	I felt criticized. It made me feel like I wasn't doing a good enough job, and that my leadership was being questioned.

Therapist's Note: Identifying the feelings is crucial for recognizing the emotional impact of the interaction. Sarah's feeling of being criticized speaks to her deeper concerns about her role and performance.

Therapist (exploring Feelings About Feelings):	And what were your Feelings about those Feelings? How did you feel about experiencing that sense of criticism?
Sarah:	I was frustrated with myself for feeling that way. I kept thinking that I should be more confident and not let things like this get to me.

Therapist's Note: This step uncovers the secondary emotional layer – Sarah's frustration with her initial emotional response. Often, feelings about feelings reveal underlying issues of self-judgment or unmet expectations of how one "should" feel.

Therapist (exploring Meaning): What Meaning did you assign to your colleague's suggestion? What did it represent to you?

Sarah: I interpreted it as them doubting my ability to lead the project. It felt like they thought I wasn't good enough for the role.

Therapist's Note: The meaning Sarah attached to the event is deeply personal, shaped by her beliefs about herself and her role as a leader. This meaning may differ greatly from the actual intention behind her colleague's suggestion, revealing how subjective interpretations can color interactions.

Therapist (exploring Underlying Beliefs): Let's take a moment to explore your Underlying Perceptions and Beliefs. How do you think these beliefs about yourself influenced the meaning you made of the interaction?

Sarah: I've always felt like I need to be perfect to earn respect. So any kind of criticism, even if it's constructive, makes me feel like a failure.

Therapist's Note: By examining Sarah's core beliefs, we can see how her perception of needing to be perfect impacts her reactions to feedback. This belief heightens her emotional response and distorts the meaning she assigns to neutral or even helpful suggestions.

Therapist (exploring Coping Mechanisms):	When you felt criticized, how did you respond? What Coping Mechanisms came into play?
Sarah:	I shut down the conversation and became defensive. I didn't want to hear any more suggestions because it just felt like an attack.

Therapist's Note: Sarah's defense mechanism – shutting down and becoming defensive – served as a protective strategy to shield herself from feelings of inadequacy. However, this response also limited her ability to engage with her colleague in a constructive way.

Therapist (introducing New Perspectives):	Considering everything we've discussed so far, what New Perspectives can you adopt when you face similar situations in the future?
Sarah (reflective):	Maybe I can start seeing feedback as a way to improve rather than as a criticism of my abilities. It could be an opportunity for growth rather than a personal attack.

Therapist's Note: Helping Sarah shift her perspective opens the door to more empowering interpretations. This shift from feeling personally attacked to viewing feedback as a growth opportunity can fundamentally change her responses in future interactions.

Therapist (discussing Change of Behavior):	How might this new perspective influence your *Behavior* in future interactions? What could you do differently the next time you encounter a similar situation?

Sarah: I could try to remain open to feedback, ask questions to clarify, and not immediately assume it's a criticism. Instead of getting defensive, I could take a moment to process what's being said and respond more thoughtfully.

Therapist's Note: Encouraging Sarah to reflect on her future behavior helps translate her insights into concrete actions. Planning these new responses allows her to practice healthier communication and congruent interactions moving forward.

Therapist (concluding with encouragement): Sarah, today we've used the Ingredients of Interaction to break down your experience at work. You've gained some valuable insights into your emotional responses and coping mechanisms, as well as some new ways of approaching feedback. Let's continue to explore and practice these elements so that you can feel more confident and empowered in your future interactions, both professionally and personally.

Final Therapist's Note: In future sessions, we will support Sarah in integrating these new perspectives and behaviors into her daily life. The goal will be to reinforce her ability to respond to interactions with greater openness, self-awareness, and congruence.

References

Eisenegger, C., Haushofer, J., Fehr, E. (2011). The role of testosterone in social interaction. *Trends in Cognitive Sciences*, *15*(6), 263–271.

Mazur, A., Booth, A. (1998). Testosterone and dominance in men. *Behavioral and Brain Sciences*, *21*(3), 353–397.

McCarthy, M.M. (1995). Estrogen modulation of oxytocin and its relation to behavior. *Advances in Experimental Medicine and Biology*, 395, 235–245.

Satir, V. (1988). *The New Peoplemaking*. Palo Alto, CA: Science and Behavior Books, Inc.
Sapolsky, R.M. (2004). *Why Zebras Don't Get Ulcers* (3rd ed.). New York: Henry Holt.
Schultz, W. (2007). Multiple dopamine functions at different time courses. *Annual Review of Neuroscience*, 30, 259–288.
Young, S.N. (2007). How to increase serotonin in the human brain without drugs. *Journal of Psychiatry and Neuroscience*, *32*(6), 394–399.

3

PRACTICAL APPLICATIONS

Triads in Therapeutic Practice

The concept of triads in therapy refers to a three-person interactional system. This model, rooted in systemic therapy, offers unique insights into relational dynamics and communication patterns. Triads can be used effectively in both group and individual therapy settings, providing a versatile tool for therapists and clients alike (Satir, 1967).

The Importance of Triads

- **Dynamic Interaction**: Triads introduce a dynamic interactional pattern that is more representative of real-world relationships than one-on-one interactions.
- **Diverse Perspectives**: They offer multiple viewpoints, enhancing understanding and empathy among participants.
- **Conflict Resolution**: Triads can simulate conflict situations, allowing for the exploration and resolution of interpersonal issues.
- **Role Flexibility**: Participants in a triad can alternate roles, gaining insights into different relational positions.

DOI: 10.4324/9781003716419-3

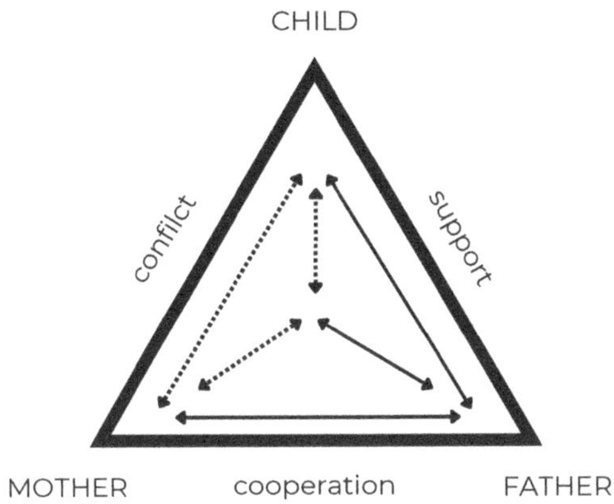

FIGURE 3.1 Triads in Therapeutic Practice

Triads in Group Work

- **Setting Up**: Form triads within the group, ideally with varying combinations over time to explore different dynamics.
- **Role Assignments**: Assign roles such as speaker, listener, and observer. Rotate these roles to give each member the experience of different perspectives.
- **Focused Interventions**: Use triads for specific exercises like role-playing, conflict resolution, or communication skills training.
- **Debriefing**: After the triad exercise, facilitate a group discussion to share insights and learning points.

Triads in Individual Therapy

- **Imaginary Triads**: Use chairs or symbols to represent significant others or different aspects of the client's inner or outer system (e.g. their inner parts or elements of their life).
- **Role-Playing**: The therapist and client can take on different roles in the triad, with an empty chair representing the third party.
- **Exploring Relationships**: Use the triad setup to explore the client's relationships with family, friends, or colleagues.
- **Dynamic Exploration**: Encourage clients to move between the chairs, experiencing and articulating the perspective of each position.

Techniques and Strategies

- **Reflective Listening**: In a triad, one member speaks, another listens, and the third observes, fostering deep listening and reflection.
- **Feedback Loop**: The observer provides feedback on the interaction, offering insights into communication patterns and relational dynamics.
- **Conflict Role-Play**: Simulate conflicts in the safety of the therapeutic setting, allowing for exploration and skill-building in managing disagreements.
- **Empathy Building**: Switching roles within the triad can foster empathy and a deeper understanding of others' perspectives.

Scientific Foundations

- **Systemic Theory**: Triads in therapy are rooted in systemic theory, emphasizing that individual behavior is part of a larger interactional system. The triad format mimics real-life social systems, providing a microcosm for exploration and intervention.
- **Communication Patterns**: Research in family systems therapy shows that triads can reveal complex communication patterns and alliances that may not be apparent in dyadic interactions.
- **Psychodrama Techniques**: The use of triads aligns with psychodrama techniques, offering a stage for enacting and resolving conflicts, a method shown to be effective in various therapeutic settings.

Integrating Satir's Models

- **Satir's Communication Stances**: Use triads to demonstrate Satir's communication stances (blamer, placater, computer, distracter, and withdrawer). This helps clients understand and shift their communication patterns.
- **Self Esteem and Congruence**: Utilize triads to explore self-esteem issues and congruence in communication. This is particularly effective in highlighting how clients present themselves versus their authentic feelings (Brothers, 1990; Lee, 2002).

Enhancing Techniques

- **Mirroring and Resonating**: In triads, use mirroring (reflecting emotions) and resonating (sharing similar experiences) to deepen empathy and connection.
- **Coping Strategies**: Explore different coping strategies within the triad setup. This can reveal how clients adapt to stressful interactions and how they can develop healthier coping mechanisms.
- **Cultural Considerations**: Adapt triads to reflect cultural dynamics and nuances, respecting diverse communication styles and family structures.

Example: Realigning Family Communication

Background: A family session involving a father, mother, and teenage daughter with communication breakdowns.

Therapist:	Let's try a role reversal. Daughter, you will play your father, and vice versa. Let's enact a typical family discussion.
Daughter (as Father):	Why haven't you finished your homework yet? You're always on your phone.
Father (as Daughter):	You don't understand me. School is hard, and I need some space.
Therapist:	Pause here. What did you each notice about being in the other's role?
Daughter:	It's stressful to be dad, always worrying.
Father:	I didn't realize how pressured she feels.

This exercise, part of the triadic interaction, brought new understanding and empathy into the family dynamics, following principles reminiscent of Satir's transformative work.

Advanced Applications and Case Studies

Case Study: Family Dynamics

- **Background**: A family therapy session where a triad consisting of a parent, a teenager, and a grandparent was formed.
- **Application**: Each member expressed their perspective on a family issue. The therapist guided the triad through Satir's communication stances, revealing underlying dynamics.
- **Outcome**: The exercise unearthed hidden emotional undercurrents and led to a breakthrough in understanding and empathy among family members.

Case Study: Workplace Conflict Resolution

- **Background**: In a group therapy session, three co-workers participated in a triad to address ongoing conflict.
- **Application**: Role-playing was used to enact typical workplace scenarios, with each member taking turns in different roles.
- **Outcome**: Participants gained insights into each other's challenges, leading to improved communication and collaboration at work.

Advanced Techniques

Expanding the Use of Triads: Building on Satir's foundational work, modern therapists have developed advanced techniques within triad therapy to address complex issues. Techniques like "sculpting" in family therapy and "role-playing" in group settings are used to unearth deeper emotional truths and foster change.

Sculpting in Action

Background: A session focusing on hidden family dynamics.

Therapist: Let's create a physical representation of your family dynamics. John, place each family member in a position that reflects your emotional experience within the family.

John:	(*Arranging the triad*) Dad is always looming over us, so he's standing. Mom seems caught in the middle, and I'm off to the side, unnoticed.
Therapist:	How does this arrangement make you feel?
John:	It's like seeing the unspoken tensions we always had.

Triad Therapy in a Workplace Context

Background: A corporate team-building session addressing communication barriers.

Therapist:	Let's use a triad to understand the team dynamics. Alice, Bob, and Carol, each of you will represent a role in your team conflict.
Alice (as Team Leader):	I need these reports done by Friday.
Bob (as Colleague):	That deadline is unrealistic. We're already swamped with work.
Carol (as Observer):	It seems like there's tension around workload management.
Therapist:	Let's pause. Carol, as the observer, what dynamics are you noticing?
Carol:	There's frustration and a lack of understanding between Alice and Bob.

[**Therapist's Note**: The triad has revealed a common workplace issue of communication breakdown and unrealistic expectations. Use this insight to explore solutions.]

Triads in Coaching

Triad coaching, an adaptation of the therapeutic triad model, has become an influential tool in the realm of personal and professional coaching. It involves three individuals engaging in a dynamic interaction to facilitate learning, reflection, and growth. This section explores how triad coaching is effectively utilized to foster personal development, enhance professional skills, and improve interpersonal dynamics (Haitoglou, 2017).

Case Example: Enhancing Leadership Skills

Background: A coaching session aimed at developing leadership skills among mid-level managers.

Coach:	In this exercise, each of you will play a different role. Mark, you'll be the manager dealing with a team conflict. Lisa, you're his team member. John, you'll observe and provide feedback.
Mark (as Manager):	I've noticed some tension in the team. Let's work together to find a solution.
Lisa (as Team Member):	I feel that my opinions aren't valued in team meetings.
John (as Observer):	Mark, I noticed you didn't ask for specific examples from Lisa. That might help understand her perspective better.
Coach:	John, that's a great observation. Mark, how could you incorporate this feedback into your approach?

Strategies for Effective Triad Coaching

- **Role Rotation**: Regularly rotate roles within the triad to ensure that each participant experiences different perspectives.
- **Guided Reflection**: Encourage participants to reflect on not only the content of the interaction but also the process and their emotional responses.
- **Skill Focus**: Each session can focus on a specific coaching skill or competency, allowing participants to practice and receive feedback in a focused manner.

Triads in coaching represent a powerful methodology for professional and personal development. They offer a unique and practical approach to learning, embodying the principles of adult education and systems thinking. As the coaching field continues to evolve, triads stand out as a versatile and impactful tool, fostering deep learning and transformational growth.

Family Mapping and Life Chronology

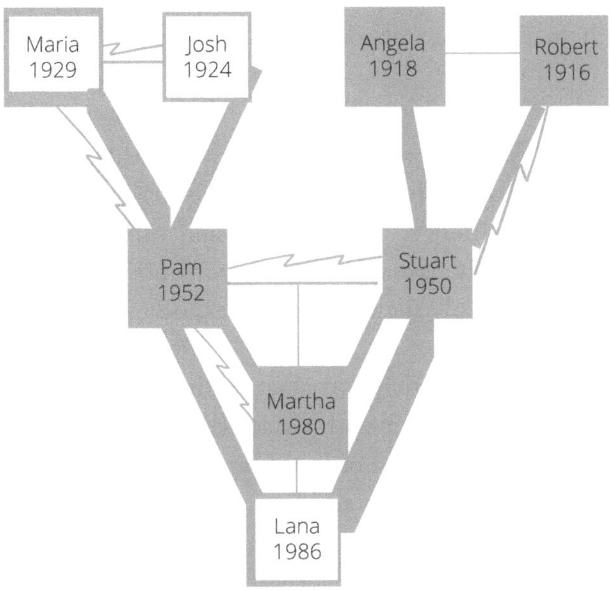

FIGURE 3.2 Family Map

In my practice of Systemic Repatterning, I frequently use Virginia Satir's powerful tools of family mapping and life chronology. These tools help unravel the intricate connections between an individual's life story and how it shapes their interactions, both in personal relationships and in professional settings. By creating visual representations of family dynamics and charting the timeline of significant life events, individuals can gain profound insights into the origins of their current behaviors, communication styles, and relational patterns.

Family Mapping

Family Mapping, a tool developed by Virginia Satir, allows individuals to visually represent their family dynamics and relationships. It uncovers hidden patterns, alliances, and conflicts within a family system, providing an opportunity to see their family-of-origin from both an objective and subjective lens (Bitter, 1988).

The Process

Satir's family mapping process occurs in two stages:

STAGE I: THE FACTUAL PRESENT

In this stage, individuals create a factual map of their family-of-origin, representing the people who shaped their upbringing. This includes parents, siblings, half-siblings, step-siblings, and other significant people who lived in the family home. Each family member is symbolically represented, and key details such as birthdates, occupations, illnesses, and relationships are added.

Drawing the Map: Participants start by drawing a family map, symbolizing each family member with circles (for females) and squares (for males). Children are placed in order of birth, and significant life events, like marriages or deaths, are noted.

Gathering Factual Information: The map becomes a repository for factual details about each person – occupations, education, religious affiliations, and significant health conditions. These factual pieces create the context for understanding the family's structure and the environment the individual grew up in.

STAGE II: THE PERCEPTUAL PAST

Once the factual map is complete, individuals shift to a more subjective lens, adding personal perceptions of their family dynamics. This part of the process is about exploring how the client experienced their family before they were 18 years old. Although current relationships may have evolved, this stage asks participants to return to their childhood mindset and consider how they felt about their family members during that time.

Personal Adjectives: Participants assign three positive and three negative adjectives to each family member, capturing the complex and nuanced way they experienced these relationships as a child. This process brings to light the dual nature of family members – how they could be both supportive and challenging.

Relationship Lines: Individuals then draw lines between family members to represent the emotional quality of relationships. Thick solid lines represent enmeshed relationships, jagged lines show conflict, broken lines indicate emotional distance, and thin solid lines are used for positive, low-conflict relationships. This visual representation helps clarify emotional patterns within the family and highlights areas of closeness, tension, or isolation.

Coping Mechanisms: Finally, participants reflect on the primary coping stances each family member used under stress. These stances – blaming, placating, being super-reasonable, or becoming irrelevant – reveal how each person navigated conflict and stress.

Life Chronology

The second tool I employ, Life Chronology, helps individuals map out the significant events of their lives, from childhood to the present day. It's a process of tracing the emotional journey through key life moments, allowing clients to connect their past experiences with their current beliefs, behaviors, and coping strategies (Satir and Baldwin, 1984).

The Process

Creating the Timeline: Participants create a timeline of key events, from early childhood memories to significant adult experiences. This timeline may include both positive and negative moments, ranging from accomplishments to traumas.

Emotional Markers: Each event is associated with specific emotions, offering insight into the emotional impact these experiences had at the time and how they continue to influence the individual today.

Identifying Patterns: By laying out these events on a timeline, participants can identify recurring themes or turning points in their lives. Patterns of behavior that have persisted since childhood become visible, helping clients understand the origins of their current struggles.

EXAMPLE IN ACTION

A client who was a successful business leader created a life chronology during a session. As we reflected on the timeline, he noticed how a childhood incident of public humiliation during a school play had shaped his fear of speaking up in board meetings. Despite his leadership role, this unresolved fear from his past continued to influence his behavior decades later.

Integrating in Group Work

In group settings, these tools become even more powerful. When used with corporate teams, for instance, family mapping and life chronology can facilitate deeper empathy and understanding among team members. Participants gain insight into how their personal histories shape their behaviors at work, and the tools help reveal the hidden dynamics that influence team interactions.

Group Exercise in Action

During one workshop, each team member was asked to create a mini family map and share one key event from their life chronology. One participant, for example, revealed that his family map showed his older sister as the central authority figure, explaining why he often took a backseat in group decision-making. Another colleague, upon hearing about a strict upbringing, gained insight into why that team member tended to enforce rules rigidly.

This exercise transformed the team's dynamics. By understanding each other's backgrounds, team members developed greater empathy and began to see each other as individuals beyond their professional roles. This newfound understanding led to more effective and compassionate communication within the team.

EXAMPLE IN ACTION

Participant: Seeing your family map, I now understand why you approach conflicts the way you do. It's similar to my own background.

Facilitator (Me): These revelations are powerful. They help us understand and support each other not just as colleagues, but as people with unique stories.

The Essence of Lines

In family mapping, the lines drawn between family members are pivotal. They represent the quality and nature of relationships.

- **Solid Lines**: Indicate strong, stable connections. When I see these lines on a map, they often suggest healthy relationships.
- **Dotted Lines**: Suggest intermittent or uncertain relationships. These often lead to discussions about trust and inconsistency in emotional connections.
- **Zigzag Lines**: Represent turbulent or conflicted relationships. They can reveal areas of strife and discord that might need addressing.
- **Broken Lines**: Often symbolize estrangement or significant emotional distance. These lines can open dialogues about loss, separation, or unresolved issues.

The Language of Colors

Colors in family mapping are more than aesthetic choices; they convey emotions and signify different aspects of relationships.

- **Warm Colors** (Red, Orange): Can indicate love, anger, or tension. The exact emotion often depends on the context in which the color is used.
- **Cool Colors** (Blue, Green): Might suggest calmness, detachment, or passive relationships. They often prompt discussions about emotional availability and support.
- **Neutral Colors** (Black, White, Grey): Can represent neutrality, indifference, or a lack of emotional connection. These colors might lead to exploring areas where emotional engagement is lacking.

Shapes and Symbols

Shapes and symbols in family maps are personalized representations that can vary greatly in their meanings.

- **Circles**: Often symbolize unity or wholeness. A circle around family members might indicate a closely-knit, protective unit.

- **Squares or Rectangles**: Can represent stability or rigidity. They might be used to describe structured or rule-bound family dynamics.
- **Triangles**: In family therapy, triangles often denote a three-person relationship dynamic, which can be either balanced or imbalanced.
- **Unique Symbols**: Clients sometimes use unique symbols (like a shield for protection or chains for bondage), which provide profound insights into their perceptions of family roles and dynamics.

Example: Emily's Family Mapping

During a session, Emily drew her family map with her parents connected by a zigzag line, colored red. Her relationship with her mother was represented by a dotted blue line, while her father was connected to her with a solid green line.

Me: Tell me about the red zigzag line between your parents.
Emily: It's their constant arguments. They love each other, but it's always been a rocky relationship.
Me: And the blue dotted line to your mother?
Emily: That's the coldness I often feel from her. It's there, but not always.

As I sat across from Emily, her family map laid out between us, the vibrant lines and symbols seemed to pulse with unspoken stories. It was time to unravel these narratives.

Me: Emily, this map is a rich representation of your family. Let's start with the overall layout. What was going through your mind as you were drawing it?
Emily: (*Reflecting*) I was thinking about how we're all connected but in such different ways. It's like we're close, but there are invisible walls.
Me: I see you've used different colors and lines to connect each family member. Let's talk about the red zigzag line between your parents.

Emily: That line… it's their love and their battles. It's passionate but always tumultuous. I grew up amidst their fiery arguments and reconciliations.

Me: (*Gently probing*): How do you feel that affected you, growing up in that environment?

Emily: It was confusing. Love meant loud words. Silence meant something was wrong. I guess it made me wary of confrontations.

Me: Moving to your connection with your mother, represented by this blue dotted line. Can you tell me more about this?

Emily: (*Hesitating slightly*) It's complicated. She's always been distant. The blue represents her cool demeanor, and the dots… the times she's been emotionally available. They're few and far between.

Me: And how has this impacted your relationship with her?

Emily: I've always craved her warmth, her approval. But I learned to keep my feelings to myself. I didn't want to seem needy.

Me: I notice a solid green line between you and your father. It's quite distinct from the others.

Emily: (*Smiling faintly*) Dad's been my rock. The green is for the stability and safety I feel with him. He's always been my safe haven amidst the chaos.

Me: (*Encouraging further insight*) It's wonderful to have that kind of support. How do you think this relationship has influenced your expectations from other relationships in your life?

Emily: (*Pondering*) I suppose I look for stability. Sometimes, I fear the chaos of my parents' relationship, so I avoid conflict, maybe too much.

Me: This map is a powerful reflection of your family dynamics and how they have shaped your perceptions and interactions. Understanding these patterns is the first step in exploring how you can relate differently, both within your family and in other relationships.

Emily: (*Nodding thoughtfully*) It's like I'm seeing my family and myself from a new perspective. I think I've been carrying these patterns without even realizing it.

As the session drew to a close, it was evident that Emily's family map had offered her new insights into her familial relationships and their profound impact on her life. Our journey through the map was not just about exploring the past; it was about understanding how these invisible threads were woven into the fabric of Emily's present interactions and perceptions. This understanding marked the beginning of a transformative journey for Emily, one where she could start to redefine her relationships and interactions based on newfound awareness and insight.

Family mapping, in its intricate and personalized nature, is a powerful tool in therapy. It's a form of visual storytelling that allows individuals to externalize and explore complex family dynamics. As a facilitator, guiding clients through this process not only helps them understand their familial relationships but also often illuminates patterns that influence their current personal and professional interactions. Every line, color, and shape woven into the map is a step toward deeper self-awareness and understanding.

The Parts Party Technique

In the chamber of self where many parts dwell,
A party unfolds, each with a story to tell.
A gathering of aspects, emotions, and roles,
In the theater of psyche, where the inner bell tolls.
First, the Critic, sharp and severe,
Whispers of doubt, judgment, and fear.
"Not good enough," their persistent chant,
In the gallery of mind, a daunting haunt.
Then comes the Child, playful and free,
Eyes full of wonder, wild with glee.
"Let's explore and dream," they cheerfully sing,
In their innocent joy, life's eternal spring.

The Protector steps forth, strong and tall,
A guardian of self, standing against all.
"I'll keep you safe," their solemn vow,
A sentinel of the soul, at the present bow.
Next, the Sage, wise and serene,
Views the world with a gaze keen.
"Seek the truth," they calmly advise,
In their profound depth, wisdom lies.
The Adventurer, restless, seeks the unknown,
Craves new experiences, far-flown.
"Let's take a risk," their daring plea,
In their bold quest, the spirit's spree.
And in the midst, the True Self shines,
A harmonious blend of these intricate lines.
"I am all these, and so much more,"
In this chorus of parts, life's rich lore.
In this Parts Party, where selves converge,
A dialogue of complexity, emotions surge.
In understanding these facets, we come to see,
The depth and richness of our full identity.

The Parts Party is a transformative therapeutic technique that involves engaging with different aspects of one's personality, often referred to as "parts" or "sub-personalities." This method is rooted in the idea that our psyche comprises various parts, each with its unique perspective and role (Satir, 2009).

Section 1: Parts Party Theoretical Foundations

Similarities with the Internal Family Systems Model

- **Origins of IFS**: Developed by Richard Schwartz, IFS is based on the concept that an individual's psyche comprises multiple sub-personalities or "parts." These parts are often formed in response to life experiences, especially during childhood, and each plays a unique role in the individual's internal system (Schwartz, 2001).
- **Roles of the Parts**: In IFS, parts are categorized typically into three roles: Managers (who control and protect), Exiles (who carry

pain and trauma), and Firefighters (who react impulsively to protect from perceived threats).
- **The "Self" in IFS**: Central to IFS is the concept of the "Self," which is the core, compassionate, and confident leader of the internal system. The Self is seen as distinct from the parts and is a resource for healing and harmony.

Virginia Satir's Influence on Understanding Internal Parts

- **Satir's Family Roles**: Satir identified specific roles in family systems, such as the blamer, placater, computer (super-reasonable), and distractor (irrelevant). These roles closely resemble the concept of internal parts, each serving a function in response to family dynamics (Satir, 1988).
- **Communication and Coping Strategies**: Satir's emphasis on communication patterns and coping strategies provides insight into how internal parts communicate and interact. Her work highlights that these patterns often develop as survival mechanisms in response to family environments.

Integration of IFS and Satir's Model in the Parts Party

- **Holistic Approach**: The Parts Party technique and the IFS structure of internal parts provides a comprehensive framework for understanding the complexity of an individual's internal world. This foundation provides a nuanced understanding of internal parts, paving the way for effective therapeutic interventions that address the complexities of the human psyche (Carlock, 2015).
- **Addressing the Whole Person**: By combining these two approaches, the Parts Party acknowledges the multifaceted nature of the human psyche. It recognizes that each part, like each family role, has a purpose and contributes to the individual's overall functioning.

Section 2: Identifying Individual Parts

The Process of Identifying Parts

The core of the Parts Party technique lies in recognizing and understanding the different parts or sub-personalities that exist within an individual.

This process is essential for clients to gain insight into their internal dynamics and the roles these parts play in their lives (Satir, 2009).

Common Parts in Individual Psychology

- **Inner Critic**: Often manifests as a voice of doubt and criticism, inhibiting actions and diminishing self-esteem.
- **Inner Child**: Represents the part that holds childhood experiences and emotions, often linked to vulnerability and creativity.
- **Protector**: A part that emerges to safeguard the individual from perceived harm, sometimes leading to defensive or controlling behaviors.
- **Adventurer**: Symbolizes the part seeking excitement, novelty, and risk-taking, reflecting a desire for freedom and exploration.
- **Caregiver**: Embodies nurturing, caring, and selflessness, but can also lead to self-neglect if overly focused on others' needs.

Techniques for Identification

1. **Introspective Exercises**: Guided meditations or visualization exercises can help clients tap into their subconscious to identify different parts.
2. **Reflective Journaling**: Clients are encouraged to journal about their thoughts, feelings, and reactions to uncover patterns that might reveal different parts.
3. **Dialogue with Parts**: Engaging in imaginary dialogues between the client and their parts can bring these parts into clearer focus.
4. **Art Therapy**: Using creative expressions like drawing or sculpting to represent different parts can provide tangible forms to abstract concepts.

Understanding the Roles and Interactions of Parts

- **Interplay of Parts**: Each part plays a unique role in the individual's psyche, often developed as a response to life experiences.
- **Conflict and Harmony**: Parts can sometimes be in conflict, leading to internal struggles, or they can work harmoniously, contributing to a well-balanced psyche.

Identifying Parts in Therapy

- **Client Scenario**: Sarah, a client, struggles with decision-making and assertiveness.
- **Application in Therapy**: Through introspective exercises, Sarah identifies her Inner Critic, which constantly undermines her confidence, and her Protector, which avoids risks to keep her safe. She also discovers an underrepresented Adventurer part, longing for more spontaneous and bold life choices.
- **Outcome**: Recognizing these parts helps Sarah understand the sources of her indecision and allows her to begin integrating her Adventurer part more into her life, leading to more balanced decision-making.

Developing an Understanding of One's Inner System

- **Empathy Towards Parts**: Clients are guided to develop empathy for each part, recognizing that each has developed for a reason and has a role to play.
- **Negotiating Between Parts**: Clients learn to mediate between conflicting parts, finding resolutions that honor the needs of each part.

Identifying individual parts in the Parts Party technique is a critical step in understanding the complexities of one's inner world. It provides insights into how various aspects of the personality interact, leading to a more integrated and harmonious self.

Section 3: Setting Up the Parts Party

Creating the Right Environment

A successful Parts Party requires a supportive and safe therapeutic environment. This setup is crucial for clients to feel comfortable exploring and expressing different aspects of their personalities (Satir, Banmen, Gerber, and Gomori, 1991).

Steps for Setting Up the Parts Party

1. **Physical Space Preparation**: Arrange the therapy room to accommodate the Parts Party. This might involve setting up chairs or designated areas representing different parts. Ensure the space is

comfortable and free from distractions. If you work online, think of virtual backgrounds or filters that can help you in the process, as well as if and how you are going to use any technological props.

2. **Introduction to the Concept**: Explain the Parts Party to the client, including its purpose and how it works. Clarify that each part is a valuable aspect of their psyche and that the goal is to understand and harmonize these parts.
3. **Identifying and Assigning Parts**: Based on the earlier identification of parts, assign each part a physical space in the room. This could be a chair or a marked area on the floor. Encourage the client to personalize each space in a way that represents the part. In a virtual setting, this can be done by graphics or objects that a client can draw and cut out of a piece of paper, or just imagine and become aware of them.
4. **Role of Props and Symbols**: Introduce props or symbols that might help the client connect with each part more tangibly. For instance, an object might represent the Protector, or a cushion might symbolize the Inner Child.

Facilitating the Parts Party

- **Guiding the Client**: As the therapist, guide the client to physically move to each part's space, encouraging them to embody that part and express its perspective and feelings.
- **Encouraging Exploration**: Promote an atmosphere of exploration and curiosity. Remind the client that there are no right or wrong responses in this process.

Practical Example: Setting Up the Parts Party

- **Client Scenario**: John, a client working on interpersonal issues, has identified several key parts, including his Inner Critic, Peacemaker, and Free Spirit.
- **Setting Up**: The therapist arranges three chairs in the room, each representing one of John's parts. John places personal items on each chair that he feels represent these parts.
- **Facilitation**: The therapist guides John to each chair, encouraging him to speak and act as each part, exploring their desires, fears, and motivations.

Ensuring Emotional Safety

- **Checking in with the Client**: Regularly check in with the client's comfort level throughout the process. Be prepared to pause or shift focus if they become overwhelmed.
- **Debriefing After Exploration**: After exploring all parts, have a debriefing session to help the client process their experiences and emotions.

Setting up the Parts Party is a critical phase in the therapeutic process. It involves creating a physical and emotional space that encourages exploration and expression. Proper setup and facilitation can lead to profound insights and promote greater self-understanding and integration (Gomori, 2015).

Section 4: Conducting the Parts Party

The Process of Engaging with Each Part

Conducting a Parts Party involves guiding the client through an immersive exploration of each identified part. This exploration is crucial for understanding the internal dynamics and fostering self-awareness.

Role-Playing Each Part

- **Encouraging Embodiment**: Instruct the client to physically move to the space designated for each part. Encourage them to embody the part, adopting its posture, tone of voice, and expressions.
- **Expressing the Part's Perspective**: Ask the client to speak from the part's perspective, expressing its thoughts, feelings, concerns, and motivations.
- **Exploring Relationships Between Parts**: Discuss how this part interacts with other parts. For example, how does the Inner Critic respond to the Adventurer? What does the Protector think of the Free Spirit?

The Therapist's Role in Facilitating the Dialogue

- **Guiding the Exploration**: Act as a mediator, guiding the client through the exploration of each part. Ask open-ended questions to deepen the understanding of each part's role and influence.

- **Ensuring Emotional Safety**: Monitor the client's emotional responses. Be prepared to provide support or redirect the session if the exploration becomes too intense.

Practical Example: A Session in Action

- **Client Scenario**: Emily, dealing with anxiety, has identified several parts, including a Worrier, a Rational Thinker, and an Optimist.
- **Conducting the Parts Party**: The therapist guides Emily to explore each part. As the Worrier, Emily expresses fears and anxieties about the future. As the Rational Thinker, she provides logical analysis of her situations. As the Optimist, she shares hopes and positive outlooks.
- **Therapist's Guidance**: The therapist helps Emily understand how these parts interact, often in conflict, contributing to her anxiety. They explore ways to bring harmony among these parts.

Navigating Complex Dynamics Between Parts

- **Identifying Conflicts and Alliances**: Recognize and discuss conflicts or alliances between parts. For instance, the Protector might be in conflict with the Adventurer.
- **Facilitating Negotiation**: Help the client negotiate between conflicting parts, finding ways to honor the needs and concerns of each part.

Integrating Insights into the Whole Self

- **Reflection on the Experience**: After exploring all parts, encourage the client to reflect on the experience. How do these parts collectively influence their behavior and feelings?
- **Connecting Parts to the Self**: Guide the client to understand how these parts relate to their core self. Encourage the integration of insights gained into a more cohesive self-understanding.

Conducting the Parts Party is a dynamic and insightful process that allows clients to deeply engage with different aspects of their psyche. This exploration can lead to significant revelations about internal conflicts, personal motivations, and the path towards greater self-integration and harmony.

Section 5: Dialogue and Interaction Between Parts

Negotiating Conflicts

In this stage, the focus is on recognizing and addressing conflicts between different parts. Often, these internal conflicts manifest as external problems or emotional distress. The therapist guides the client to explore the nature of these conflicts, helping them understand the underlying reasons and needs of each part.

Therapist: Let's look at the conflict between the part of you that wants to please others and the part that seeks independence. How do these parts interact with each other?

Client (Anna): The pleaser in me always says yes to everyone. But then, the independent part feels trapped and angry.

Therapist: It sounds like both parts have important roles, yet they're in conflict. What does each part need to feel heard and respected?

Anna: The pleaser needs to feel valued, while the independent part wants freedom.

Therapist: How can these needs be addressed in a way that both parts feel fulfilled? Can we find a compromise that honors both?

Fostering Empathy Among Parts

This stage involves encouraging the client to develop empathy towards all their parts. This means understanding the positive intentions of each part, even when their actions might seem counterproductive or harmful. The goal is to create a harmonious internal environment where all parts feel understood and valued.

Therapist: Let's try to see things from each part's perspective. What positive intention might the pleaser part have?

Anna: It wants to make sure I'm liked and accepted. It's scared of rejection.

Therapist: That's an important role. It's trying to protect you from feeling left out. How about the independent part? What is its positive intention?

Anna: It wants me to be true to myself, to make sure I'm not losing my identity in pleasing others.

Therapist: So both parts are actually trying to protect and care for you, but in different ways. Can you see how they might be working towards the same goal – your well-being?

Anna: I never thought of it that way. They both want what's best for me, just... differently.

Therapist: Exactly. Now, how can we help these parts understand and support each other? Perhaps the pleaser part can learn that saying 'no' sometimes is also a way of caring for yourself. Meanwhile, the independent part might see that seeking connections doesn't always mean losing oneself.

Creating Dialogue Between Parts

Therapist: Imagine if these two parts could talk to each other. What might they say? Let's have a dialogue between them.

Anna (as the Pleaser): I'm just trying to keep us safe from being alone.

Anna (as the Independent): And I'm trying to keep us true to who we are. We don't always have to please others to be okay.

Therapist: This dialogue is a great start. It helps each part understand the other's fears and hopes. By acknowledging and addressing these concerns, you can find a balance that honors both your need for acceptance and your desire for independence.

In this expanded section of the Parts Party process, the therapist facilitates a deeper understanding and negotiation between conflicting parts. Through empathy and dialogue, Anna begins to appreciate the intentions of her different parts and learns how to integrate them harmoniously. This approach not only resolves internal conflicts but also leads to greater self-compassion and holistic well-being.

Section 6: Integration and Resolution

Harmonizing the Internal System

In this stage of the Parts Party process, the focus shifts to harmonizing the internal system, aiming for a balanced and cohesive sense of self. The therapist helps the client integrate the various parts, ensuring that each part's needs and roles are recognized and respected in a way that contributes positively to the client's overall well-being.

Therapist: Now that we understand the roles and needs of your different parts, let's explore how they can work together harmoniously. How can each part contribute to a more balanced you?

Client (Anna): I think if the pleaser part can learn to set boundaries, and the independent part can appreciate the value of relationships, I can find a middle ground.

Therapist: That's a great insight. It's about finding balance. Let's visualize your internal system as a team where each member has a unique but essential role. How can this team coordinate to make decisions that are good for you as a whole?

Applying Insights to Real Life

The final part of the process involves translating the insights gained from the Parts Party into real-life changes. The therapist guides the client to apply these insights to their daily behavior and decision-making, fostering a more integrated and authentic way of living.

Therapist: Let's take these insights and think about how they can be applied in your daily life. Can you think of a recent situation where understanding these parts could have changed your response or decision?

Anna: Last week at work, I agreed to a project that I didn't really have time for. Understanding these parts now, I could have balanced my desire to please my boss with my own capacity and needs.

Therapist: That's a practical application of what you've learned. Moving forward, how can you use this understanding to make decisions that honor all parts of you?

Anna: I need to pause and consult my different parts – to check in with my pleaser side, my independent side, and any other feelings that come up before making a decision.

Therapist: That sounds like a thoughtful approach. Remember, it's a process and takes practice. Each decision is an opportunity to learn and grow. Let's explore some strategies to remind you to check in with your parts in different situations.

Integration and Resolution are crucial in ensuring that the work done in understanding the different parts leads to tangible improvements in the client's life. By harmonizing the internal system and applying these insights to everyday situations, the client can achieve a more balanced and authentic way of being. This stage solidifies the changes and ensures that the client is equipped to maintain this new, integrated sense of self.

Section 7: Advanced Applications

Couples Therapy: Exploring Relationship Dynamics

In couples therapy, the Parts Party can be an invaluable tool for exploring how each partner's internal parts influence their relationship dynamics. This approach helps partners understand not only their own internal conflicts but also how these conflicts interact with and impact their partner (Oz, 1988). Research into "couple congruence" highlights that when partners engage with each other's parts spiritually and authentically, it significantly deepens their relational bond (Bentheim, 2006; Bentheim, 2007).

Therapist (to Couple – Mark and Sarah): Let's each identify the parts that are most active in your relationship. Mark, which part of you is most present when you're with Sarah?

Mark: I think it's my protective part. I always feel like I need to be the strong one.

Sarah: And for me, it's my anxious part. I constantly worry about the relationship.

Therapist: Now, let's see how these parts interact. Mark, when your protective part is active, how does Sarah's anxious part respond?

Mark: I think it makes her more anxious because she feels I'm not listening to her worries.

Sarah: Yes, and then my anxiety triggers Mark's need to be even more protective.

Therapist: This insight is valuable. It shows a cycle where your parts are reinforcing each other. How can we find a way for these parts to support rather than escalate each other's reactions?

Group Therapy: Collective Insights and Shared Experiences

Conducting group Parts Party sessions can be incredibly beneficial in a group therapy setting. It allows for shared experiences and collective insights, as individuals see common patterns and learn from each other's processes.

Therapist (to Group): Today, we're going to share our parts and see how they resonate with each other. Let's start with someone sharing a part they've been exploring.

Group Member 1: I've been working with my perfectionist part. It always demands that I do everything flawlessly.

Group Member 2: I can relate to that. My perfectionist part makes me procrastinate because I'm afraid of not being perfect.

Therapist: It seems like the perfectionist part is a common theme here. How does recognizing this part in others help you understand your own?

Group Member 3: Hearing others talk about it makes me feel less alone. It's also interesting to see how the same part can act out differently in each of us.

Therapist: What can we learn from each other about managing this perfectionist part? Let's share strategies that have worked for us.

The advanced applications of the Parts Party process in both couples and group therapy settings offer deeper insights into interpersonal dynamics and shared human experiences. In couples therapy, it helps partners understand how their internal worlds affect their relationship. In group therapy, it fosters a sense of community and shared learning, as members reflect on their own parts and learn from the experiences of others.

Section 8: Challenges and Considerations

Managing Overwhelm

One of the challenges in the Parts Party process is ensuring clients do not become overwhelmed by intense emotions or conflicts between their internal parts. This process can unearth deep-seated emotions and conflicts, which, if not carefully managed, can lead to distress rather than healing.

EXPANDED STRATEGIES FOR MANAGING OVERWHELM

- **Establishing Safety**: The therapist must create a safe and supportive environment where clients feel comfortable expressing themselves without fear of judgment or retribution.
- **Pacing the Process**: The therapist should carefully pace the session, allowing clients to explore their parts without rushing, which can help prevent feelings of overwhelm.
- **Checking in Regularly**: Regular check-ins during the session can help the therapist gauge the client's emotional state and adjust the process accordingly.
- **Using Grounding Techniques**: If a client becomes overwhelmed, the therapist can use grounding techniques to help them return to a calmer, more centered state.

Therapist: I'm noticing some distress as we explore this part. Let's pause for a moment. I want you to take a deep breath and feel your feet on the ground. Remember, you're in a safe space.

Continued Support

Another important consideration is providing ongoing support and guidance as clients work to integrate their insights from the Parts Party process into their daily lives. This integration is crucial for lasting change and personal growth.

STRATEGIES FOR CONTINUED SUPPORT

- **Follow-Up Sessions**: Regular follow-up sessions can help clients maintain the progress they've made and continue to explore their parts in a supportive environment.
- **Developing Action Plans**: The therapist can help clients develop action plans that translate insights from therapy into practical steps for daily living.
- **Providing Resources**: Offering clients additional resources, such as reading materials or exercises, can support their journey outside of therapy sessions.
- **Encouraging Self-Care**: The therapist should emphasize the importance of self-care practices to help clients manage any emotional turbulence that may arise from the process.

Therapist: Let's build on the insights you've gained today. What are some steps you can take this week to nurture the parts we've discussed? Remember, it's important to also take time for self-care. What activities help you feel grounded and balanced?

The Parts Party process, while immensely valuable, requires careful navigation to manage potential overwhelm and ensure ongoing support for clients. Therapists must be attuned to their clients' emotional states and equipped with strategies to help them navigate the complexities of exploring their internal parts. With the right support and guidance, clients can successfully integrate their insights into their daily lives, leading to meaningful and lasting personal growth.

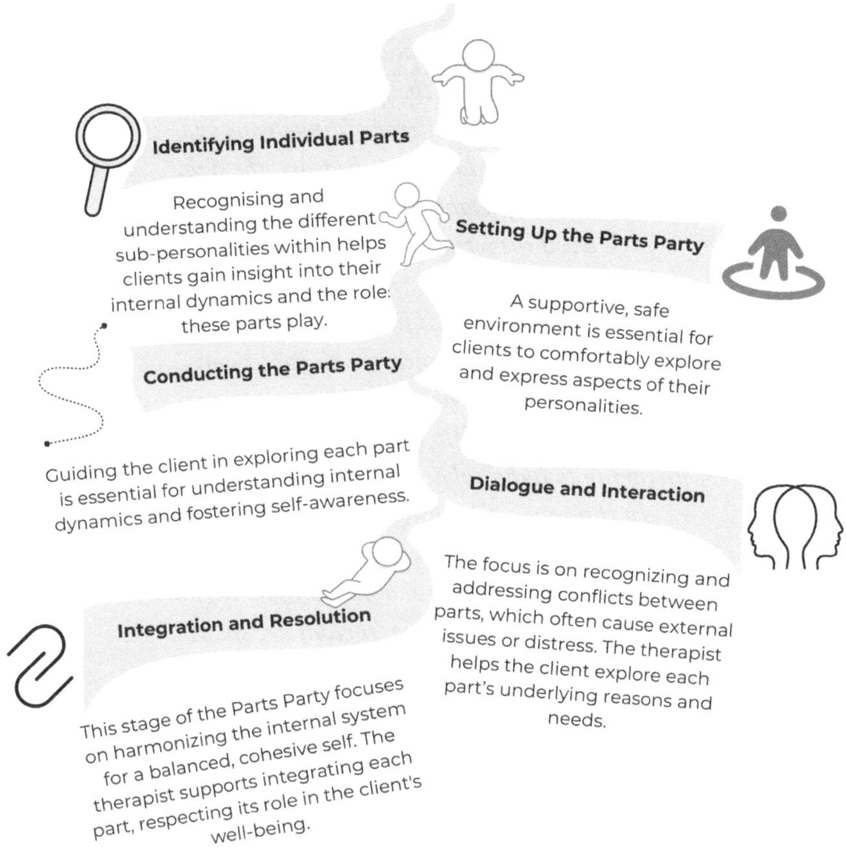

FIGURE 3.3 Parts Party Technique

The Family Reconstruction

In the tapestry of time, where threads intertwine,
Lies a story of kin, a familial design.
Through the lens of the past, with wisdom to construct,
Unravels the dance of Family Reconstruction.
From roots deep and tangled, stories untold,
Emerge shadows of ancestors, in patterns bold.
Generations whisper, in a silent recollection,

Their joys and their sorrows, in quiet reflection.
In the present's embrace, the family stands,
Holding the past in their outstretched hands.
Each member, a mirror of times gone by,
Reflecting the laughter, the tears, the sigh.
Roles long established, in history's play,
Unveil the scripts that still hold sway.
The dutiful child, the rebel, the peacemaker,
Each a character, a familial undertaker.
With gentle guidance, the therapist's art,
Weaves through the narrative, part by part.
Seeking to heal, to understand, to mend,
Bringing to light, what the shadows tend to bend.
In this space of healing, truths are revealed,
Wounds of the past, no longer concealed.
Forgiveness whispered, a new chapter begun,
In the web of healing, threads are spun.
From the ruins of the old, a new structure rises,
Built on understanding, it harmonizes.
A family reborn, in connection and affection,
Embracing each member, in their unique perfection.
In this journey of reconstruction, love is the key,
Unlocking doors, setting old burdens free.
In the heart of the family, a newfound connection,
Bound by the threads of introspection and affection.

The Process of Family Reconstruction

Family Reconstruction is a transformative process used in therapy and coaching to explore and understand family dynamics. In a group therapy setting, this method takes on an added dimension, as participants are not only exploring their own family histories but also actively engaging in the representation of others' family members. This approach provides a unique perspective, allowing individuals to step into the roles of family members from different families, thereby facilitating deeper empathy and insight (Nerin, 1991). Each participant may be called upon to represent a family member of another group member, a role-playing aspect that is crucial for the externalization of family dynamics. It provides a unique opportunity for individuals to experience family roles from a different perspective, which can be enlightening and therapeutic. This method brings to light patterns and relational dynamics that might remain hidden in traditional one-on-one sessions (Taylor, 2002). Virginia Satir's therapy model emphasizes communication, self-worth, and the importance of understanding family systems. In group Family Reconstruction, these principles are vividly brought to life. By participating in the reconstruction of another's family, individuals gain insights into their own family systems and communication patterns, leading to a greater understanding of how individual behavior is influenced by family dynamics and how these dynamics shape communication and self-perception (Satir, Bitter, and Krestensen, 1988).

Benefits of Group Dynamics

The group setting offers several benefits for Family Reconstruction:

- **Shared Experience**: There's a collective energy and support in a group setting that can foster deeper emotional safety and openness.
- **Multiple Perspectives**: Participants gain insights not only from their own family reconstruction but also from the experiences of others in the group.
- **Dynamic Interaction**: The interaction between group members during the reconstruction process can mirror real-life family dynamics, providing valuable real-time insights.

Challenges in a Group Setting

Conducting Family Reconstruction in a group setting also presents unique challenges:

- **Complexity of Dynamics**: Managing the complex dynamics with multiple participants acting out different family roles requires skillful facilitation.
- **Emotional Intensity**: The process can evoke strong emotions, and the therapist must be adept at navigating and containing these feelings within the group.

- **Time Constraints**: Given that we are focusing on a brief, 2-hour session, there's a need for effective time management to ensure that the process is both thorough and contained.

1. Pre-session Preparation

Effective pre-session preparation is crucial, especially when time is limited. It ensures that the brief time available for the group Family Reconstruction session is used efficiently and meaningfully. The preparation involves two main components: creating family maps and compiling life chronologies.

FAMILY MAPS: A TOOL FOR VISUALIZING RELATIONSHIPS

- **Objective**: Family maps are visual representations of family relationships and dynamics. They help both the therapist and the client understand the family structure, including key relationships and emotional connections.
- **Guidance for Clients**: Before the session, clients are instructed to create their family maps. This may include immediate family members and significant extended family members, indicating the nature of their relationships (close, strained, distant, etc.) and any relevant emotional or behavioral patterns.
- **Utilizing Family Maps in the Session**: In the group setting, these maps will serve as a foundation for understanding each participant's family dynamics. They provide a starting point for the reconstruction process and help other group members step into specific family roles more effectively.

LIFE CHRONOLOGY: DOCUMENTING SIGNIFICANT LIFE EVENTS

- **Objective**: A life chronology is a timeline of significant events and experiences in a client's life. It helps in identifying patterns and pivotal moments that have shaped the client's perceptions and behaviors (Satir and Baldwin, 1984).
- **Instructions for Clients**: Clients should be encouraged to reflect on and document major life events, both positive and negative, that have impacted their development and family relationships.

- **Application in the Session**: The life chronology assists in contextualizing the family map. It offers insights into how certain family dynamics may have evolved or been influenced by life events. This background information is vital for a nuanced understanding during the reconstruction process.

2. Preparing Participants for Representing Others
   - **Sensitizing Participants**: Before the session, it's important to sensitize participants to the responsibility and sensitivity involved in representing someone else's family member. This includes discussions on empathy, respect, and maintaining a non-judgmental stance.
   - **Role-Playing Guidance**: Provide basic guidelines on role-playing, emphasizing the importance of observation and reflection rather than performance.

3. Time Management Strategies
   - **Briefing on Process**: At the beginning of the session, quickly brief participants on the process and the importance of adhering to time constraints.
   - **Structured Phases**: Divide the session into structured phases – introduction, family sculpting, discussion, and closure – and allocate specific time slots for each.

4. Initiating the Session
   - **Introduction and Ground Rules**: Begin by introducing the purpose and process of Family Reconstruction. Establish ground rules to create a safe and respectful environment, emphasizing confidentiality and emotional support.
   - **Overview of Prepared Materials**: Quickly review the pre-prepared materials (family maps and life chronologies) to ensure everyone is familiar with the essential background information.

5. Creating Family Sculpts
   - **Dividing Time**: Allocate specific time for each participant's sculpt, ensuring everyone has an equal opportunity to engage in the process.

- **Process of Sculpting**: Guide the client whose family is being sculpted to choose group members to represent their family members, based on their family map. The client then arranges these representatives in a way that reflects the family dynamics and relationships (Satir, Bitter, and Krestensen, 1988).
- **Dynamic Engagement**: Encourage interaction among the participants in their roles. This may involve role-playing specific family scenarios or expressing emotions and relationships as perceived on the family map.

6. Facilitating Dialogue and Interaction
   - **Guided Reflection**: After the sculpt, lead a guided reflection. Ask the client to share their insights and feelings about what was represented. Encourage the group to offer observations and feedback, focusing on the emotional and relational dynamics observed.
   - **Time Management**: Be mindful of the time during these discussions to ensure that the session remains focused and productive.

7. Focusing on Key Insights
   - **Highlighting Transformative Moments**: During the sculpting and discussion, identify and highlight moments that reveal significant insights into the family dynamics.
   - **Encouraging Personal Insights**: Guide the client to connect these insights to their current life situations, relationships, and personal growth goals.

8. Integrating New Perspectives
   - **Facilitate Understanding**: Help the client integrate the insights gained from the sculpt into their broader understanding of their family and personal history.
   - **Future Steps**: Discuss how these new perspectives can be applied in their current life and relationships.

9. Guiding Participants to Transformative Insights
   - **Deepening Understanding**: The key to a successful Family Reconstruction is guiding participants to gain profound insights

into their family of origin. This involves exploring patterns, roles, and dynamics that have shaped their current beliefs and behaviors.

- **Facilitating Aha Moments**: During the sculpting process, therapists should pay close attention to significant reactions and interactions. These moments often reveal underlying issues and offer opportunities for transformative insights (Gomori, 2015).

10. Fostering Personal Connections

- **Connecting Past to Present**: Encourage participants to connect their experiences within the sculpt to their present life. This can illuminate how past family dynamics continue to influence current relationships and personal challenges.
- **Personal Growth Pathways**: Guide participants to identify steps they can take towards personal growth, based on the insights gained. This might involve challenging old patterns, enhancing communication skills, or developing new coping strategies.

11. The Power of Group Dynamics

- **Learning from Others**: Emphasize the value of learning from each other's experiences. Observing and participating in others' Family Reconstructions can offer parallel insights into one's own life.
- **Emotional Resonance and Support**: The group setting provides a unique space for emotional resonance and support. Participants often find comfort and validation in realizing that others share similar experiences and struggles.

12. Reflecting on the Process

- **Structured Debriefing**: Conclude each Family Reconstruction with a structured debriefing session. This allows participants to process their emotions and thoughts and to articulate their takeaways from the exercise.
- **Integrating Insights into Therapy**: Discuss how the insights gained from the Family Reconstruction can be integrated into ongoing therapy or personal development work.

13. Ensuring a Safe and Supportive Environment
    - **Navigating Emotional Intensity**: Be prepared to navigate and contain strong emotions that may arise during the session. It's crucial to maintain a safe and supportive environment for all participants.
    - **Closure and Continuity**: Ensure that the session ends with a sense of closure, while also acknowledging that the journey of understanding and growth is ongoing.

Case Studies and Practical Applications

This section provides real-world examples and practical applications of brief Family Reconstruction sessions in a group setting, illustrating the process and the transformative impact they can have on participants.

Case Study 1: Revisiting Childhood Roles

- **Background**: A participant, Sarah, had difficulty asserting herself in personal relationships, often feeling overshadowed.
- **Family Reconstruction Process**: During the sculpting, Sarah observed a group member portraying her younger self, constantly overshadowed by a dominant family member.
- **Insights and Application**: Sarah recognized how this childhood dynamic influenced her current behavior. Post-session, she worked on assertiveness skills and redefining her self-image, guided by the insights from the session.

Case Study 2: Healing from Parental Absence

- **Background**: Mark struggled with feelings of abandonment due to an absent father during his upbringing.
- **Family Reconstruction Process**: In the session, seeing another participant enact the role of his father provided Mark with a new perspective on his father's absence.
- **Insights and Application**: Mark began to explore and understand his father's challenges, which led to a shift in his feelings of abandonment and initiated a journey towards forgiveness and healing.

Case Study 3: Understanding Intergenerational Patterns

- **Background**: Emily, dealing with relationship issues, was unaware of the intergenerational patterns in her family.
- **Family Reconstruction Process**: Through the session, Emily saw clear parallels between her relationship patterns and those of her mother and grandmother.
- **Insights and Application**: Recognizing these patterns, Emily took steps to break the cycle, seeking to establish healthier relationships and communicate more effectively.

Practical Applications in Therapy and Coaching

- **Broadening Perspectives**: Use Family Reconstruction to help clients see beyond their immediate family experiences, understanding broader patterns and influences.
- **Enhancing Group Therapy**: Incorporate Family Reconstruction as a regular feature in group therapy sessions, allowing participants to learn from each other's experiences and insights.
- **Building Emotional Resilience**: Through observing and participating in others' reconstructions, clients can build empathy and emotional resilience, understanding their experiences in a wider context.

The journey of Family Reconstruction in a group therapy setting, as outlined in this chapter, underscores the profound impact of understanding and reinterpreting family dynamics. This therapeutic approach, deeply rooted in Virginia Satir's principles, provides a unique opportunity for individuals to explore their family histories, uncover hidden patterns, and embark on a path of personal transformation.

EMPHASIZING THE VALUE OF BRIEF SESSIONS

While traditional Family Reconstruction can be a lengthy process, the adaptation to a brief, structured format in a group setting has shown to be both effective and impactful. This approach respects the time constraints of modern therapy contexts while still delivering significant insights and emotional breakthroughs. It demonstrates that even within a limited timeframe, meaningful and transformative work can be accomplished.

THE ROLE OF PREPARATION AND PARTICIPATION

The effectiveness of brief Family Reconstruction sessions hinges on thorough preparation and active participation. The pre-session work involving family maps and life chronologies sets a strong foundation, allowing for a more focused and profound exploration during the actual session. The willingness of participants to engage in the process, both as representatives of others' family members and in exploring their own family dynamics, is crucial to the success of the session.

LEARNING FROM GROUP DYNAMICS

The group setting of Family Reconstruction brings an added dimension of communal learning and support. It allows participants to not only gain insights into their own family systems but also to learn from the experiences of others. This shared journey fosters a sense of empathy, understanding, and connection among group members, enriching the therapeutic experience.

THE THERAPIST'S ROLE

The therapist plays a pivotal role in guiding the session, managing the dynamics, and ensuring a safe space for all participants. Their skill in facilitating the sculpting process, encouraging reflective dialogue, and helping integrate insights into ongoing personal growth is fundamental to the success of the session.

ONGOING JOURNEY BEYOND THE SESSION

Family Reconstruction is not just a singular event but a starting point for ongoing exploration and growth. Insights gained in these sessions often spark further reflection and development in subsequent therapy or personal contemplation. Therapists should encourage clients to continue exploring the themes and patterns uncovered during the session, integrating them into their broader journey of self-discovery and healing.

In conclusion, brief Family Reconstruction sessions in a group setting are a powerful and adaptable tool in the field of therapy. They embody the essence of Satir's transformational therapy – fostering self-awareness,

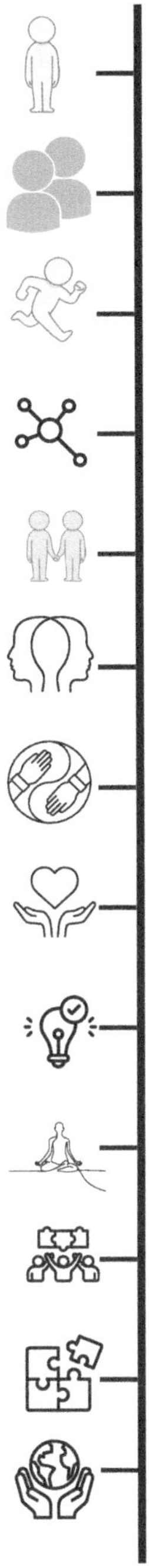

Pre-Session Preparation
Family maps visually represent relationships and dynamics to clarify family structure and emotional connections.

Preparing Participants for Representing Others
Before the session, participants should be guided to empathetically and respectfully represent others' family members.

Time Management Strategies
At the session start, briefly explain the process and stress time limits.

Initiating the Session
Introduce Family Reconstruction's purpose and process, set ground rules for a safe, respectful, and confidential environment.

Creating Family Sculpts
Ensure equal time for each participant's sculpt.

Facilitating Dialogue and Interaction
After the sculpt, guide reflection by asking the client to share insights and feelings, and invite group feedback on observed dynamics.

Focusing on Key Insights
Highlight key moments revealing family dynamics during sculpting and discussion.

Integrating New Perspectives
Help the client integrate sculpt insights into their understanding of family and personal history.

Guiding Participants to Transformative Insights
Successful Family Reconstruction involves exploring family origins, patterns, roles, and dynamics shaping beliefs and behaviors.

Fostering Personal Connections
Encourage links between the sculpt and present life to reveal ongoing influences.

The Power of Group Dynamics
Highlight the value of learning through observing and participating in others' Family Reconstructions.

Reflecting on the Process
Conclude with a debrief to process emotions and share takeaways.

Ensuring a Safe and Supportive Environment
Be ready to manage strong emotions and ensure a safe, supportive environment.

FIGURE 3.4 Family Reconstruction

understanding systemic patterns, and catalyzing personal growth. As therapists and clients alike navigate the complexities of family dynamics, this approach offers a path to deeper understanding and lasting change. A case study in the sixth chapter further illustrates the profound impact of this method, providing real-life insights into its application and benefits.

Navigating Challenging Scenarios with Satir's Tools

In my practice, not all journeys are smooth. Some cases are particularly challenging, presenting complex dynamics and deep-seated issues. Through these, I've learned the importance of adaptability and the power of Satir's tools in facilitating breakthroughs. Let's explore some of these tougher examples and how Satir's methods can be adapted to navigate them effectively.

Scenario 1: The Resistant Family

The Challenge: A family came in with deep-rooted resentment. The parents were on the verge of separation, and the teenage children were disengaged, each member resistant to the process.

Satir's Tool Adapted: I turned to Satir's family sculpting, but with a twist. Instead of traditional sculpting, I asked each family member to create an individual clay sculpture representing their view of the family.

Verbatim in Session:

Father: I don't see the point in this.

Me: It's about expressing your perspective in a different way. There's no right or wrong here.

As they sculpted, defenses started to lower, and a dialogue began to emerge.

Scenario 2: The Silent Executive Team

The Challenge: An executive team, proficient in hiding their conflicts behind corporate decorum. Their communication was superficial, impeding genuine collaboration.

Satir's Tool Adapted: I employed Satir's communication stances but integrated them into a mock board meeting setup. Each executive was assigned a stance to exaggerate during a simulated meeting.

Verbatim in Role-Play:

CEO (as Blamer): This project's delay is unacceptable!
CFO (as Placater): We'll do whatever it takes to get back on track.

The exaggeration of these stances helped them see the absurdity and inefficiency of their usual communication patterns.

Scenario 3: Addressing a Team Paralyzed by Past Trauma

One of the most challenging cases I encountered was with a team still reeling from the aftershocks of a corporate scandal. The scandal had eroded trust and left a lingering fear of taking risks. This team's journey to recovery was a delicate process, requiring a careful blend of empathy and strategic intervention.

Initial Assessment: Understanding the Depth of Trauma

During our initial sessions, I observed a pervasive atmosphere of caution and mistrust among team members. Conversations were guarded, and decision-making was hindered by an overwhelming fear of repeating past mistakes.

Me: I sense a lot of hesitation in this room. Can you share how the past events have impacted your approach to work?

The responses revealed a deep-seated trauma.

Using Satir's Iceberg Metaphor and Narrative Therapy

To address these issues, I turned to Satir's iceberg metaphor, combined with elements of narrative therapy. This approach allowed team members to articulate their experiences and feelings related to the scandal, exploring the unseen "underwater" parts of their emotional icebergs.

Team Member 1: When the scandal broke, it was like a betrayal. Now, I double-check everything, afraid of making a mistake.
Me: Let's delve into that feeling of betrayal. What's beneath that fear?

As team members shared, it became evident that the scandal had deeply impacted their sense of security and trust, both in themselves and in their colleagues.

Narrative Exploration: Rewriting the Story

I guided the team through a narrative exploration, encouraging them to reframe their experience of the scandal from a different perspective.

Me: Imagine you're a narrator of this story. How would you retell the event to highlight the learning and growth that emerged from it?

This exercise helped shift their focus from blame and fear to learning and resilience.

Team Member 2: In retelling this story, I see us not just as victims of the scandal but as a group that has learned valuable lessons about accountability and transparency.

Implementing Change: Strategies for Moving Forward

With new insights, the team began to develop strategies to rebuild trust and embrace a culture of healthy risk-taking.

Me: Based on our discussions, what are some steps we can take to foster a more trusting and open environment?

The team brainstormed ideas, such as implementing regular transparent communication sessions and creating a "safe space" for expressing concerns and ideas.

Team Leader: Let's start a monthly forum where we can openly discuss our challenges and brainstorm solutions without judgment.

Over time, the team started to shed the paralysis of their past. They began to view the scandal not as a defining moment of failure but as a turning point towards a more robust, transparent, and resilient future. This journey highlighted the power of narrative therapy and the iceberg metaphor in transforming a team's collective trauma into a foundation for growth and renewed collaboration.

Scenario 4: Cross-Cultural Misunderstandings

The Challenge: A culturally diverse team struggling with misunderstandings and stereotyping, leading to tension and ineffective collaboration.

Satir's Tool Adapted: I introduced a cultural mapping exercise, where team members mapped out their cultural backgrounds and values. We then used Satir's model of congruent communication to discuss these cultural differences respectfully.

Team Member from Culture A: In my culture, being direct is seen as rude.

Team Member from Culture B: I see. In mine, directness is valued as honesty. Let's find a middle ground.

These scenarios underscore the versatility of Virginia Satir's tools in addressing a wide range of challenges. By adapting these tools to fit the unique context of each situation, practitioners can facilitate understanding, healing, and transformation even in the most challenging scenarios. As a practitioner, these experiences have reinforced my belief in the resilience of individuals and groups and the power of empathetic, creative therapeutic approaches.

Meditation, Centering, and Metaphors

In the realm of therapeutic healing and personal growth, certain tools stand out for their profound impact on the individual's journey toward self-discovery. Meditation, centering, and the use of metaphors are among these powerful techniques, each playing a unique role in enhancing self-awareness, reducing stress, and facilitating the exploration of deep-seated emotions.

Meditation: Cultivating Mindfulness and Awareness

Meditation is more than just a practice; it is a pathway to mindfulness and self-reflection. By encouraging individuals to quiet their minds and focus on the present moment, meditation creates a space where thoughts and emotions can be observed without judgment. This practice is particularly beneficial for those who struggle with anxiety, stress, or the overwhelming pressures of daily life.

In therapeutic settings, meditation is often introduced as a means to help clients reconnect with their inner calm. For example, when working with individuals who feel constantly overwhelmed by their thoughts, guiding them through a meditation exercise can offer immediate relief. The simple act of focusing on the breath, of grounding oneself in the present moment, can transform the chaotic whirlwind of the mind into a more peaceful, manageable state.

Clients often describe this experience as finding an oasis of calm within themselves, a place they can return to whenever the external world becomes too demanding. As they continue to practice, this inner calm becomes more accessible, allowing them to approach their challenges with greater clarity and resilience.

Meditation Script

Setting the Scene:

Find a quiet, comfortable space where you can sit undisturbed for a few minutes. Allow yourself to settle into a relaxed position, either sitting or lying down. Close your eyes, and take a deep breath in, then slowly exhale. Let's begin our journey of mindfulness and self-discovery.

Focusing on the Breath:

Gently bring your attention to your breath. Notice the natural rhythm of your breathing. Feel the air entering through your nostrils, filling your lungs, and then gently leaving your body. With each breath, allow yourself to sink deeper into relaxation.

Body Awareness:
Now, shift your focus to your body. Starting from the top of your head, slowly scan down through your body. Notice any areas of tension or discomfort. As you breathe in, imagine drawing in calmness and peace. As you exhale, let go of any tension or stress. Allow relaxation to wash over you, moving gently down to your toes.

Centering the Mind:
As you continue to breathe deeply, bring your awareness to your mind. Observe any thoughts that come to you. Instead of engaging with them, simply acknowledge their presence and let them float away like leaves on a stream. Return your focus to your breath.

Embracing the Present Moment:
In this moment, there's nothing you need to do, nowhere you need to be. Just be here, in the now, with your breath and your body. Feel the sense of peace that comes from being fully present.

Connecting with Your Inner Self:
Imagine a space deep within you, a place of wisdom and serenity. Each breath takes you closer to this inner sanctuary. In this place, you are whole and complete. Here, you can tap into your inner strength and intuition.

Reflecting on Gratitude:
Think about something in your life that you are grateful for. It could be a person, a moment, or a simple aspect of your daily life. Allow the feeling of gratitude to fill your heart, and let it radiate through your entire being.

Slow Return to Awareness:
As this meditation session comes to a close, slowly bring your awareness back to the room. Wiggle your fingers and toes, gently stretch your body, and when you feel ready, open your eyes.

Closing Thought:
Carry the sense of calm and mindfulness from this meditation into your day. Remember, you can always return to this place of inner peace whenever you need it.

Spiritual Meditation Script

Creating a Sacred Space:
Find a quiet and comfortable place where you won't be disturbed. This is your sacred space for healing and introspection. Sit or lie down in a comfortable position. Gently close your eyes and take a deep, cleansing breath. As you exhale, let go of the external world and begin to journey inward.

Connecting with the Breath:
Turn your attention to your breathing. Feel each breath as a wave of divine energy, washing over you, cleansing and renewing your spirit. With each inhale, draw in peace and serenity. With each exhale, release any thoughts or concerns that may be weighing on your spirit.

Body and Spirit Unification:
As you continue to breathe deeply, visualize a luminous energy enveloping you. This light represents the unification of your body and spirit. Feel the light as it touches each part of your body, from the top of your head to the tips of your toes, bringing harmony and tranquility.

Journey to the Heart:
Now, bring your focus to the center of your chest, to your heart space. This is the seat of your spiritual essence. Imagine a radiant, glowing light in your heart, growing brighter with each breath. Feel its warmth and love.

Embracing Universal Connection:
In this sacred heart space, recognize your connection to the universe and all living beings. Feel the interconnectedness of all things. You are a part of this magnificent tapestry of existence, a unique and beautiful thread in the weave of the universe.

Reflecting on Inner Wisdom:
Within you is an ocean of wisdom. Take a moment to listen to the whispers of your inner self. Here, in this space of deep connection,

you may receive insights, answers, or simply the peace of understanding your own truth.

Gratitude and Love:
Let feelings of gratitude and love wash over you. Be thankful for the journey of life, with all its lessons and blessings. Feel the love that surrounds you, the love of the universe that supports and nurtures your spiritual growth.

Gently Returning:
As this meditation draws to a close, take a few more deep breaths. Gently wiggle your fingers and toes, bringing awareness back to your physical body. When you feel ready, open your eyes, returning to the world around you, carrying with you the sense of peace and spiritual connection from this meditation.

Closing Affirmation:
"I am a part of the divine tapestry of the universe. I carry within me peace, wisdom, and an ever-present connection to all that is."

Centering: Achieving Emotional Balance

Emotional balance is crucial for navigating the complexities of life, and centering is a technique designed to help individuals find this equilibrium. Centering involves grounding oneself emotionally, particularly during times of stress or when making important decisions. This practice helps to stabilize emotions, making it easier to respond to situations with a clear and balanced mind (Gabriel, 2014).

In group settings, centering exercises can be particularly effective. For instance, in a team environment where conflicts may arise, guiding the group through a centering exercise can diffuse tension and foster a more cooperative atmosphere. Members are encouraged to pause, take deep breaths, and focus on their own sense of grounding. This brief moment of reflection can shift the dynamic of the entire group, leading to more thoughtful and measured interactions.

The effects of centering are often immediate and palpable. Participants frequently report feeling more composed and focused, better able to engage in productive discussions. This emotional balance not only enhances the quality of the conversation but also strengthens the overall group dynamic, making it a vital tool for both personal and collective growth.

Metaphors: The Anchors of Awareness

The use of metaphors in therapy offers a creative and insightful way to explore complex emotions and experiences. Metaphors allow individuals to articulate feelings that might be difficult to express directly, providing a bridge between the conscious mind and the deeper, often hidden layers of the psyche (Baron, 2009).

In therapy, clients are often encouraged to describe their emotions or situations through metaphorical imagery. This process can lead to profound revelations, as metaphors tend to bypass the rational mind and tap into deeper emotional truths. For example, a client might describe feeling trapped in a maze, constantly searching for a way out. This metaphor not only vividly captures their current emotional state but also opens up new avenues for exploration in therapy.

The exploration of such metaphors can lead to a deeper understanding of the underlying issues that the client is facing. It allows both the therapist and the client to explore these feelings in a safe, non-threatening way. Through this process, clients often gain new perspectives on their challenges, discovering insights and solutions that might have remained hidden through more direct approaches.

Metaphors are also powerful in their ability to evolve. As therapy progresses, the initial metaphor a client used might change, reflecting their growth and transformation. The maze, for instance, might gradually become a path, a journey with a clearer destination. These shifts in metaphorical imagery can be as significant as the changes they represent, marking milestones in the client's therapeutic journey.

Integration and Impact

Together, meditation, centering, and metaphors form a trio of techniques that offer diverse pathways to healing and self-discovery. Each technique complements the others, creating a holistic approach that addresses both the mind and the emotions, the conscious and the subconscious. Whether used individually or in combination, these tools empower individuals to navigate their inner landscapes with greater confidence and clarity.

In practice, the impact of these techniques is profound. Clients who engage in meditation often find that it enhances their ability to remain present and mindful, reducing the grip of anxiety and stress. Centering helps them maintain emotional balance, particularly in challenging situations, enabling more thoughtful and deliberate actions. The use of metaphors unlocks deeper emotional layers, revealing insights that can lead to transformative change.

As these techniques become integrated into one's life, they foster a greater sense of self-awareness and emotional intelligence. The individual becomes better equipped to handle the complexities of life, finding within themselves the resources needed for growth and healing. Through meditation, centering, and the exploration of metaphors, the journey toward personal transformation becomes not only possible but profoundly enriching.

References

Banmen, J. (Ed). (2006). *Applications of the Satir Growth Model.* Seattle, WA: Avanta, the Virginia Satir Network.

Baron, S. (2009). Metaphor and the Satir therapist. *The Satir Journal, 3*(1), 49–60.

Bentheim, S. (2006). Couple congruence and spirituality: Expanding Satir's model through seven couple narratives. *Dissertation Abstracts International Section A: Humanities and Social Sciences, 66,* 10A.

Bentheim, S. (2007). Couple congruence and spirituality: Part I. *The Satir Journal, 1*(3), 27–63.

Bitter, J.R. (1988). Family mapping and family constellation: Satir in Adlerian context. *Individual Psychology: Journal of Adlerian Theory, Research and Practice, 44,* 106–111.

Brothers, B.J. (1990). Self esteem and congruent communication: Virginia Satir's road to integration. *Advanced Development, 2,* 23–34.

Carlock, J. (2015). The solo parts party. *Satir International Journal, 3,* 36–57.

Gabriel, C. (2014). I am. *Satir International Journal, 2,* 29–31.

Gomori, M. (2015). *Satir Family Therapy in Action.* The Haven Institute Press.

Haitoglou, D. (2017). The Satir Systemic Coaching Model. *The Satir International Journal, 5*(1), 4–18.

Lee, B.K. (2002). Congruence in Satir's model: Its spiritual and religious significance. *Contemporary Family Therapy: An International Journal, 24*(1), 57–81.

Nerin, W.F. (1991). Family reconstruction: The masterpiece of Virginia Satir. *Journal of Couples Therapy, 2*(1–2), 103–118.

Oz, S. (1988). A modified "Parts Party" for couples work. *Contemporary Family Therapy, 10*(3), 183–193.
Satir, V. (1967). Family systems and the approach to family therapy. *Journal of Fort Logan Mental Health Center, 4*(2), 81–93.
Satir, V. (1988). *The New Peoplemaking*. Palo Alto, CA: Science and Behavior Books, Inc.
Satir, V. (2009). *Your Many Faces: The First Step to Being Loved* (3rd ed.). Berkeley, CA: Celestial Arts.
Satir, V., Baldwin, M. (1984). *Satir Step-by-Step: A Guide to Creating Change in Families.* Palo Alto, CA: Science and Behavior Books, Inc.
Satir, V., Banmen, J., Gerber, J., Gomori, M. (1991). *The Satir Model: Family Therapy and Beyond.* Palo Alto, CA: Science and Behavior Books, Inc.
Satir, V., Bitter, J.R., Krestensen, K.K. (1988). Family Reconstruction: The family within – a group experience. *Journal for Specialists in Group Work, 13*(4), 200–208.
Schwartz, R.C. (2001). *Introduction to Internal Family Systems.* New York: Guilford Press.
Taylor, G. (2002). Family reconstruction. *Contemporary Family Therapy: An International Journal, 24*(1), 129–138.

4

SATIR'S KEY METAPHORS

Metaphors of Satir

Virginia Satir, renowned for her work in family therapy, frequently used metaphors to help clients understand and articulate their experiences and feelings. Here is a list of some of the notable metaphors and analogies she often employed:

1. **Iceberg Metaphor**: Used to illustrate how a person's behavior (the tip of the iceberg) is just a small, visible part of a larger underlying structure of feelings, perceptions, expectations, and desires.
2. **Jigsaw Puzzle**: Used to illustrate how each family member is a unique piece of the larger family picture, each with their own place and importance.
3. **Cooking Pot Analogy**: Satir likened family tension and conflict to a pot on the stove, where the heat represents the stress or problems simmering within the family.
4. **Mirrors and Reflections**: This metaphor is used to explain how individuals often mirror behaviors, emotions, or attitudes seen in significant people in their lives, especially during childhood.

DOI: 10.4324/9781003716419-4

5. **Life's Balance Sheet**: A metaphor used to help clients evaluate the positives and negatives in their life, similar to how one would balance assets and liabilities in accounting.
6. **Life River**: Referring to the journey of life with its ebbs and flows, this metaphor helps individuals understand and navigate the changes and transitions in life.
7. **Mobile**: Used to represent family systems, illustrating how movement (change or stress) in one part of the family system affects all other parts.
8. **Gardening Analogy**: Satir often used this to describe the nurturing process needed for personal growth, emphasizing that just like plants, people need care, attention, and a conducive environment to thrive.
9. **Scarecrow Metaphor**: Used to illustrate how people, like scarecrows, can become stuck in one place, unable to move or grow, often due to fear or learned behaviors.
10. **Survival Rules Metaphor**: This metaphor helps clients understand the unspoken family rules they learned to survive emotionally in their childhood environment, which may no longer serve them in adulthood. These adaptive behaviors solidify into "rules" that the individual follows unconsciously. For instance, "I must not express anger," "I should always put others first," or "It's dangerous to trust others." These rules serve to protect the individual from perceived threats or emotional pain in their family environment.
11. **Five Freedoms**: While not a metaphor, this is a significant concept in Satir's work. It describes the freedoms of seeing and hearing what is here and now, saying what one feels and thinks, feeling what is inside of oneself, asking for what one wants, and taking risks on one's own behalf.
12. **Hand Model**: Satir used the parts of the hand as a metaphor for the components of communication – words, tone of voice, timing, body language, and the true meaning/intent.
13. **Open Door Analogy**: This metaphor is used to illustrate the idea of open communication within a family or group, emphasizing the importance of allowing thoughts and feelings to be expressed freely.

14. **"As If" Technique**: Satir encouraged clients to act "as if" they are already in the state they wish to be (confident, calm, etc.), using this as a tool for change and growth.
15. **Ingredients of Interaction**: This analogy is used to break down the elements of communication and interaction into smaller, more manageable parts.
16. **Dance Metaphor**: Often used to describe the dynamics of relationships and interactions, comparing them to a dance where each person has a role and rhythm.
17. **"Yearning Pot" Metaphor**: This analogy was used to describe the deep, often unacknowledged desires and needs that drive individual behavior.
18. **"Peoplemaking"**: Satir used this term, which is also the title of one of her books, to describe the process of growing and developing as individuals within the context of relationships and family life.
19. **"Your Own Best Friend" Concept**: This idea encourages individuals to treat themselves with the same kindness, compassion, and understanding that they would offer to a close friend.
20. **"Rules of the Game" Analogy**: This metaphor was used to describe the often unspoken rules that govern family interactions and dynamics.
21. **"Becoming More Fully Human"**: While not a metaphor, this concept was central to Satir's philosophy, emphasizing the goal of therapy as helping people become more authentic, compassionate, and fully realized versions of themselves.
22. **"Inner Child" Concept**: Satir often spoke of nurturing the "inner child" within each individual – a concept used to address deep-seated emotional needs from childhood.
23. **"Communication Stances as Dance Steps"**: Expanding on the dance metaphor, Satir likened different communication styles to dance steps, each with its own rhythm and impact on the relational "dance."
24. **"Family Soul" Concept**: This idea suggests that each family has a collective soul or essence, shaped by the emotions, experiences, and histories of its members.

25. **"Healing from the Inside Out"**: This metaphor captures Satir's belief in the intrinsic ability of individuals to heal and grow, emphasizing inner resources and resilience.
26. **"Living in Process"**: Satir viewed life as a process of continuous growth and change, rather than a series of static states.
27. **"Family Tree" Metaphor**: Used to explore the roots and branches of family history, helping clients understand how past generations influence present dynamics.
28. **"Building Bridges" Metaphor**: Used to describe the process of creating understanding and connection between individuals or within oneself.
29. **"Weather Patterns" in Families**: This analogy compares family dynamics and moods to changing weather patterns, acknowledging the fluid and sometimes unpredictable nature of relationships.
30. **"Symphony Orchestra" Analogy**: Used to describe how a family functions like an orchestra, with each member playing a distinct part that contributes to the overall harmony or discord.
31. **"Life Scripts" Concept**: Refers to the idea that people live out narratives based on early family interactions and expectations, often unconsciously.
32. **"Healing Space" Metaphor**: Refers to the therapeutic setting as a safe and sacred space for growth and healing.
33. **"Journey of Self-Discovery"**: An analogy for the therapeutic process, emphasizing exploration, learning, and the unfolding of one's authentic self.
34. **"Windows of Opportunity"**: This metaphor is used to describe moments in therapy where significant insight, change, and healing can occur.
35. **"Peace Within, Peace Between, Peace Among"**: This powerful mantra encapsulates Satir's philosophy of inner and outer harmony. It suggests that inner peace leads to peaceful relationships, which in turn contribute to a peaceful society. It reflects her belief in the interconnectedness of personal healing and broader social harmony.
36. **"Making Contact"**: This concept involves establishing a genuine connection with oneself and others, emphasizing the importance of authentic communication in building meaningful relationships.

37. **"Life Energy" Concept**: This idea revolves around the understanding that each person possesses a unique energy that drives their growth, interactions, and life choices.
38. **"New Leaf" Metaphor**: This metaphor is used to represent the process of personal growth and renewal, akin to a tree shedding old leaves and growing new ones.
39. **"Healing Inner Conflicts"**: A significant aspect of Satir's work focused on resolving internal conflicts and achieving a state of internal harmony and balance.
40. **"Yearning Pot" Metaphor**: This analogy was used to describe the deep, often unacknowledged desires and needs that drive individual behavior.
41. **"Your Own Best Friend" Concept**: This idea encourages individuals to treat themselves with the same kindness, compassion, and understanding that they would offer to a close friend.
42. **Temperature Reading**: A technique for families or groups to openly express thoughts, feelings, and concerns. By creating a structured space, it encourages honest communication, reduces misunderstandings, and builds trust, helping to strengthen emotional connections within the group.
43. **Mandala**: Represents wholeness and the integration of self, used in self-exploration and healing. The Mandala reflects how each part of a person's life – physical, mental, emotional, and spiritual – contributes to their sense of balance and completeness.
44. **Hologram**: Reflects the interconnectedness of personal and relational experiences, where each part mirrors the larger whole. This metaphor helps individuals see how their actions, beliefs, and emotions influence and are influenced by their relationships.

These metaphors and analogies are powerful tools that Satir employed to help individuals and families understand complex emotional concepts in a more relatable and simpler way. They continue to be widely used in therapy for their effectiveness in facilitating insights, healing, and growth. Below, we will explore some of them, such as the Iceberg, Temperature Reading, Hologram, and Mandala.

Iceberg

The Iceberg Metaphor offers a profound understanding of the complex layers of human experience and behavior. In practice, this metaphor has proven invaluable for exploring and addressing the deeper issues that clients often face. This chapter will delve into the Iceberg Metaphor, unpacking its significance and practical applications across various professional fields, including coaching, organizational development, education, and healthcare.

Imagine an iceberg floating in the ocean. What we see above the surface – the visible tip – is just a small fraction of the entire structure. Beneath the waterline lies the vast majority of the iceberg, hidden from view but critical to its existence and stability. This imagery is used to

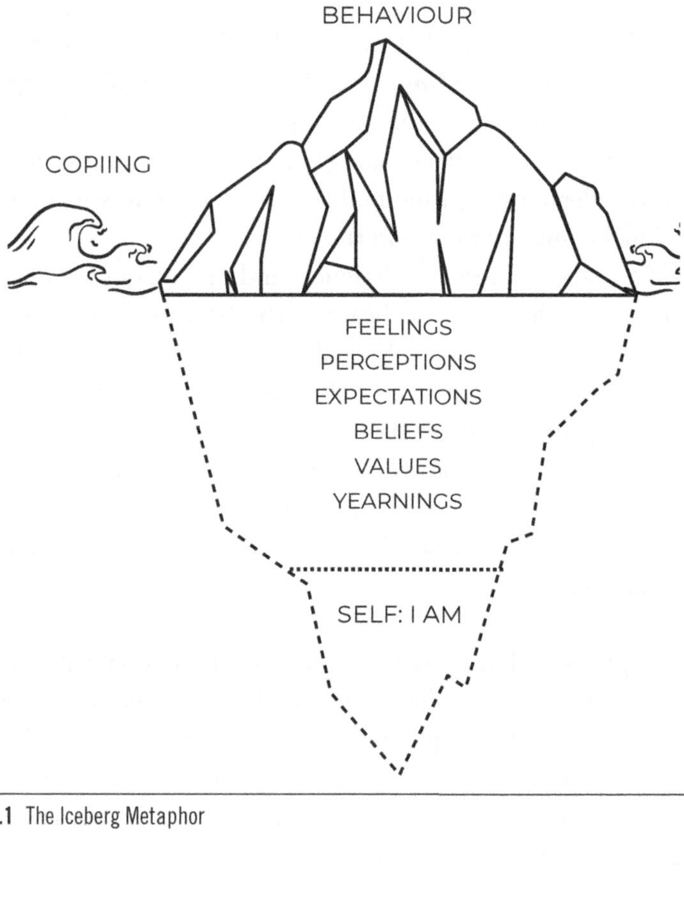

FIGURE 4.1 The Iceberg Metaphor

explain human behavior and experience: what we observe on the surface is only a small part of the whole picture, with much of what drives our feelings and actions lying beneath the surface, unseen but deeply influential.

The Iceberg Metaphor invites us to look beyond the obvious and explore the hidden depths of our inner world. By doing so, we can better understand the underlying motivations, beliefs, and emotions that shape our behavior and interactions.

Surface Level: Behaviors and Coping Strategies

At the top of the iceberg – the part visible above the surface – are our **behaviors** and **coping strategies**. These are the actions, reactions, and outward expressions that we and others can observe in everyday life. They include how we respond to stress, interact with others, and manage challenges.

- **Overview**: The surface level represents the easily observable aspects of our lives. These behaviors are often the first things we notice in ourselves and others, but they are just the tip of the iceberg.
- **Example in Coaching**: Consider a client who frequently procrastinates. Procrastination is a visible behavior – a coping strategy that the client uses to manage deeper, often unrecognized issues. Understanding that procrastination is merely the surface level prompts a deeper exploration into what lies beneath.

Middle Level: Feelings and Perceptions

Beneath the surface, we find the layer of **feelings, feelings about feelings**, and **perceptions**. This level includes our emotions and the ways we perceive ourselves, others, and the world around us. It's more difficult to see this layer because it's internal and often not directly expressed.

- **Overview**: The middle level of the iceberg consists of the emotional undercurrents that influence our behaviors. These feelings can range from joy, sadness, and anger to more complex emotions like shame, guilt, or anxiety.

- **Example in Coaching**: In the case of the procrastinating client, further exploration may reveal that their avoidance behavior is rooted in feelings of overwhelm or a perception of inadequacy. These emotions drive the visible behavior of procrastination, making it crucial to address them to effect meaningful change.

Deeper Level: Beliefs and Expectations

At this deeper level, we encounter our **beliefs** and **expectations**. These are the internal assumptions and anticipations that drive our emotions and behaviors. Beliefs are the ideas we hold about ourselves, others, and the world, often unconscious, yet they exert a powerful influence on our actions. Expectations are the hopes or predictions we have about how things should be, which can guide our behavior in subtle and significant ways.

- **Overview**: This level represents the underlying beliefs and expectations that shape how we interact with the world. These can often go unexamined, but they have a profound impact on our emotional state and interactions.
- **Example in Professional Development**: Imagine a manager who struggles with delegating tasks. Upon closer examination, it becomes clear that this reluctance stems from a belief that their worth is tied to their indispensability and an expectation that they must handle everything themselves to be valued. These beliefs and expectations shape their leadership style and the way they engage with their team.

Core Level: Yearnings and Values

At the very core of the iceberg lie our **yearnings** and **values**. These are the foundational desires and principles that define who we are at our deepest level. Yearnings are the deep-seated needs for connection, acceptance, success, and love. Values are the guiding principles that shape our decisions, relationships, and how we see our place in the world. These are the most fundamental aspects of our identity and motivation.

- **Overview**: The core level of the iceberg is where our most deeply held yearnings and values reside. These are the central forces that influence every aspect of our behavior and self-concept.
- **Example in Personal Relationships**: In a romantic relationship, one partner may exhibit jealousy or clinginess. At the surface level, these behaviors might seem possessive or insecure. However, delving deeper reveals that these behaviors are rooted in a core yearning for love and acceptance and a value placed on deep, meaningful connections. Addressing these core aspects can lead to healthier and more secure behaviors in the relationship.

This structure acknowledges that while beliefs and expectations are powerful drivers of behavior, it is the deeper yearnings and values that form the true core of our motivations and identity.

Application in Various Fields

The Iceberg Metaphor is not just a theoretical construct; it has practical applications in a variety of fields. By understanding the different layers of the iceberg, professionals can develop more effective strategies for helping individuals and teams overcome challenges and achieve their goals.

- **Coaching**: The Iceberg Metaphor is used to uncover the deeper motivations behind a client's actions. By understanding the underlying feelings, expectations, and beliefs, coaches can more effectively guide clients towards meaningful change.
- **Organizational Development**: In a corporate setting, understanding the Iceberg Metaphor can enhance team dynamics and leadership. Leaders can use this metaphor to appreciate the underlying factors influencing team behavior and morale.
- **Education**: Educators can apply the Iceberg Metaphor to understand student behaviors and motivations, leading to more empathetic and effective teaching methods.
- **Healthcare**: Healthcare professionals, including mental health therapists, can use the Iceberg Metaphor to comprehend the deeper emotional and psychological factors affecting a patient's well-being.

Strategies for Exploring the Iceberg

Exploring the different layers of the iceberg requires a thoughtful and patient approach. Here are some strategies that can help uncover the deeper aspects of the iceberg:

- **Active Listening and Inquiry**: Use active listening and open-ended questions to explore each layer of the iceberg. This approach encourages individuals to express their feelings, expectations, and beliefs in a safe and supportive environment.
- **Reflective Exercises**: Encourage clients or team members to engage in reflective exercises that uncover deeper feelings, beliefs, and desires. Journaling, mindfulness practices, and guided self-reflection can be effective tools for this purpose.
- **Visualization Techniques**: Visualization can help individuals imagine their "iceberg" and gain insights into their inner workings. This technique can be particularly powerful in helping people identify and articulate the deeper layers of their experience.

The Iceberg provides a powerful framework for understanding the complexities of human behavior and motivation. Its application extends beyond therapy and coaching into numerous fields, offering a tool for deeper empathy, understanding, and effective intervention. By exploring beneath the surface, we can address the root causes of behaviors and foster lasting change.

This metaphor reminds us that there is always more beneath the surface than meets the eye. Whether in personal growth, professional development, or therapeutic settings, taking the time to explore the depths of the iceberg can lead to profound insights and transformative outcomes.

Temperature Reading

In the realm of hearts, where emotions sway,
A tool emerges, lighting the way.
Temperature Reading, Satir's gentle art,

A process to connect, to open the heart.
First, Appreciations, like morning dew,
Gratitude spoken, heartfelt and true.
"I value your kindness," softly said,
A stream of warmth, where goodwill is bred.
Then New Information, the day's fresh light,
Sharing of news, bringing insight.
"Here's what's happening," spoken with ease,
In the exchange, minds find their peace.
Puzzles come next, clouds of query and thought,
Questions like mazes, answers sought.
"I wonder why," the curious voice,
In seeking to know, we make a choice.
Complaints with Recommendations, like rain's steady flow,
Voicing concerns, letting them show.
"Here's my grievance, and a way through,"
In this constructive space, solutions brew.
Lastly, Wishes, Hopes, and Dreams, stars in the night,
Aspirations shared, shining bright.
"I dream of peace," whispered with yearning,
In these hopes, the soul's fire burning.
Temperature Reading, a journey of five,
In this dance of dialogue, relationships thrive.
A tool for connection, for understanding's seed,
In Satir's garden, a nurturing deed.

Virginia Satir's "Temperature Reading" is a remarkable tool for improving communication within relationships, particularly within families and teams. It's a structured way of checking in with each other, promoting open and honest communication, and addressing issues constructively. The process of Temperature Reading comprises five distinct steps.

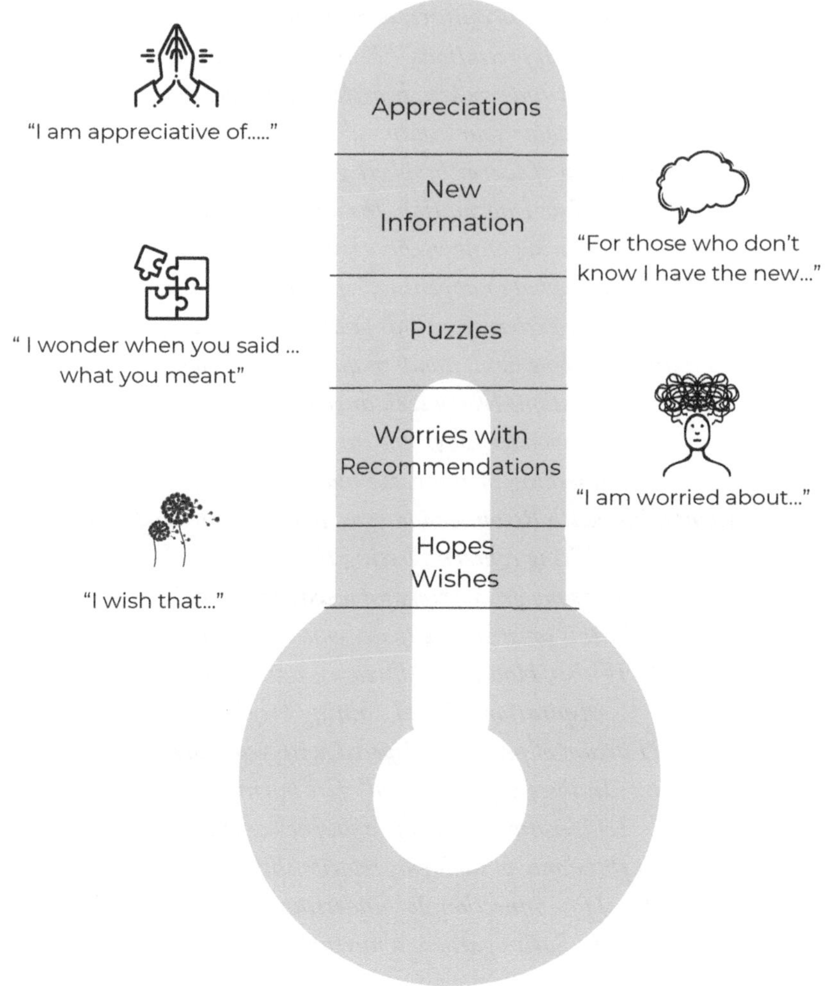

FIGURE 4.2 Temperature Reading

1 Appreciations

Purpose: To express gratitude or appreciation for each other.
Verbatim Example:

Family Member: I appreciate how you helped me with my project yesterday. It meant a lot to me.

Team Member: I'm grateful for your support during the meeting. Your insights really helped clarify our objectives.

2 *New Information*

Purpose: To share any new information relevant to the family or team.

Parent: I want to let you all know that I'll be working late this Thursday.
Manager: There's an update on the project timeline I need everyone to be aware of.

3 *Puzzles*

Purpose: To express anything that is unclear or confusing, without expecting an immediate solution.

Teenager: I'm puzzled about why we can't have later curfews on weekends.
Employee: I'm unclear about the new client's requirements. Can we discuss this further?

4 *Complaints with Recommendations*

Purpose: To voice complaints or issues, but importantly, to also offer a constructive recommendation for resolving them.

Spouse: I feel frustrated when you don't help with household chores. Could we create a chore schedule?
Colleague: I've noticed our meetings often run over time, which affects my other commitments. Could we try sticking more closely to the agenda?

5 *Wishes, Hopes, and Dreams*

Purpose: To share aspirations, hopes, or dreams, which helps deepen understanding and connection.

Child: I hope one day to go to college and study marine biology.
Team Leader: My dream for our team is to not just meet our targets but to exceed them in a way that boosts everyone's professional growth.

Application and Benefits

In a therapy or coaching session, the Temperature Reading process can be facilitated as follows:

- **Introduce the Process**: Explain each of the five steps to the participants.
- **Facilitate Each Step**: Allow each person time to speak, ensuring all steps are covered.
- **Encourage Active Listening**: Make sure everyone listens without interrupting or responding defensively.
- **Summarize and Reflect**: At the end, summarize key points and reflect on the process.

Benefits:

- Enhances communication and understanding within the group.
- Allows for regular check-ins and prevents small issues from escalating.
- Fosters a positive atmosphere through appreciation.
- Encourages problem-solving through recommendations.
- Strengthens bonds by sharing personal aspirations.

Temperature Reading is an effective tool for creating a safe and structured environment for open communication. Whether in a family setting, a team, or a therapeutic context, it encourages a holistic approach to communication, balancing the expression of needs, concerns, and positive aspirations. This process can be particularly transformative in environments where open and honest communication has been a challenge.

Application of Temperature Reading for a Divorcing Couple

Applying Satir's Temperature Reading to a divorcing couple can be a powerful tool for facilitating respectful and constructive communication during a challenging transition. It helps the couple navigate their changing relationship by providing a structured way to express emotions, share information, and acknowledge each other's perspectives.

1. Appreciations

Purpose: To acknowledge the positive aspects of each other or the relationship, even amidst difficulties.
Session Example:

Partner 1: I appreciate the years of support you've given me, especially during my career change.
Partner 2: I am grateful for the way you've always been involved with our children's activities and school life.

2. New Information

Purpose: To share any relevant updates that impact either partner or the process of divorce.
Session Example:

Partner 1: I want to let you know that I'll be moving into a new apartment next week.
Partner 2: I've started looking into a different health insurance plan now that our situation is changing.

3. Puzzles

Purpose: To express confusion or uncertainty without the pressure of immediate resolution.
Session Example:

Partner 1: I'm puzzled about how we'll manage shared custody during holidays.
Partner 2: I'm unclear about how we're dividing our joint assets.

4. Complaints with Recommendations

Purpose: To voice concerns or issues, accompanied by suggestions for addressing them.

Session Example:

Partner 1: I get frustrated when discussions about finances become heated. Maybe we can have a mediator help us with this part.

Partner 2: I feel overwhelmed by the legal paperwork. Perhaps we can set aside a time each week to go through it together or with our attorneys.

5. Wishes, Hopes, and Dreams

Purpose: To share aspirations for the future, fostering a sense of goodwill and mutual respect.

Session Example:

Partner 1: I hope we can both find happiness and fulfillment in our lives after this. I wish for a peaceful co-parenting relationship.

Partner 2: My dream is for us to maintain a respectful relationship and for our children to see us handle this transition with maturity.

Benefits for the Divorcing Couple

- **Fosters Respectful Communication**: Helps maintain dignity and respect in conversations.
- **Reduces Conflict**: By structuring communication, it minimizes misunderstandings and conflicts.
- **Supports Co-parenting**: Establishes a foundation for effective co-parenting post-divorce.
- **Facilitates Closure**: Encourages a sense of closure and understanding about the relationship's end.
- **Promotes Positive Future Relations**: Lays groundwork for a cooperative and possibly friendly relationship in the future.

For a divorcing couple, the Temperature Reading process can provide a valuable framework for navigating the complexities of their changing relationship. It helps them communicate effectively, address practical issues, and acknowledge each other's worth and contributions, all of which are crucial during the emotionally charged process of divorce.

Combined Session: Temperature Reading and Meditation

Combining Virginia Satir's Temperature Reading with a meditation practice creates a powerful, holistic approach to communication and self-awareness. This combination allows individuals or couples, like in the context of a divorcing couple, to not only communicate effectively but also to connect deeply with their internal emotional states. Here's how it can be structured.

Part 1: Guided Meditation for Centering and Awareness

Purpose: To bring participants into a mindful, present state, preparing them for open and honest communication.
Session Example:

- **Begin with Deep Breathing**: "*Let's start by taking deep, slow breaths. Inhale peace and calm, exhale tension and stress.*"
- **Body Scan for Relaxation**: "*Focus on each part of your body, from your toes to your head, releasing any tension you find.*"
- **Mindful Awareness**: "*Now, bring your attention to your thoughts and feelings. Observe them without judgment, just acknowledging them as they are.*"

Part 2: Temperature Reading

After the meditation, when both partners are centered and more aware of their inner states, proceed with the Temperature Reading process.

Appreciations: In a calm, mindful state, expressing gratitude can be more heartfelt.

Partner 1: In this moment of peace, I realize and appreciate your efforts in co-parenting during this tough time.

New Information: Sharing updates becomes less reactive and more thoughtful.

Partner 2: I've been thinking about our housing situation, and I'd like to discuss some possible solutions.

Puzzles: A meditative state allows for expressing confusion without frustration.

Partner 1: I'm still trying to understand how our weekly schedules will work. Let's explore this together.

Complaints with Recommendations: Meditation helps in addressing issues without heightened emotions.

Partner 2: I feel we sometimes miscommunicate about finances. Maybe we can set a specific time to discuss this calmly.

Wishes, Hopes, and Dreams: Meditation opens up space for positive, forward-looking thoughts.

Both Partners: We hope to move forward in a way that's healthy for us and the best for our children.

Part 3: Closing Meditation for Reflection and Peace

End the session with a short meditation to help internalize the conversation and maintain a sense of calm.

Session Example:

- **Reflective Silence**: "*Let's spend a few moments in silence, reflecting on our conversation.*"

- **Positive Affirmations**: "*Repeat to yourself: 'I am capable of respectful communication. I am open to understanding and being understood.'*"
- **Closure**: "*Take a deep breath and, as you exhale, gently open your eyes, carrying forward this sense of peace and understanding.*"

Combining Temperature Reading with meditation provides a comprehensive approach to communication, especially for couples navigating challenging transitions like divorce. It allows for a deeper connection with one's own emotions and thoughts, and facilitates a more empathetic, understanding interaction with the other person. This approach can be powerful in any relationship or team setting, fostering a climate of mutual respect, mindfulness, and effective communication.

Hologram

Satir's introduction of the "Hologram" concept has significantly enriched the landscape of therapeutic concepts. This metaphor, rooted in the world of science and imagery, provides a profound framework for comprehending individuals and family systems in the context of therapy. The essence of the hologram concept lies in the idea that every part of a system contains information about the whole, much like a fragment of a holographic image encapsulates the entirety of the picture (Satir, 1983).

In the realm of family therapy, the hologram concept holds particular significance. It underscores the interconnectedness of individuals within a family unit and highlights the idea that understanding one member of the family can offer valuable insights into the dynamics of the entire family system, and vice versa. Just as a holographic fragment allows us to reconstruct the complete image, delving into the experiences, emotions, and interactions of a single family member can shed light on the broader familial context (Goldenberg and Goldenberg, 2013).

Satir's "Hologram" metaphor invites therapists and counselors to adopt a holistic perspective when working with families. It encourages them to recognize that change and growth within one family member can reverberate throughout the entire system, potentially leading to transformative shifts in family dynamics. Conversely, by addressing systemic issues and improving family interactions, therapists can contribute to the well-being and personal growth of individual family members (Boyatzis, Goleman, and Rhee, 2013).

This concept challenges therapists to move beyond surface-level observations and delve into the interconnected web of relationships, emotions, and experiences that characterize family systems. It emphasizes the need to approach therapy with an open and perceptive mindset, recognizing that each family member's narrative contributes to the broader story of the family.

In essence, Satir's "Hologram" concept serves as a powerful reminder of the depth and complexity inherent in family therapy. It encourages therapists to explore the multifaceted nature of family dynamics, understanding that every individual within the system plays a vital role in shaping the overall narrative. By embracing this metaphor, therapists can unlock new avenues for facilitating positive change and fostering healthier, more resilient family systems.

The Hologram in Family Systems

The concept of the "Hologram" in the context of family systems therapy offers a profound perspective on how families function as interconnected entities. Within the framework of this metaphor, a family is akin to a holographic entity, where every member acts as a reflection of the dynamics, health, and patterns of the entire family unit. This holistic viewpoint provides therapists with a valuable lens through which to understand and work with family systems (Satir, 1967).

Consider the scenario where a child's behavior appears to be disruptive or problematic within the family. In a traditional view, this behavior might be solely attributed to the child's individual characteristics or issues. However, when viewed through the lens of the family hologram, therapists recognize that the child's behavior is not isolated but is, in fact, a reflection of the broader family dynamics.

In this context, the child's behavior can be seen as a mirror that reflects the unspoken tensions, unresolved conflicts, or hidden issues within the family. It serves as a visible manifestation of the underlying family patterns and dynamics that may be affecting the entire unit. By closely examining these individual expressions within the family system, therapists can gain profound insights into the family's deeper dynamics.

Therapists who embrace the "Hologram" concept understand that addressing the child's behavior alone may provide temporary relief but is unlikely to lead to lasting change. Instead, they recognize the importance of delving deeper into the family's collective narrative. By exploring how each family member's thoughts, emotions, and actions contribute to the overall family dynamic, therapists can uncover the root causes of challenges and conflicts.

This approach fosters a more comprehensive and systemic understanding of family functioning. It encourages therapists to investigate not only the overt behaviors but also the underlying beliefs, communication patterns, and emotional dynamics that shape the family's interactions. By doing so, therapists can identify areas of intervention that have the potential to create transformative change within the family unit as a whole.

In summary, the "Hologram" concept in family systems therapy invites therapists to view families as intricate and interconnected systems. It emphasizes that each family member, whether through their behaviors or emotional expressions, reflects the larger family dynamic. By exploring and addressing these individual reflections, therapists can gain valuable insights into the underlying issues that impact the family as a whole, ultimately facilitating more effective and lasting therapeutic interventions.

Expanding Beyond the Family

While primarily used in family therapy, the hologram concept can be applied in broader contexts, such as organizations or communities. It reminds us that individual actions and attitudes often reflect larger systemic issues and that changes at the individual level can have a ripple effect (Burke and Litwin, 1992).

Application in Therapy and Coaching

- **Identifying Patterns**: In therapy, when a member displays certain behaviors or emotions, these are not viewed in isolation. Instead, they are seen as reflections of broader family patterns or issues.
- **Therapeutic Interventions**: Working with one family member can lead to changes in the entire family system. Therapists use this interconnectedness to facilitate healing and transformation.

- **Empathy and Understanding**: Recognizing that each individual's behavior is a part of a larger picture fosters empathy and a deeper understanding within the family.

> ***Example: The Johnson Family***
>
> The Johnson family came to therapy due to conflicts between the parents and their teenage son, Michael. Through the lens of the hologram, the therapist observed that Michael's rebellious behavior was not just an individual issue but a reflection of the parents' unresolved marital conflicts. As therapy progressed, addressing the couple's relationship indirectly helped alleviate the tension between Michael and his parents.

Satir's Hologram concept offers a powerful perspective in therapy and personal growth. It teaches us that we are not just isolated beings but part of a larger, interconnected system. This understanding fosters a deeper sense of empathy, responsibility, and the potential for holistic change, both within families and in the wider world.

Mobile

In the realm of Satir's groundbreaking family therapy approach, the metaphor of the "Mobile" takes center stage as a profound representation of family dynamics and relationships. The Mobile, a simple yet evocative concept, serves as a powerful symbol for understanding the intricate and interdependent nature of family systems (Wetchler and Piercy, 1996).

Imagine a mobile hanging delicately in a room, with its various components artfully balanced and interconnected. Each element of the mobile, no matter how small or seemingly insignificant, plays a crucial role in maintaining its delicate equilibrium. Similarly, within the context of family systems, the Mobile metaphorically represents the intricate web of connections and relationships that binds family members together.

The Mobile in Family Systems

The Mobile in the context of family systems therapy embodies the idea that every family member's actions, emotions, and interactions are interconnected and have a significant impact on the entire family unit. Just as when one element of a mobile is set in motion it causes a ripple effect throughout the structure, any change or behavior exhibited by one family member can reverberate throughout the entire family system (Middelburg and Gross, 1979).

Consider a scenario where a teenager in a family begins to exhibit signs of withdrawal and isolation. In a conventional perspective, this behavior might be viewed solely as the teenager's individual struggle. However, when viewed through the lens of the Mobile metaphor, therapists recognize that the teenager's actions are not isolated but are intimately connected to the broader family dynamics.

In this context, the teenager's withdrawal may be seen as a response to underlying family tensions, communication patterns, or unresolved conflicts. Like a subtle movement of one element on a mobile causing the entire structure to sway, the teenager's behavior reflects and is influenced by the family's collective emotional landscape.

Therapists who embrace the Mobile concept understand that addressing the teenager's isolation necessitates a systemic approach. They recognize that to bring about lasting change, it is essential to explore how the teenager's behavior is entwined with the family's interactions, emotions, and communication patterns. By doing so, therapists can uncover the deeper issues that contribute to the family's challenges.

This holistic perspective fosters a more profound understanding of family dynamics and relationships. It encourages therapists to examine not only the visible behaviors but also the underlying emotional currents and relational dynamics that shape the family's experiences. By addressing these underlying factors, therapists can work towards restoring balance and harmony within the family system.

In summary, the "Mobile" metaphor in family systems therapy invites therapists and families alike to recognize the interconnectedness of family members and their profound influence on one another. It underscores the idea that family dynamics are not isolated incidents but are part of a delicate and interdependent structure. By understanding and addressing these interconnections, therapists can guide families toward more harmonious and fulfilling relationships.

Application in Therapy and Coaching

- **Understanding Interconnectedness**: The Mobile helps families understand how each member's behavior influences and is influenced by others, fostering a systemic perspective.
- **Identifying Patterns of Influence**: It can be used to identify which family member's actions or emotions are currently causing the most movement (change) within the family system.
- **Restoring Balance**: The goal in therapy becomes not just addressing individual issues, but also restoring balance to the entire family system.

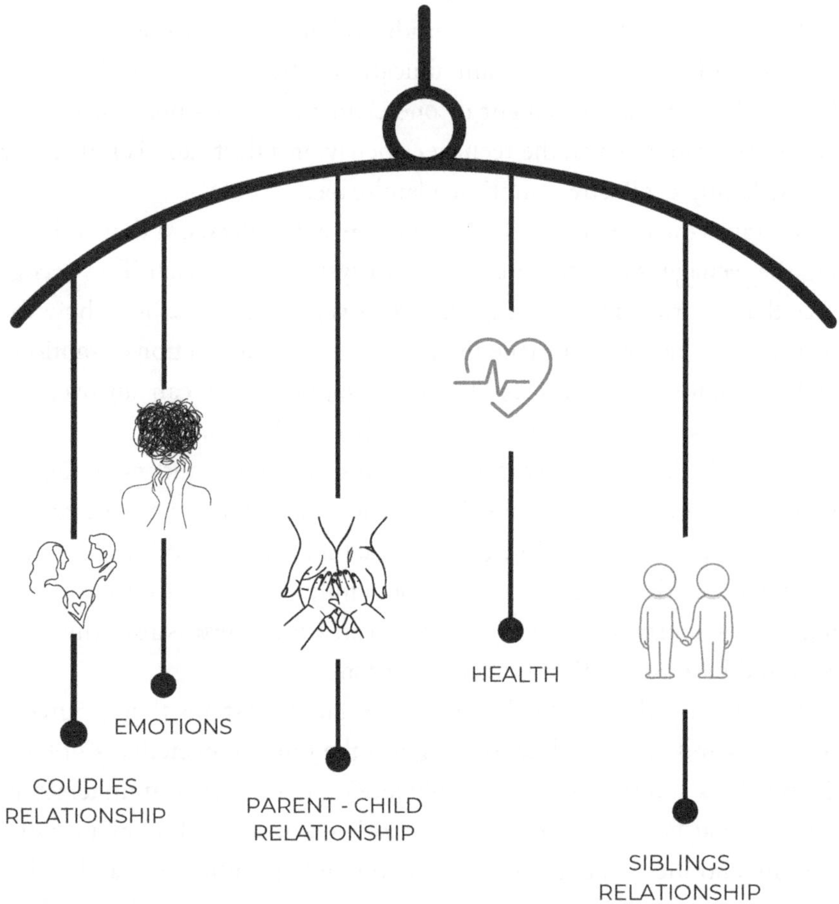

FIGURE 4.3 Mobile Metaphor

Example: Session Using the Mobile Metaphor

The Thompson family, consisting of parents (John and Linda) and two children (Emily, 16, and Max, 12), are in a therapy session addressing conflicts arising from Emily's recent behavioral changes. The therapist introduces the Mobile concept to explore family dynamics.

Therapist: Imagine your family as a mobile hanging from the ceiling. Each of you is a different element that contributes to the mobile's balance. Let's explore how changes in one part affect the whole. John, can you share how you've been feeling in the family lately?

John (Father): Ever since Emily started acting out, I feel like I've had to be the strict one, always enforcing rules.

Therapist: So, in our family mobile, your role has been to add a sense of order. How does this role affect the rest of the family? Linda, what do you think?

Linda (Mother): I find myself trying to soften John's strictness, to keep peace. I guess I'm trying to balance the mobile in my own way.

Therapist: That's an insightful observation, Linda. You're compensating to maintain balance. Emily, how do you see your role in this family mobile?

Emily: I feel like I'm the one everyone's always looking at, like I'm the problem. It's like I'm the part of the mobile that's always moving and causing imbalance.

Therapist: It sounds like you feel you're at the center of the family's challenges. Max, how about you? How do you fit into our family mobile?

Max (Brother): I try to stay out of the way, to not make things worse. I guess I'm like the part that doesn't move much.

Therapist:	It seems like each of you is playing a role that you believe helps maintain some form of balance in the family, yet it's leading to tension. What if we tried adjusting these roles slightly? John, what could happen if you eased some of the strictness?
John:	Well, I might feel less stressed, but I worry about losing control.
Therapist:	Understandable concern. Linda, if John eases his approach, how might that affect your role?
Linda:	Maybe I wouldn't have to always be the mediator. I could be more of myself.
Therapist:	And Emily, if there's less tension between your parents, how might that change your behavior?
Emily:	I might not feel so cornered all the time. I could be more open with them.
Therapist:	And Max, what would change for you?
Max:	I might feel like I can actually be part of the family, not just someone on the sidelines.
Therapist:	This is a great start. Adjusting each of your roles can bring a new balance to your family mobile, one that's more harmonious and reflective of each person's needs. Let's explore more ways to achieve this balance.

In this session, the Mobile metaphor helps the Thompson family understand how each member's behavior impacts the family dynamics. It encourages them to consider how small changes in their roles can lead to a more balanced and healthier family system.

Each part of the Mobile can represent different roles family members play. Understanding these roles can lead to insights into how family members might be maintaining or disrupting the family balance.

The Mobile metaphor extends beyond family therapy. In organizational psychology, social groups, or community dynamics, it illustrates how actions of individuals can affect the larger group, emphasizing the importance of considering systemic impacts in any intervention.

The Mobile metaphor in Satir's work is a powerful tool for visualizing and understanding the complex interplay within families. It emphasizes that in a system where everything is connected, interventions must consider the whole system, not just the individual parts. By recognizing and adjusting these interconnected dynamics, families can achieve a more harmonious and balanced relationship.

Mandala

The Mandala, a Sanskrit word meaning "circle," has been a significant symbol in various cultures and spiritual practices for centuries. At its core, a Mandala represents the universe, wholeness, and the infinite cycle of life. In the context of psychology, Carl Jung, a prominent figure in the early development of psychotherapy, identified Mandalas as a profound tool for personal insight and self-integration. Jung's exploration of Mandalas as reflective of the inner psyche provides a foundational understanding for their use in modern therapeutic practices.

Creating a Mandala can be a deeply introspective process, allowing individuals to express emotions, thoughts, and experiences that may be difficult to articulate verbally. This creative process engages both the conscious and unconscious aspects of the psyche, often revealing insights about one's internal conflicts, dreams, fears, and desires. The act of drawing, coloring, or even simply observing Mandalas can serve as a meditative practice, fostering mindfulness and inner tranquility (Buckbee and Dupont, 2016).

In Satir's therapeutic model, Mandalas illustrate the interconnectedness of an individual's internal and external worlds. Clients explore how their thoughts, emotions, and behaviors affect their relationships (Piddocke, 2010). This aligns closely with other projective techniques in the Satir model, such as Sand Tray therapy, where externalizing internal worlds helps transform trauma and facilitate healing (De Little, 2012; Wang and Peng, 2017).

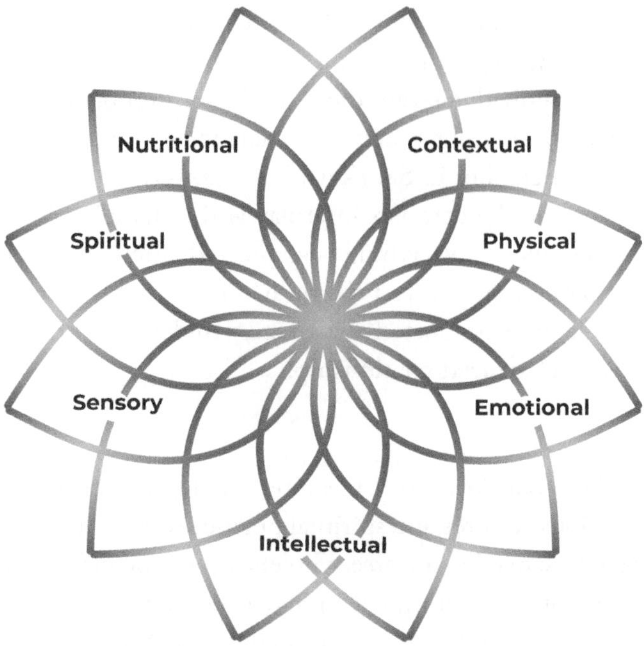

FIGURE 4.4 Self Mandala

The process of creating a Mandala can be a therapeutic journey in itself. For clients undergoing transformational therapy, the act of designing a Mandala serves as a form of non-verbal expression, allowing emotions and thoughts to flow onto paper without the constraints of language. This form of expression is particularly valuable in uncovering emotions and thoughts that clients may not yet be ready or able to articulate verbally. The shapes, colors, and patterns chosen unconsciously reflect the creator's inner emotional state, providing valuable insights to both the client and the therapist.

For therapists practicing Satir's methods, Mandalas offer a unique window into the client's subconscious. By analyzing the elements of a client's Mandala, therapists can glean insights into their inner conflicts, fears, joys, and aspirations. This reflection can be particularly powerful in addressing deep-seated issues. The symmetry and balance inherent in Mandalas also help clients visualize harmony and balance in their lives, often a goal in transformational therapy.

Therapists can facilitate the Mandala creation process by providing a safe and supportive environment. It's essential to encourage clients to let go of any artistic self-judgment and focus on the process rather than the outcome. Therapists can guide clients in selecting themes or focal points for their Mandalas, such as a current emotion, a significant life event, or a personal goal. This directed focus helps clients channel their thoughts and feelings more effectively into their art.

Once a client has created a Mandala, the therapist and client can explore its meanings together. This exploration is not about imposing interpretations but rather about opening a dialogue. Questions like "What does this color say about how you're feeling?" or "What does the center of the Mandala represent for you?" can help clients delve deeper into their psyche. This process not only aids in self-discovery but also strengthens the therapeutic relationship, building trust and understanding.

Incorporating Mandala exercises into therapy sessions can be a flexible and dynamic process. Therapists can use Mandala creation as a regular part of sessions or as an occasional tool to deepen understanding or overcome specific hurdles. It's also beneficial to adapt the approach to fit the client's comfort level with art and their stage in therapy. For some, simple coloring of pre-drawn Mandalas can be a starting point, gradually moving towards more personal and complex creations (Nesbit, 2012).

Case Study 1: Navigating Family Dynamics

Background: A client, Emily, was struggling with her role within her family system, feeling both overwhelmed and underappreciated. Despite numerous verbal therapy sessions, she found it challenging to articulate her emotions fully.

Mandala Exercise: Emily was guided to create a Mandala that represented her family system. She used different colors and shapes to symbolize various family members and their relationships with each other.

Outcome: Through her Mandala, Emily identified a pattern of being on the periphery of her family, represented by placing herself as small circles on the Mandala's edge. This visual representation led to a breakthrough in understanding her feelings of isolation and initiated a discussion on ways to strengthen her presence within her family dynamics.

Case Study 2: Addressing Personal Trauma

Background: John, a client with a history of trauma, found it difficult to speak about his past experiences, leading to blocked emotional expression.

Mandala Exercise: The therapist introduced Mandala drawing as a non-verbal way to explore his inner world. John was asked to create a Mandala focusing on his feelings and memories associated with his trauma.

Outcome: John's Mandala featured chaotic patterns and dark colors in the center, moving towards brighter colors and organized patterns towards the edges. This progression visually represented his journey from turmoil to healing, providing a starting point for discussing his trauma and recovery process.

Case Study 3: Enhancing Self-Esteem and Personal Growth

Background: Lisa sought therapy for low self-esteem and difficulty in decision-making. She often felt lost in defining her identity.

Mandala Exercise: The therapist suggested creating a Mandala that represented Lisa's ideal self. She was encouraged to incorporate elements that symbolized her strengths, aspirations, and values.

Outcome: Lisa's Mandala was vibrant and contained symbols of strength, such as a lion in the center and rays of sunlight. This exercise helped her visualize her potential and discuss ways to bridge the gap between her current self and ideal self.

Application in Therapy and Coaching

- **Group Therapy Sessions**: Mandalas can be used in group settings to foster a sense of community and shared experience. Each member creates their own Mandala, followed by group discussions about the process and insights gained.
- **Self-Awareness Workshops**: In workshops focusing on self-awareness and personal development, participants can be guided

through Mandala exercises to explore their inner thoughts and feelings.

- **Stress Reduction Programs**: Mandalas can be incorporated into stress reduction and mindfulness programs, providing a meditative and calming activity that aids in emotional regulation.

Mandala Exercises

Mandala exercises in therapy and coaching can be tailored to suit various needs and objectives. These exercises aim to facilitate self-expression, introspection, and personal growth. Below are detailed descriptions and instructions for a range of Mandala-based exercises.

EXERCISE 1: THE EMOTION WHEEL MANDALA

Objective: To help clients identify and express their emotions.
Instructions:

1. Provide the client with a blank Mandala template that has concentric circles and divided sections, resembling a wheel.
2. Ask the client to think of different emotions they have experienced recently and allocate each emotion a color.
3. Instruct them to fill in each section of the Mandala with colors corresponding to their emotions, focusing on the intensity and frequency of these emotions.
4. After completion, discuss the Mandala, exploring the prevalence and interplay of various emotions.

EXERCISE 2: THE LIFE JOURNEY MANDALA

Objective: To assist clients in reflecting on their life journey and significant events.
Instructions:

1. Encourage the client to think of their life as a story and imagine how they would represent this story in a circular form.
2. Provide art materials like colored pencils, markers, and paints.

3. Guide them to depict their life journey in the Mandala, using symbols, colors, and patterns to represent different life stages and key events.
4. Reflect on the completed Mandala, discussing the patterns, changes, and any insights that emerge.

EXERCISE 3: THE FUTURE SELF MANDALA

Objective: To help clients envision their future selves and goals.
Instructions:

1. Ask the client to imagine where they see themselves in the future – personally, professionally, emotionally, and spiritually.
2. Encourage them to represent these aspirations in a Mandala, using symbols and colors that resonate with their vision.
3. After the Mandala is created, explore the elements within it, discussing how they relate to the client's hopes, dreams, and steps needed to achieve them.

EXERCISE 4: THE STRESS RELEASE MANDALA

Objective: To provide a calming and meditative exercise for stress relief.
Instructions:

1. Offer the client a pre-drawn Mandala with intricate patterns.
2. Encourage them to color the Mandala, focusing on the process and the sensations of coloring, rather than the outcome.
3. Use this as a mindfulness exercise, guiding the client to notice their breath and any physical or emotional sensations as they color.

TIPS FOR THERAPISTS AND COACHES

- **Adaptability**: Adjust the complexity and nature of the exercises based on the client's comfort with art and their therapeutic needs.
- **Non-judgmental Approach**: Emphasize that the process is more important than artistic skill. Encourage clients to express themselves freely without fear of judgment.

- **Active Listening and Exploration**: During discussions, actively listen and encourage clients to delve deeper into the meanings and symbolism in their Mandalas.
- **Cultural Sensitivity**: Be aware of cultural meanings attached to symbols and colors. This is particularly crucial when applying Satir's model to diverse populations, such as Hispanic families or Asian contexts, where symbols may hold specific communal significance (Bermudez, 2008; Cheung and Chan, 2002). Additionally, tools like "Say It Straight" can be integrated here to help clients verbalize the insights they gain from their visual creations (Englander-Golden, Elconin, and Satir, 1986).

Mandalas, in their multifaceted nature, serve as a powerful tool in transformational therapy, resonating deeply with Satir's emphasis on self-awareness and personal growth. The creation and interpretation of Mandalas can facilitate a deeper understanding of oneself and one's place in the broader system of relationships and environments. As we move forward, the practical application of Mandalas in therapeutic settings will be explored, demonstrating their effectiveness in aiding emotional expression and uncovering deep-seated issues.

References

Bermudez, D. (2008). Adapting Virginia Satir techniques to Hispanic families. *The Family Journal*, *16*(1), 51–57.

Boyatzis, R.E., Goleman, D., Rhee, K. (2013). Emotional and social intelligence competencies: Cross-cultural implications. *Cross Cultural Management: An International Journal*, *20*(1), 20–30.

Buckbee, S., Dupont, M. (2016). The Mandala, a model for teaching and therapy. *Satir International Journal*, *4*(1), 56–58.

Burke, W.W., Litwin, G.H. (1992). A causal model of organizational performance and change. *Journal of Management*, *18*(3), 523–545.

Cheung, G.Y.K., and Chan, C. (2002). The Satir model and cultural sensitivity: A Hong Kong reflection. *Contemporary Family Therapy: An International Journal*, *24*(1), 199–215.

De Little, M. (2012). Transformation in the sand tray: Examples of the Satir model in sand tray therapy. *The Satir Journal*, *5*(1), 49–64.

Englander-Golden, P., Elconin, J., Satir, V. (1986). Assertive/leveling communication and empathy in adolescent drug abuse prevention. *Journal of Primary Prevention*, *6*(4), 231–243.

Goldenberg, I., Goldenberg, H. (2013). *Family Therapy: An Overview*. Boston, MA: Cengage Learning.

Middelburg, C., Gross, S. (1979). Families' affective rules and their relationship to the families' adjustment. *The American Journal of Family Therapy*, 7(2), 37–45.

Nesbit, C. (2009). Ingredients of our internal process: A series of meditations from Virginia Satir. *The Satir Journal*, *3*(3), 71–75.

Nesbit, C. (2012). Love and light. *The Satir Journal*, *5*(1), 75–77.

Piddocke, S. (2010). The self: Reflections on its nature and structure according to the Satir model. *The Satir Journal*, *4*(1), 109–154.

Satir, V. (1967). Family systems and the approach to family therapy. *Journal of Fort Logan Mental Health Center*, *4*(2), 81–93.

Satir, V. (1983). *Conjoint Family Therapy*. Palo Alto, CA: Science and Behavior Books, Inc.

Wang, E.N., Peng, X. (2017). Intervention effect of group counseling on meaning of life: A therapy based on sand play and the Satir model. *Chinese Journal of Clinical Psychology*, *25*, 315–318.

Wetchler, M., Piercy, F. (1996). Experiential family therapies. In Piercy, F., Sprenkle, D., Wetchler, M., et al. (1996), *Family Therapy Sourcebook* (2nd ed.). New York: Guildford Press.

5
Advanced Concepts and Integration

Systemic Repatterning: An Innovative Approach for Group Dynamics

Introduction to Systemic Repatterning in Group Settings

Systemic Repatterning is tailored for group dynamics, particularly effective in corporate teams and executive groups. It innovatively integrates family reconstruction concepts with systemic organizational theory, addressing patterns that impede group functionality and cohesion. This method facilitates the discovery and remodeling of interactional patterns within professional groups, enhancing collective performance and interpersonal relations (Haitoglou, 2022).

Core Concepts

- **Systemic Understanding**: Recognizes that group behaviors are influenced by complex systems, mirroring family dynamics (Burke and Litwin, 1992).
- **Pattern Disruption**: Focuses on identifying and disrupting unproductive patterns that hinder group effectiveness.
- **Role Dynamics**: Explores individual roles within the group and their impact on group interactions and outcomes.
- **Collective Repatterning**: Engages the group in exercises that foster new, more productive ways of interacting and decision-making.

DOI: 10.4324/9781003716419-5

Protocol for Systemic Repatterning in Groups

1. **Group Assessment**: Conduct a comprehensive assessment of group dynamics, communication styles, and role distributions.
2. **Identification of Systemic Patterns**: Through observations and guided discussions, identify key behavioral and communicative patterns within the group.
3. **Designing Interventions**: Develop specific interventions, such as systemic constellations, role-plays, and feedback exercises, aimed at addressing identified patterns.
4. **Interactive Repatterning Sessions**: Facilitate sessions where group members participate in structured activities to experience and practice new interaction patterns.
5. **Integration and Reflection**: Conclude with a group reflection, discussing insights gained and strategies for integrating new patterns into workplace dynamics.

Example: Systemic Repatterning in a Corporate Team

Background: A corporate team struggling with siloed communication and unclear leadership roles.

Facilitator: Let's set up a constellation representing your current team structure. Position yourselves as you perceive your role and relation to others in the team.

(*The team arranges themselves, revealing isolated clusters and a lack of clear leadership.*)

Facilitator: Observe this physical representation of your team. Let's discuss what this setup reveals.

Team Member: It's clear we're fragmented. I'm far from others, indicating how isolated I feel in my role.

Facilitator: Now, let's rearrange this constellation to represent a more cohesive and functional team dynamic. Consider communication flow and leadership.

(*The team repositions, creating a more interconnected formation.*)

Facilitator:	(*After the repositioning*) Reflect on how this new arrangement feels and how it might translate into your day-to-day interactions.

Innovative Applications

- **Virtual Reality and AI Integration**: Utilize virtual reality technology for remote teams to engage in systemic repatterning. Recent studies have even applied machine learning algorithms to classify Satir's coping stances, offering data-driven insights into communication patterns that were previously subjective (Wang et al., 2022).
- **Digital Health Platforms**: The integration of Satir's model into digital platforms has shown remarkable success. For instance, combining health education with the Satir model via platforms like **WeChat** has been proven to improve self-management behaviors and social adaptation in patients, demonstrating the model's versatility in the digital age (Feng et al., 2021).
- **Feedback Loops with Real-Time Analytics**: Incorporate real-time feedback tools to provide analytics on communication patterns during exercises, enhancing awareness and learning.
- **Cross-Functional Team Dynamics**: Apply systemic repatterning across different departments to improve interdepartmental collaboration and understanding.

Outcomes and Benefits

- **Enhanced Team Cohesion**: Fosters a deeper understanding among team members, leading to improved cohesion and collaboration (Boyatzis, Goleman, and Rhee, 2013).
- **Effective Communication**: Breaks down communication barriers, promoting a culture of open dialogue and constructive feedback.
- **Leadership Development**: Clarifies and strengthens leadership roles within the group, enhancing overall team direction and purpose.

Conclusion: Revolutionizing Group Dynamics

Systemic Repatterning represents a cutting-edge approach to reshaping group dynamics in professional settings. By applying principles of family reconstruction and systemic theory to group and organizational contexts, this method offers a unique pathway to enhancing team functionality and interpersonal relationships. Its innovative applications promise to revolutionize how teams and organizations address systemic challenges, paving the way for more integrated, effective, and cohesive group interactions (Strider, 2013).

Navigating Group Dynamics

As I developed the Systemic Repatterning method, my goal was to bring about transformative change in team dynamics. Drawing on my extensive experience with executives and businesses, I crafted a process that not only identifies but also actively reshapes the patterns that define group interactions. Let me walk you through the journey of this method.

1. **Unveiling the Group's Core: Assessment Phase**

In my early encounters with teams, I start by peeling back the layers of their interaction. This phase is all about observation and listening. I use surveys and interviews, but most importantly, I observe their natural interactions in meetings or group sessions. It's like being a detective in a world of unspoken words and hidden emotions, where each gesture and pause speaks volumes.

My Observation: During one team meeting, I noticed that when certain members spoke, others visibly withdrew. This observation was the key to understanding their underlying dynamics.

2. **The Revelation: Identifying Systemic Patterns**

The next step is about connecting the dots. I sit down with the team and lay out the patterns I've observed. It's often an eye-opening moment. Using visual tools, I help them see the "dance" they unknowingly participate in every day.

A Pivotal Session: In one session, when I mapped out the communication flow, the team was stunned to see how their interaction mirrored a hierarchical structure, stifling open communication.

3. **The Blueprint for Change: Designing Interventions**

This is where creativity meets psychology. I tailor activities that directly address the team's unique challenges. These interventions are not just exercises; they are experiences designed to shift perspectives and provoke introspection.

My Approach: For a team struggling with hierarchical barriers, I designed a role-reversal exercise. It wasn't just about changing places; it was about stepping into each other's worlds.

4. **The Transformation Begins: Interactive Repatterning Sessions**

During these sessions, the magic happens. The team engages in the activities, and I guide them through the experience. It's a process of unlearning and relearning, of breaking down barriers and building new bridges.

A Memorable Moment: In a session, a usually reserved team member assumed the leader's role. The shift in his demeanor was remarkable, illuminating the untapped potential within the team.

5. **Cementing the Change: Integration and Reflection**

Change is only as good as its sustainability. In this final phase, we reflect on the insights gained and develop strategies for integrating the new patterns into daily practice. It's about turning short-term revelations into long-term evolutions.

Our Collective Journey: In one team, we decided to introduce regular open forums. This small step marked the beginning of a new era of communication for them.

Systemic Coaching and Mentoring

As psychotherapy pivots from compartmentalized medical models towards ecological perspectives acknowledging personal, relational, and collective dimensions of wellbeing, coaching philosophies revolutionized by Satir's systemic insights help integrate her lifespan growth vision across more holistic conversations (Banmen, 2006). Satir Systemic Coaches and Mentors are trained to illuminate the ripple effects of self-concept, communication patterns, and contextual dynamics in shaping the situations clients face. Then experientially, they guide mapping parts, sculpting burdens, and reconstructing narratives towards coherent alignment between one's inner and outer worlds. Altogether, Satir Systemic Coaching and Mentoring expands clinical spaces into creative containers for societal healing (Haitoglou, 2017).

In the ever-evolving landscape of coaching and personal development, Systemic Coaching and Mentoring has emerged as a powerful approach that delves deep into the interconnected web of human experience. Drawing inspiration from various fields, including family therapy, organizational psychology, and systems thinking, Systemic Coaching and Mentoring offers a holistic framework for facilitating profound transformation.

A Holistic Perspective: At the core of Systemic Coaching is the recognition that individuals are not isolated entities but are embedded within larger systems. These systems encompass family dynamics, organizational structures, cultural influences, and more. Coaches operating within this paradigm understand that personal growth and change are intimately linked to these broader systems.

Navigating Complexity: In a world characterized by complexity and rapid change, Systemic Coaching and Mentoring equips individuals with the tools to navigate the intricate web of relationships and influences. Coaches guide clients in exploring the dynamics that impact their lives, helping them uncover hidden patterns and connections.

Unearthing Unconscious Influences: One of the key tenets of Systemic Coaching is the exploration of unconscious influences. Clients are encouraged to delve deep into their belief systems, values, and family histories. By bringing these hidden forces to light, individuals gain greater self-awareness and the ability to make conscious choices.

Relationship-Centered: Systemic Coaching places a strong emphasis on relationships. Whether it's improving communication within a family, enhancing teamwork in an organization, or fostering healthier connections in personal relationships, the coaching process revolves around building and nurturing these vital connections.

Systemic Tools: Coaches in this field utilize a rich toolbox of systemic tools and techniques. These may include genograms to map family dynamics, organizational constellations to explore workplace issues, and various forms of dialogue and role-play to facilitate understanding and change.

Embracing Diversity: Systemic Coaching recognizes the diversity of human experiences and contexts. It embraces individuals from all walks of life and acknowledges that each person's journey is unique. Coaches in this field are skilled at adapting their approach to meet the specific needs and backgrounds of their clients.

Empowering Change: Ultimately, Systemic Coaching is about empowering individuals to enact positive change within themselves and their systems. It's a collaborative journey where clients gain not only greater self-awareness but also the tools and insights needed to transform their lives (Loeschen, 2005).

As we venture further into an era defined by interconnectedness and interdependence, Systemic Coaching stands as a beacon of guidance. It offers individuals and organizations a profound means of navigating the complex terrain of the human experience, fostering growth, resilience, and meaningful transformation.

Sharon Loeschen has developed a coaching program that incorporates elements of Virginia Satir's work. Her program, often referred to as the "Satir Coaching" program, draws inspiration from Satir's systemic approach to family therapy and applies it to the coaching context.

Loeschen's Satir Coaching and Mentoring program emphasizes the following key aspects.

1. **Systemic Perspective**: Similar to Satir's approach in family therapy, Satir Coaching takes a systemic perspective. It recognizes that individuals are influenced by their family systems, personal history, and social context. Coaches using this approach explore how these factors impact clients' thoughts, behaviors, and goals.
2. **Communication and Self-Expression**: Satir Coaching places a strong emphasis on effective communication and self-expression. Clients are encouraged to explore and improve their communication skills, as well as to express their emotions and needs openly and authentically.
3. **Transformation and Growth**: The program aims to facilitate personal transformation and growth. Coaches work with clients to identify areas where they seek personal development, whether it's in relationships, self-esteem, or other aspects of life. The goal is to help clients achieve positive change and self-discovery.

4. **Empathy and Connection**: Just as Satir highlighted the importance of empathy and connection within families, Satir Coaching prioritizes building a strong coaching relationship based on empathy and trust. Coaches strive to create a safe and supportive space for clients to explore their challenges and aspirations.
5. **Practical Tools and Techniques**: Satir Coaching provides clients with practical tools and techniques to navigate life's challenges. These tools may include visualization exercises, role-play, and other experiential methods aimed at fostering personal insight and growth.

It's important to note that while Loeschen's program is inspired by Satir's work, it has evolved into its own unique approach to coaching. Coaches who incorporate Satir Coaching principles into their practice aim to empower individuals to overcome obstacles, improve their relationships, and lead more fulfilling lives.

If you're interested in learning more about the Satir Coaching program, I recommend exploring resources, as well as considering training or certification programs offered by the Satir Global organization or affiliated institutions.

Emotional Intelligence and Self-Leadership

In a rapidly evolving world, where personal and professional growth is paramount, the Satir Coaching and Mentoring Program stands as a beacon of transformation. This comprehensive program is designed to enhance emotional intelligence, foster self-leadership, and empower individuals to navigate the intricate web of human relationships and experiences (Loeschen and Jendrusakova, 2015).

A Holistic Approach: At the heart of the Satir Coaching and Mentoring Program lies a holistic approach to personal development. It recognizes that growth is not a solitary journey but an interconnected exploration of self and others. Whether you're embarking on this journey for personal enrichment or to become a certified Satir Coach and Mentor, the program offers a structured path to self-discovery and empowerment.

Learning Objectives: The program is structured into three levels, each tailored to support your growth and knowledge acquisition while providing ample opportunities for practice and skill development. Here are the key learning objectives for each level:

Level 1 – Enriching Your Relationship with Your Self and Others

- Making Contact: Learn to pause, slow down, and pay attention to your thoughts and feelings.
- Validating: Acknowledge and accept your feelings while highlighting your inner resources and values.
- Facilitating Awareness: Develop an understanding of your behaviors and what drives them.
- Promoting Acceptance: Gain greater acceptance of your disliked parts and those of others.
- Making Changes: Make positive choices and changes in your life.
- Reinforcing Changes: Seek support during times of stress and change.
- Deepening Connection: Strengthen your connection with yourself and others.
- Deepening Self-Value: Enhance your sense of self-worth.
- Deepening Awareness: Recognize defensive behaviors and their drivers.
- Opening to Greater Acceptance: Embrace disliked parts and encourage others to do the same.
- Integrating Skills: Bring together the skills and knowledge gained in the previous lessons.

Level 2 – Satir's Theoretical Concepts and her Process

- Explore Satir's foundational concepts, including the Use of Self and a Growth Mindset.
- Dive into the understanding of families and individuals as systems.
- Uncover the power of the Self-Mandala and the Inner Levels of Experience.
- Delve into the pivotal role of Self-Esteem and Self-Worth in communication.
- Explore the spiritual dimension of personal growth.

Level 3 – Satir Coaching and Mentoring Specialist Training

- Understand the phases of helping in Satir Coaching and Mentoring.
- Master the art of making contact with yourself and others.
- Develop the skill of validating yourself using your inner resources.
- Affirm your values and learn to highlight a coachee's resources.
- Cultivate empathy in responding to both yourself and coachees.
- Deepen your ability to respond empathically to coachees.
- Become aware of defensive behaviors and their drivers.
- Facilitate coachee awareness of defensive behaviors.
- Accept your disliked parts and promote coachee acceptance of theirs.
- Learn to make changes within yourself and seek support.
- Elicit and reinforce changes in coachees.
- Guide coachees in choosing to live by their values.
- Apply all phases of helping and review growth readiness for certification.

The Satir Coaching and Mentoring Program is sponsored by the Virginia Satir Global Network. And it is through this international body that the certifications for the program are awarded, ensuring that you receive top-quality training in the Satir approach.

Flexibility and Accessibility: The program offers flexibility, allowing you to participate fully online through Zoom or in person, making it accessible to individuals from diverse backgrounds and locations.

A Journey of Self-Discovery: Whether you're embarking on this journey for personal growth or to become a certified Satir Coach and Mentor, the program offers a profound exploration of self, relationships, and the art of transformation.

Join us on this transformative journey, where you'll not only enhance your emotional intelligence but also become a catalyst for positive change in your own life and the lives of others (The Virginia Satir Institute, n.d.).

Compatibility with Other Therapeutic Approaches

In the ever-evolving field of psychotherapy, the compatibility with different therapeutic approaches has become increasingly important. This section of our book delves into how the timeless techniques of Virginia Satir are being effectively combined with contemporary therapeutic modalities, such as Emotion-Focused Therapy (EFT), Cognitive Behavioral Therapy (CBT), and mindfulness practices. We explore the synergistic potential of these integrations, offering both therapists and clients new avenues for growth and healing (Haber, 2002).

Cognitive Behavioral Therapy (CBT)

The compatibility of Cognitive Behavioral Therapy (CBT) and Satir's family therapy approach offers a holistic framework for addressing both individual and systemic issues within a therapeutic context. CBT, renowned for its effectiveness in altering dysfunctional thoughts and behaviors, complements Satir's emphasis on enhancing family communication and deepening emotional connections.

This synergy becomes particularly potent in addressing issues where individual cognitive patterns impact family dynamics. For instance, CBT's focus on identifying and challenging irrational or harmful thought patterns can be invaluable in a family setting where such thoughts contribute to dysfunctional interactions. Satir's approach, which concentrates on open and honest communication and nurturing self-esteem, can then be utilized to facilitate healthier and more understanding interactions among family members (Banmen, 2002).

In a typical therapy session that combines these two approaches, the therapist might begin by employing CBT techniques to help individual family members identify specific negative thoughts that are contributing to issues within the family. For example, a family member who consistently feels unloved or unappreciated may hold a core belief that they are unworthy of love. CBT strategies can help them challenge and reframe these thoughts.

Once these individual patterns are identified and addressed, Satir's techniques can be introduced to improve the ways in which these thoughts and emotions are communicated within the family. Satir's methods, such as using "I" statements and family sculpting exercises, can help family members express their newfound understanding of their personal thought patterns and how these affect their interactions with others. This not only enhances individual self-awareness but also fosters empathy within the family unit.

Moreover, CBT's structured approach to problem-solving can be effectively combined with Satir's more experiential techniques. For instance, once a family member has worked through their individual cognitive distortions using CBT techniques, Satir's methods can be used to role-play new ways of interacting based on these insights. This can help the entire family practice and solidify healthier communication patterns.

However, combining CBT and Satir's approach requires careful navigation. The therapist must balance the individual-focused nature of CBT with the systemic focus of Satir's approach. This involves ensuring that while individual thought patterns are addressed, the overall goal of enhancing family communication and connection is not lost. Moreover, therapists need to be mindful of not letting the structured nature of CBT overshadow the more fluid and dynamic aspects of Satir's methods (Satir, 1983).

In conclusion, combining CBT with Satir's family therapy approach creates a comprehensive therapeutic model that addresses both individual cognitive processes and family interaction patterns. This fusion approach not only helps in resolving current family issues but also equips family members with skills and techniques that promote long-term emotional health and stronger family relationships.

Example: Satir's Family Therapy with Cognitive Behavioral Therapy (CBT) in Managing Family Anxiety

Consider a family therapy session with the Thompsons, a family of four where each member is dealing with anxiety manifesting in different ways. The combination of Satir's methods with CBT aims to address both individual anxiety symptoms and dysfunctional family communication patterns.

INITIAL SESSION: ESTABLISHING THE FRAMEWORK

Therapist: Welcome, Thompson family. Our goal here is to create a space where each of you can explore your feelings and learn healthier ways to communicate and support each other. We'll be combining some strategies from Cognitive Behavioral Therapy, which helps in understanding and managing your thoughts and behaviors, with Satir's family therapy approach, focusing on improving how we connect and communicate as a family.

IDENTIFYING PATTERNS: A CBT AND SATIR COMBINED APPROACH

Therapist: Let's start by talking about moments when anxiety is most present. I'd like each of you to share what you feel and think during these moments.

Mr. Thompson (Father): I worry constantly about providing for the family. It feels like a pressure that never goes away.

- **CBT Technique**: The therapist works with Mr. Thompson to identify specific thoughts and how they contribute to his anxiety. For instance, identifying thoughts like "I must be perfect" and understanding how they are unrealistic and unhelpful.

Mrs. Thompson (Mother): When he's stressed, he becomes distant. We all feel it. I try to keep the kids calm, but it's hard.

- **Satir's Communication Exercise**: The therapist guides Mrs. Thompson in expressing her feelings more openly to her husband using "I" statements, a technique from Satir's method, to facilitate clearer and more empathetic communication.

ROLE-PLAYING SESSION: PRACTICING NEW COMMUNICATION SKILLS

Therapist: Let's try a role-playing exercise. Mr. Thompson, express your worry about work as you would at home. Mrs. Thompson and kids, respond as you typically would, and then we'll try some new ways of communicating about it.

- After the initial role-play, the therapist highlights patterns and introduces new communication strategies.

INTRODUCING CBT AND SATIR TECHNIQUES

Therapist: Now, let's try that again, but this time, Mr. Thompson, I want you to pause and consider a more balanced thought before you speak. Mrs. Thompson, acknowledge his effort to communicate differently, and express your feelings using "I" statements.

- **Practical Application**: The family engages in the role-play again, this time incorporating the new techniques. Mr. Thompson practices cognitive restructuring by reframing his anxious thought, and Mrs. Thompson uses Satir's communication techniques to express her feelings.

HOMEWORK AND APPLICATION

Therapist: For the next week, I'd like each of you to practice these techniques. Mr. Thompson, whenever you notice an anxious thought, write it down and reframe it. Mrs. Thompson, continue using "I" statements to express your feelings to your family.

REFLECTING AND BUILDING UPON PROGRESS

In subsequent sessions, the therapist reviews the homework with the family, discussing challenges and successes. The therapist continues to blend CBT and Satir's methods, tailoring techniques to the family's evolving dynamics.

VERBATIM FROM A FOLLOW-UP SESSION

Emily (Daughter): I tried telling Dad how I felt when he missed my recital, using what we practiced. It was hard, but I think he understood.

Therapist: That's a big step, Emily. Mr. Thompson, how did it feel hearing Emily express herself this way?

Mr. Thompson: It was eye-opening. I didn't realize how my anxiety was affecting her. It made me want to work harder at managing my thoughts and being there for her.

CONCLUSION

This extended example provides a detailed view of how Satir's family therapy can be combined with CBT to address family anxiety. The verbatim extract from sessions offers insight into the practical application of these techniques, demonstrating their effectiveness in improving both individual and family functioning.

Dialectical Behavior Therapy (DBT)

Combining Dialectical Behavior Therapy (DBT) with Satir's family therapy approach presents a unique opportunity to address both individual and family dynamics in a comprehensive manner. DBT, with its core components of mindfulness, emotional regulation, distress tolerance, and interpersonal effectiveness, offers tools for individuals to understand and manage their emotions and behaviors. On the other hand, Satir's approach, with its focus on enhancing communication, nurturing self-esteem, and understanding family roles and systems, provides a framework for improving family interactions and dynamics.

The synergy between these two approaches becomes particularly evident when addressing issues like emotional dysregulation within families. For instance, DBT's mindfulness techniques can significantly enhance family members' awareness of their emotions and reactions during interactions. When family members become more mindful of their emotional states, they can communicate more effectively and empathetically, aligning well with Satir's emphasis on open and honest communication (Banmen and Banmen, 1991).

Moreover, DBT's emotional regulation strategies can be employed to help family members manage intense emotions, contributing to healthier family dynamics. Such strategies can be integrated into Satir's family therapy sessions, where families can learn to express their emotions in a constructive manner. For example, in a scenario where a family member feels overwhelmed by anger or frustration, employing DBT's emotional regulation techniques can help them to approach the situation more calmly, thus enabling a more productive conversation using Satir's communication tools.

Distress tolerance, another key component of DBT, is particularly useful in managing family conflicts. These skills can help family members cope with stressful situations without resorting to destructive behaviors. Integrating these skills into Satir's family sculpting exercises can enhance the family's ability to navigate and resolve conflicts. In such exercises, family members can physically represent their emotional states and relationships, and employing distress tolerance skills can help them stay grounded and focused, even when discussing difficult or triggering topics.

Interpersonal effectiveness, a crucial aspect of DBT, focuses on improving relationships and communication skills. This aspect of DBT can be seamlessly integrated with Satir's communication stances to foster more effective and empathetic communication within the family. For instance, role-playing scenarios that blend DBT's interpersonal effectiveness skills with Satir's family therapy techniques can be particularly effective. In these scenarios, family members can practice asking for what they need and saying no when necessary, in a manner that respects both their own needs and those of other family members.

However, integrating these approaches is not without challenges. Resistance to mindfulness practices, balancing individual and family needs, and ensuring that each family member's voice is heard and valued are some of the potential hurdles. Moreover, ethical considerations, particularly around consent when introducing new techniques, are paramount. Therapists must navigate these challenges thoughtfully, ensuring that they maintain ethical standards and cater to the unique needs of each family.

In conclusion, the integration of DBT with Satir's family therapy offers a rich, multifaceted approach to therapy. By combining DBT's focus on individual skills with Satir's emphasis on family systems, therapists can provide more holistic and effective treatment. This approach not only addresses individual emotional and behavioral issues but also fosters healthier and more constructive family dynamics.

Example: Satir's Family Therapy with Dialectical Behavior Therapy (DBT) for the Henderson Family

The Hendersons are dealing with heightened emotional volatility and communication breakdowns, particularly between the teenage children, Emily and Josh, and their parents.

STAGE 1: ESTABLISHING A THERAPEUTIC FOUNDATION

Therapist: I'm glad to see all of you today. Our goal is to create a space where each of you feels heard and understood. We'll be combining DBT, which is excellent for understanding and managing emotions, with Satir's family therapy to enhance how you connect and communicate. Let's start by sharing how each of you currently feels within the family.

- After each member shares, the therapist acknowledges their feelings, setting a tone of empathy and understanding.

STAGE 2: INDIVIDUAL AND FAMILY DYNAMICS

Therapist: Emily, you mentioned feeling overwhelmed during family arguments. Let's explore those feelings. What goes through your mind during these moments?

Emily: I just feel like everything is falling apart. I think I should fix it, but I don't know how.

- **DBT Technique**: The therapist teaches Emily mindfulness techniques to observe her emotions without immediately reacting.
- **Satir's Technique**: The therapist helps Emily articulate her feelings using "I feel" statements.

STAGE 3: ROLE-PLAYING FOR SKILL INTEGRATION

Therapist: Let's recreate a recent argument. Pay attention to your thoughts and feelings, and try to use the skills we discussed.

- **Role-Play Example**:

Emily (using mindfulness): I notice my heart racing and I'm thinking it's all my fault.

Therapist: Excellent observation, Emily. Now, express that using an "I feel" statement.

Emily: I feel anxious and overwhelmed when we argue. I feel like it's up to me to fix it.

- The family discusses the new communication dynamic, with the therapist providing guidance.

STAGE 4: ADVANCED INTEGRATION – EMOTIONAL REGULATION AND COMMUNICATION

Therapist: Now, let's use DBT to manage your emotions during these conflicts. We'll follow it with a family sculpting exercise to explore how we physically and emotionally position ourselves in these situations.

- **DBT Emotional Regulation**: The therapist guides the family through identifying and managing their immediate emotional responses.
- **Family Sculpting**: Each family member positions others to represent the emotional landscape of a typical argument.

STAGE 5: HOMEWORK AND CONTINUOUS PRACTICE

Therapist: This week, practice your DBT skills when you feel strong emotions. During family interactions, use the communication techniques we've worked on.

REFLECTING ON PROGRESS

- The family shares their experiences with practicing the techniques, discussing successes and challenges.

DETAILED VERBATIM FROM A FOLLOW-UP SESSION

Josh: I realized I get angry quickly. Mindfulness helped me pause before reacting.

Therapist: Josh, that's a great step. How did you communicate differently after pausing?

Josh: I told my dad, "I feel angry when you dismiss my opinions."

Father: Hearing Josh say it that way, instead of him just storming off, made me listen. I didn't realize how my actions came across.

Therapist: This is a significant shift in your family communication. You're not only managing your emotions better but also expressing them more constructively.

This extensive example provides a detailed view of integrating DBT with Satir's family therapy. The verbatim sections from various stages of the therapy offer a practical illustration of how these techniques can be applied to foster emotional understanding and improve communication within the family.

Emotion-Focused Therapy (EFT)

Combining Satir's family therapy approach with Emotionally Focused Therapy (EFT), developed by Dr. Sue Johnson, creates a powerful amalgam for therapy, particularly in dealing with relational and emotional issues. While Satir's approach emphasizes communication, self-esteem, and family systems, EFT focuses on attachment and bonding in relationships, primarily in couples and families. This combination allows therapists to work simultaneously on improving communication skills, understanding family dynamics, and deepening emotional connections (Brubacher, 2006; Littlewood, 2009).

In Satir's model, the emphasis is on fostering healthier communication, enhancing self-worth, and transforming unhelpful patterns within family systems. EFT, meanwhile, delves into the emotional underpinnings of relationships, seeking to create secure emotional bonds and improve attachment styles. When these two approaches are combined, therapists can address both the systemic aspects of family interactions and the emotional bonds that underlie these interactions.

A therapy session combining these two approaches might begin with Satir's techniques to open up communication channels within the family or couple. For instance, using role-plays or the family sculpting technique, a therapist can help family members or partners articulate their feelings and perceptions. This sets the stage for EFT's focus on emotional responses and attachment needs.

Once communication is more open, and family members or partners begin to express their deeper feelings and needs, EFT techniques can be employed to explore and strengthen emotional bonds. This might involve identifying and discussing attachment styles or patterns, and how these are playing out in the relationship. The therapist might guide the couple or family through EFT's "hold me tight" conversations, which aim to address and soothe attachment-related fears and insecurities.

An important aspect of integrating these approaches is maintaining a balance between improving communication (Satir) and focusing on emotional bonding (EFT). The therapist needs to ensure that while family members or partners learn to communicate more effectively, they also work on understanding and responding to each other's emotional needs and attachment signals.

One challenge in integrating these methods is ensuring that the focus on individual patterns within the family (as emphasized by Satir) harmonizes with the focus on emotional bonds between partners or within the family (as emphasized by EFT). The therapist must skillfully navigate between these two focuses, ensuring that they complement rather than conflict with each other.

In conclusion, combining Satir's family therapy approach with EFT offers a comprehensive framework for therapists. This integrative approach not only enhances communication and understanding within families and couples but also deepens the emotional connections that are fundamental to healthy, secure relationships. By addressing both the systemic and emotional aspects of relationships, this combined approach offers a robust method for facilitating lasting change in family and couple dynamics.

Here's a verbatim example of a therapy session integrating Satir's family therapy approach with Emotionally Focused Therapy (EFT):

Therapist: Thank you all for coming in today. Let's start by creating a space where each of you can share how you've been feeling in the family lately. Remember, this is about expressing yourselves openly and safely.

Anne (Mother): I just feel like we're not connected anymore. Like everyone is in their own world.

Therapist: Anne, it sounds like you're longing for a deeper connection with the family. Let's explore that. Can you tell me more about these feelings of disconnection?

Mark (Father): I think we all just got busy with life. It's not like we don't care.

Therapist: Mark, it's clear you care deeply. Sometimes, our daily lives can create distances in our relationships. Let's try an exercise from Satir's approach. I'd like each of you to position yourselves in the room in a way that represents how you feel in the family.

(The family engages in a family sculpting exercise, physically positioning themselves in relation to each other.)

Therapist: Now, let's reflect on this sculpt. Emily, you've positioned yourself quite far from everyone else. Can you share what this represents for you?

Emily (Daughter): It's like I'm there, but not really part of the family. I just feel alone even when I'm with everyone.

Therapist: That sounds really tough, Emily. Let's shift to an EFT perspective. I want to understand the emotions tied to this feeling of being alone. What do you need from your family in these moments?

Emily: I guess I just want to feel like I matter to them.

Therapist: It's important to feel valued and seen. Mark, Anne, how does it feel to hear Emily express this need?

Anne: It's heartbreaking. I didn't know she felt that way.

Therapist: Let's use this moment to practice responding to each other's emotional needs. Anne, can you express to Emily how important she is to the family?

Anne: Emily, you are so important to us. I hate that you feel this way. I want to be there for you more.

Therapist: Thank you, Anne. Emily, how does it feel to hear your mother say this?

Emily: It feels good… and a bit surprising. I didn't think she noticed.

Therapist: This is an excellent start. By communicating openly about our feelings and needs, like in Satir's model, and responding to our emotional bonds, as emphasized in EFT, we can start to heal and strengthen our family connections.

Narrative Therapy

Narrative Therapy, a modality that focuses on the stories people construct about their lives, can be harmoniously integrated with Satir's family therapy approach. While Satir's methods emphasize communication, self-worth, and family dynamics, Narrative Therapy offers a way to explore and reframe the narratives that individuals and families create about their experiences and relationships (Bentheim, 2006). This aligns with social construction theory, which posits that reality is co-created through language and interaction, a concept Satir intuitively practiced (Cheung, 1997).

Example of a Therapy Session Integrating Satir's Approach with Narrative Therapy

Therapist: Today, we'll explore the stories that each of you hold about your family and yourselves. These narratives shape how we see our world and interact with each other. Let's start by sharing how each of you perceives the current situation in the family.

David (Father): I feel like I'm always portrayed as the bad guy. Whenever there's an issue, it feels like the family story is that I'm to blame.

- **Narrative Therapy Technique**: The therapist invites David to elaborate on this "bad guy" narrative, exploring its origins and impact on his relationships within the family.

Therapist: David, let's delve deeper into this narrative. When do you feel this story began, and how has it influenced your interactions with the family?

- **Satir's Technique**: The therapist then uses Satir's communication methods to help David express how this narrative affects his self-esteem and family role.

Sarah (Mother): I think we all play a part in supporting that narrative, maybe without even realizing it.

Therapist: Sarah, that's an insightful observation. Let's use Satir's family sculpting exercise to physically represent this narrative and how each of you relates to it.

- **Combining Techniques**: The family engages in the sculpting exercise, positioning themselves to represent the "bad guy" narrative. This physical representation helps make the abstract narrative more concrete and easier to discuss.

Therapist: Now, let's work on reshaping this narrative. How can we rewrite this story to be more empowering and reflective of the family you want to be?

- **Narrative Redefinition**: The therapist guides the family in deconstructing the negative narrative and collaboratively constructing a new, more positive and empowering story.
- **Incorporating Satir's Methods**: The family is then encouraged to communicate how this new narrative resonates with them and to express their commitment to reinforcing it in their daily interactions.

Emily (Daughter): In our new story, I see my dad not as the bad guy, but someone who cares deeply, even if he doesn't always show it.

Therapist: Emily, how can you and the rest of the family support this new narrative?

- **Narrative and Systemic Integration**: The family discusses practical ways to reinforce this new narrative, using both Narrative Therapy techniques to reshape their story and Satir's communication methods to ensure these changes are deeply rooted in their interactions.

This session illustrates how integrating Satir's family therapy with Narrative Therapy can provide a comprehensive approach. While Satir's methods enhance family communication and connection, Narrative Therapy offers a framework for understanding and reshaping the stories that families create about themselves, leading to transformative changes in both individual and family narratives.

Solution-Focused Brief Therapy (SFBT)

Combining Satir's family therapy approach with Solution-Focused Brief Therapy (SFBT) offers an innovative and pragmatic method for facilitating change in family therapy. While Satir's approach emphasizes communication, self-worth, and understanding family systems, SFBT focuses on identifying and enhancing existing strengths and solutions. This integration allows therapists to address the systemic and relational issues within the family while simultaneously harnessing and building upon the family's existing resources and capabilities.

Example of a Therapy Session Integrating Satir's Approach with SFBT

Therapist: Today, we're going to focus on what's working well in your family and how we can build on these strengths. Let's start by discussing a recent time when you felt things were going well in the family.

Julia (Mother): Last week, we had a great evening where everyone was talking and sharing about their day. It felt really connected.

- **SFBT Technique**: The therapist explores this positive experience further, encouraging the family to identify what contributed to this successful interaction.

Therapist: That sounds like a wonderful experience, Julia. What do you think made that evening different?

- **Satir's Technique**: The therapist then uses Satir's methods to delve deeper into the emotions and communication patterns that facilitated this positive experience.

Brian (Father): I think we all made an effort to listen more and not interrupt each other.

Therapist: Listening is a key component of healthy communication. How can we apply this success to other areas where you're facing challenges?

- **Integrating Techniques**: The therapist helps the family identify and amplify their successful strategies (SFBT) while using Satir's approach to enhance their communication skills.

Michael (Son): We could try having more family dinners where everyone gets a chance to speak.

Therapist: That's a great idea, Michael. Let's plan how we can make this a regular part of your family life. We can use some of Satir's communication exercises to ensure that everyone feels heard and valued during these dinners.

- **Solution-Building and Communication Enhancement**: The family works together to develop a plan for more family dinners, incorporating Satir's communication exercises to improve their interactions.

Therapist: I'd like you to notice and jot down moments during the week when you feel heard and connected as a family. We'll use these observations in our next session to continue building on your successes.

This session illustrates how integrating Satir's family therapy techniques with SFBT can create a focused and strengths-based approach in family therapy. While Satir's methods enrich the family's communication skills and emotional connections, SFBT directs the family to recognize and build upon their existing strengths and successful interactions. This integrated approach not only addresses current family issues but also empowers the family to continue developing and applying successful strategies in the future.

Gestalt Therapy

Merging Satir's family therapy approach with Gestalt Therapy offers an insightful and experiential pathway for enhancing family therapy sessions. Satir's model, emphasizing communication, emotional expression, and family systems, can be complemented by Gestalt Therapy's focus on awareness, the here-and-now experience, and the holistic view of individuals within their environment. This integration enables therapists to work on improving family dynamics while also focusing on each member's personal awareness and present-moment experiences.

Example of a Therapy Session Integrating Satir's Approach with Gestalt Therapy

Therapist: In our session today, we're going to focus on how each of you experiences your family interactions in the present moment. We'll use techniques from Gestalt Therapy to heighten your awareness and Satir's methods to facilitate communication and understanding.

Emma (Daughter): I often feel like I'm invisible in our family. It's like no one sees me or what I need.

- **Gestalt Technique**: The therapist invites Emma to explore her feelings of invisibility, focusing on her immediate physical and emotional sensations. This is done to enhance her awareness of her experience in the present moment.

Therapist: Emma, let's delve into these feelings. How do you experience this invisibility right now, in this room, with your family?

- **Satir's Technique**: The therapist then guides the family to respond to Emma's sharing, using Satir's communication techniques to express their feelings and thoughts in response to Emma's revelation.

Tom (Father): Hearing you say that makes me feel sad. I didn't realize you felt this way.

Therapist: Tom, that's an important acknowledgment. Let's use a Gestalt exercise called "the empty chair." Imagine Emma's feelings of invisibility are in that empty chair. What would you like to say to those feelings?

- **Combining Techniques**: Tom engages in a dialogue with "the empty chair," expressing his feelings and thoughts. This is followed by a family discussion using Satir's methods to further explore these emotions and improve their communication.

Susan (Mother): I want to understand better and be there for you, Emma.

Therapist: Susan, expressing this desire is crucial. Now, let's use Satir's mirroring exercise. Emma, can you mirror back what your mom just said? This will help ensure that everyone understands and feels understood.

- **Integration in Action**: The family participates in the mirroring exercise, enhancing their understanding and empathy for each other's experiences.

Therapist: As we continue, I encourage you to stay present with these feelings and observations. Notice how acknowledging and expressing these experiences impact your interactions.

This session demonstrates how the integration of Gestalt Therapy with Satir's family therapy approach can deepen the therapeutic process. By combining Gestalt's emphasis on present awareness and experiential techniques with Satir's focus on communication and emotional expression, therapists can facilitate a profound exploration of family dynamics and individual experiences within the family context. This integrated approach not only addresses the immediate issues in the family but also fosters a deeper understanding and connection among family members.

Psychodynamic Therapy

Merging Satir's family therapy approach with Psychodynamic Therapy creates a multifaceted therapeutic framework. While Satir's approach emphasizes open communication, self-esteem, and systemic family dynamics, Psychodynamic Therapy delves into the unconscious, exploring deep-seated emotional conflicts, past experiences, and internalized family roles. This integration allows therapists to address not only the overt interaction patterns within a family but also the underlying psychological processes that drive these patterns.

Example of a Therapy Session Integrating Satir's Approach with Psychodynamic Therapy

Therapist: Today, let's explore some deeper feelings and histories that may influence how you relate to each other. To begin, I'd like us to use a technique called family reconstruction, which will help us look at past family dynamics to understand how they might shape your current interactions. Linda, could you share a bit about your experience growing up?

Linda (Mother): I often felt overwhelmed and unnoticed as a child, like I wasn't really seen or heard.

Therapist: Thank you for sharing that, Linda. As you think about these feelings from the past, do you notice any similarities in how you feel in your family now?

- **Family Reconstruction in Practice**: The therapist guides Linda in reflecting on her family history, helping her connect early experiences of feeling unnoticed with her current sense of being unsupported.

Linda: Yes, I think I bring that same feeling here. It's why I often feel unseen and overwhelmed in my own family.

Therapist: That's an important insight. Let's share this with the family through a temperature reading. Each of us will take turns sharing something in a few different areas: appreciations, new information, puzzles, worries with recommendations, and hopes or wishes. Linda, would you like to start?

- **Temperature Reading**: The therapist initiates a structured temperature reading, where each family member can share in these specific areas to encourage openness and a well-rounded view of each other's thoughts.

Linda: For appreciation, I want to thank everyone for being here today – it means a lot to me. New information: I'm realizing that I've been carrying these feelings of being unnoticed since childhood, and it impacts how I feel here too. For my puzzle, I wonder if any of you noticed this about me. A worry is that if things don't change, I'll keep feeling unsupported. My hope is that we can work on being more aware of each other's needs.

Greg (Father): Thank you, Linda. For my appreciation, I want to acknowledge how open you're being with us today. New information: I'm realizing that I may have been less attentive than I thought. A puzzle for me is understanding how I can be more supportive. A worry I have is that I might fall back into old habits without realizing it. My hope is that I can be more present with you and the kids.

Therapist: Thank you, Greg. This is a wonderful start. Sarah, would you like to share your thoughts for each part of the temperature reading?

Sarah (Daughter): For appreciation, I'm grateful that we're talking about this together. New information: I didn't know Mom felt that way, but it makes sense. My puzzle is understanding how I fit into this, especially when I feel like

I have to be the strong one. A worry is that I'll always feel like I'm stepping into the adult role. My wish is that we can be more balanced as a family.

Therapist: Thank you, Sarah. That's insightful. Now, let's explore this further through parts work. Sarah, I'd like you to describe different parts of yourself – maybe a responsible part and any other parts that feel differently about your role in the family.

- **Parts Work in Dialogue**: The therapist guides Sarah to explore her different parts, allowing her to name and express the "responsible" part and any conflicting parts, giving her a more comprehensive way to articulate her experience.

Sarah: The responsible part of me feels like I have to keep everything together, but another part feels tired and wishes someone else would take over.

Therapist: Thank you, Sarah. Finally, let's try congruent communication, where each of you shares something you wish you could express more openly. I'd like each of you to speak from a place of authenticity, without holding back or playing a role.

- **Congruent Communication in Practice**: The family members practice congruent communication, sharing their honest feelings and needs without pretense, which deepens mutual understanding.

Greg: I wish I had been more present and aware of what Linda was feeling all along.

Therapist: Thank you, Greg, for being so genuine. Reflecting on our family reconstruction, temperature reading, parts work, and congruent communication, do you notice any patterns connected to family roles or past experiences?

Greg: It's clear we're unconsciously repeating some of these roles from our past, but now I feel hopeful that we can change them.

Therapist: That's a great insight, Greg. How can you use this awareness to create more supportive interactions with each other moving forward?

- **Integrating Techniques for Change**: The family discusses practical steps for applying these insights, planning to use regular temperature readings and congruent communication to continue fostering openness and support in their daily interactions.

This session showcases the integration of Satir's family reconstruction, temperature reading, parts work, and congruent communication with psychodynamic exploration. By addressing both the psychological roots and visible dynamics within the family, this approach provides a pathway for meaningful and lasting change.

Humanistic Therapy

Combining Satir's family therapy with Humanistic Therapy offers a holistic approach that focuses on the individual's potential, personal growth, and self-actualization within the context of family dynamics. Satir's approach, which emphasizes communication, empathy, and systemic understanding, aligns well with Humanistic Therapy's focus on personal experience, autonomy, and the intrinsic value of each individual. Together, they create a therapeutic environment that fosters personal growth while enhancing family relationships.

Example of a Therapy Session Integrating Satir's Approach with Humanistic Therapy

Therapist: Today, let's focus on understanding and expressing your individual experiences within the family, while also considering how these experiences influence the family as a whole. We'll blend Satir's methods for enhancing communication with Humanistic Therapy's emphasis on personal growth and self-awareness.

Alex (Son): I feel like I'm always trying to meet expectations, losing track of what I really want.

- **Humanistic Exploration**: The therapist encourages Alex to explore his feelings and aspirations, focusing on his personal experiences and perceptions.

Therapist: Alex, tell us more about these feelings. What are your own aspirations and how do they differ from the expectations you feel are placed upon you?

- Satir's Communication Exercise: Alex is guided to express his feelings to his family using Satir's "I" statements, fostering clarity and vulnerability.

Karen (Mother): I didn't realize you felt this way, Alex. I guess we've been focusing more on achievements than on what truly makes you happy.

Therapist: Karen, it sounds like Alex's sharing is providing new insights for you. How does it feel to hear his perspective?

- **Enhancing Self-Awareness and Autonomy**: The therapist uses Humanistic techniques to help each family member explore their personal goals and how these goals interact with family expectations.

Mike (Father): I think we all have different ideas of success and happiness. Maybe we need to communicate more about what each of us truly values.

Therapist: That's a valuable observation, Mike. Let's use a Humanistic approach to explore these values. I'd like each of you to share one personal value that is important to you and how you feel it fits within the family.

- **Sharing Personal Values**: Each family member shares, leading to a deeper understanding of individual needs and aspirations.

Therapist: Now, let's incorporate Satir's mirroring exercise. After each person shares, another family member will mirror back what they heard. This will help ensure everyone understands each other's values and needs.

- **Mirroring Exercise**: The family engages in mirroring, enhancing their understanding and empathy for each other's personal values and experiences.

Therapist: Reflecting on this exercise, how can we support each other's personal growth while nurturing our family connections?

- **Combining Techniques for Growth and Connection**: The family discusses how to apply their newfound insights into their daily interactions, using both Humanistic principles to support individual growth and Satir's methods to maintain healthy communication.

This session demonstrates how integrating Satir's family therapy techniques with Humanistic Therapy can lead to a deeper understanding of individual experiences and aspirations while maintaining healthy family dynamics. The therapist uses Humanistic principles to explore each family member's personal growth and values, and Satir's communication techniques to ensure these individual needs are expressed and understood within the family context. This integrated approach fosters personal development and enhances familial bonds.

Cognitive Analytic Therapy (CAT)

Blending Satir's family therapy with Cognitive Analytic Therapy (CAT) offers a dynamic approach to understanding and improving family dynamics. While Satir's model emphasizes communication, emotional expression, and systemic understanding within the family, CAT focuses on understanding maladaptive patterns of behavior and thinking, and their roots in past relationships. This combination allows therapists to address the family's current communication and interaction patterns while also exploring and modifying the ingrained behavioral patterns of individual members.

Example of a Therapy Session combining Satir's Approach with CAT

Therapist: In our session today, we'll work on understanding the patterns that you each bring into family interactions, drawing from both your personal histories and your experiences as a family. We'll use Satir's methods to enhance your communication, and CAT's approach to identify and modify unhelpful patterns.

Daniel (Teenage Son): I always feel like I need to be perfect. If I'm not, I worry my parents will be disappointed.

- **CAT Exploration**: The therapist guides Daniel to explore how this pattern of needing to be perfect might have developed, perhaps linked to past experiences or relationships.

Therapist: Daniel, let's explore this need for perfection. Can you think of earlier times in your life when you felt this pressure?

- **Satir's Communication Exercise**: Daniel is encouraged to express these feelings using Satir's "I" statements, helping his parents understand his internal pressures.

Rachel (Mother): Hearing this makes me realize we might have set the bar too high for Daniel. I never wanted him to feel he had to be perfect.

Therapist: Rachel, it's important to acknowledge this realization. Let's use a CAT technique called "mapping out." We'll map out Daniel's pattern of needing to be perfect and how it interacts with the family's expectations.

- **Mapping Exercise**: The therapist helps the family visually map out Daniel's need for perfection and the family's responses, providing insight into how these patterns interact.

John (Father): This map shows how our expectations might contribute to Daniel's pressure. We need to change our approach.

Therapist: John, that's a proactive thought. Let's consider how we can communicate differently. Using Satir's family sculpting, let's physically represent how we can support Daniel's need for growth without the pressure of perfection.

- **Family Sculpting**: The family engages in sculpting, positioning themselves in a way that represents supportive and non-pressuring relationships.

Therapist: Reflecting on this sculpt, how do you think you can implement these changes in your daily interactions?

- **Combining Techniques for Change**: The family discusses practical ways to apply the insights from the mapping and sculpting exercises, using CAT to understand and modify patterns and Satir's methods to enhance communication and emotional support.

This session exemplifies how combining Satir's family therapy techniques with CAT can create a comprehensive approach for understanding and improving family dynamics. The therapist uses CAT to explore and address individual behavioral patterns and their interaction with family dynamics, while employing Satir's methods to improve communication and emotional expression. This integrated approach provides a deeper understanding of both individual and family processes, facilitating meaningful change in family relationships.

Acceptance and Commitment Therapy (ACT)

In a family session with the Martins, where each member struggles with individual anxieties and its impact on the family dynamics, the combination of Satir's family therapy with ACT provides a comprehensive approach.

Example of a Therapy Session combining Satir's Approach with ACT

STARTING THE SESSION

Therapist: Today, let's bring our focus to how individual experiences, especially around anxiety, are impacting our family interactions. We'll combine Satir's methods for communication with ACT's focus on acceptance and committed action based on your values.

EXPLORING INDIVIDUAL STRUGGLES WITHIN THE FAMILY CONTEXT

Lucas (Teenage Son): I feel like I'm always worried about messing up, and it's like I shut down around everyone.

- **ACT Technique – Cognitive Defusion**: The therapist invites Lucas to observe his thoughts about "messing up" without becoming entangled in them.

Therapist: Lucas, let's take a step back and notice these thoughts. Imagine them as leaves floating down a stream, separate from you. How does it feel observing them this way?

COMBINING SATIR'S COMMUNICATION TECHNIQUES

Elaine (Mother): I didn't realize Lucas felt so anxious. I thought he was just being aloof.

- **Satir's Technique – Validating Communication**: The therapist guides Elaine to communicate her new understanding to Lucas.

Therapist: Elaine, let's practice an "I" statement to share this realization with Lucas. It can help deepen your connection.

COMBINING ACT'S VALUES CLARIFICATION WITH SATIR'S FAMILY ROLES

Derek (Father): I worry I'm too hard on Lucas. I guess I'm trying to push him to succeed.

- **ACT Technique – Values Clarification**: The therapist helps Derek explore his values around parenting.

Therapist: Derek, what values do you want to guide your parenting? Let's explore and articulate these values.

FAMILY SCULPTING INCORPORATING ACT PRINCIPLES

Therapist: Let's do a family sculpting exercise. Position yourselves in a way that represents how you currently interact as a family. Then, we'll adjust the sculpt to reflect how you'd like to interact, based on your values.

(*The family arranges themselves, with Lucas appearing isolated.*)

Therapist: Now, let's rearrange based on how you'd like to support each other, keeping in mind your individual values and the acceptance strategies from ACT.

BRINGING IN MINDFULNESS AND COMMITTED ACTIONS

Therapist: As a final exercise, I'd like us to practice a mindfulness technique. Focus on your breathing, and observe your thoughts and feelings in this moment.

(*The family engages in a brief mindfulness exercise.*)

Therapist: Let's end by each of you stating a committed action that you will take this week, something that aligns with your values and supports the family.

WRAPPING UP THE SESSION

Therapist: Great work today. Remember, the goal is not to eliminate anxiety but to understand it and make room for it, so it doesn't dominate your individual experiences or family interactions.

This session showcases how Satir's family therapy, with its emphasis on open communication and validation, can be effectively integrated with ACT's focus on acceptance, mindfulness, and values-based action. The therapist skillfully combines techniques from both modalities to address the individual and collective needs of the family, promoting healthier interactions and personal growth.

Eye Movement Desensitization and Reprocessing (EMDR)

Blending Satir's approach with EMDR addresses deep-seated trauma by acknowledging the biological reality of stress. Satir's "survival stances" (like Blaming or Placating) can be understood through the lens of neurobiology:

- **Blaming** correlates with testosterone and dominance behaviors often seen in stress responses (Mazur and Booth, 1998).
- **Placating** may relate to the "tend-and-befriend" response mediated by **oxytocin**, particularly in how estrogen modulates social bonding behaviors during stress (McCarthy, 1995).
- **Stress Responses**: Understanding the physiological toll of chronic stress – why "zebras don't get ulcers" but humans do – validates Satir's goal of reducing internal incongruence to lower physiological wear and tear (Sapolsky, 2004).

Integrating these biological insights with EMDR helps clients understand that their "stances" are not just psychological choices but biological survival mechanisms that can be reprogrammed.

Example of a Therapy Session combining Satir's Approach with EMDR

Therapist: Today, we're going to explore how individual experiences, particularly traumatic ones, are influencing our family interactions. We'll use EMDR to address these personal traumas and Satir's techniques to improve communication and understanding within the family.

Dan (Father): I have these flashbacks from my military service that I think affect how I react to everyone at home.

- **EMDR Technique – Processing Trauma**: The therapist works individually with Dan, using EMDR techniques to help him process his traumatic memories. This involves bilateral stimulation, such as eye movements, while recalling traumatic experiences to reduce their emotional intensity.

Therapist: Dan, as you recall this memory, follow my hand with your eyes. Notice what thoughts and feelings come up as we do this.

Carol (Mother): I sometimes feel like I'm walking on eggshells. I'm afraid of triggering Dan's flashbacks.

- **Satir's Technique – Open Communication**: The therapist encourages Carol to express her feelings to Dan using "I" statements, enhancing clarity and reducing blame.

Therapist: Carol, let's communicate this to Dan using an "I" statement. How does his reaction affect you?

Carol: Dan, when you suddenly get angry, I feel scared and unsure of how to support you.

COMBINING EMDR INSIGHTS WITH SATIR'S FAMILY ROLES

Therapist: Now that we've worked on processing some of Dan's traumatic experiences with EMDR, let's explore how this impacts our family roles and communication.

- **Family Sculpting Incorporating EMDR Insights**: The family engages in Satir's family sculpting, positioning themselves to represent their roles and relationships in light of Dan's trauma.

Therapist: Let's create a physical representation of your family. Place yourselves in a way that shows how you feel in the family, considering what we've processed today.

Emily (Daughter): I feel like I need to be the peacemaker when things get tense.

Therapist: (*Reflecting and guiding*) Emily, that's a powerful role. How does this role affect you, and how can we communicate this impact to the family?

EXPLORING NEW COMMUNICATION PATTERNS

Therapist: Based on our EMDR work and the family sculpting, let's discuss new ways of communicating. How can we support each other, keeping in mind the trauma and its impact?

- **Developing New Family Dynamics**: The family discusses new communication strategies, considering both the trauma processed through EMDR and their roles identified in the sculpting exercise.

Therapist: I'd like each of you to think of one change you can make in how you interact with each other, considering our work today. Let's share these commitments.

WRAPPING UP THE SESSION

Therapist: Today's session brought important insights into how individual trauma affects our family system. Remember, healing is a journey, both individually and as a family. Let's continue to use these new insights and communication strategies to support each other.

This session illustrates the combination of EMDR and Satir's family therapy, addressing both individual trauma and its ripple effects on family dynamics. The therapist uses EMDR to help Dan process his traumatic experiences, then employs Satir's methods to enhance family communication and understanding, facilitating a more supportive and empathetic family environment.

In the context of combining Satir's family therapy with Eye Movement Desensitization and Reprocessing (EMDR), the EMDR process, particularly the bilateral stimulation, typically happens during individual sessions with the family member who has experienced trauma. This is because EMDR is a highly specialized and individual-focused therapy that requires a controlled environment to address and process traumatic memories.

EXAMPLE OF WHEN EMDR BILATERAL STIMULATION HAPPENS IN A SESSION

During a session that combines both therapies, the therapist might first use Satir's methods for a part of the session to enhance family communication and understanding. Then, they might move into an individual session with the family member who has experienced trauma for the EMDR process.

Therapist (to Dan, the father with military trauma): Dan, we've talked as a family about how your experiences in the military might be affecting your interactions at home. Now, let's take some time to focus specifically on processing some of these memories. We'll use EMDR for this part.

The therapist then engages Dan in the EMDR process:

Therapist: As you bring up a specific traumatic memory, I want you to follow my hand with your eyes. This bilateral stimulation can help in processing and reducing the emotional intensity of the memory.

Dan follows the therapist's hand movements while recalling a specific traumatic experience. The therapist checks in periodically:

Therapist: As you're following my hand, notice what thoughts, emotions, or physical sensations come up for you. Just observe them without judgment.

This portion of the session focuses on Dan individually, allowing him to engage in the EMDR process in a safe and controlled environment. The bilateral stimulation, a core component of EMDR, is conducted in this individual setting rather than in the group family therapy context.

After completing the EMDR portion with Dan, the therapist can reconvene with the entire family:

Therapist: Now that we've worked individually on some of Dan's experiences, let's come back together as a family. We can talk about how we might support each other and communicate effectively, considering what we've learned and processed today.

In this fusion approach, the EMDR process is carefully woven into the broader therapeutic journey, ensuring that the individual trauma work complements and informs the family therapy goals. This method allows for addressing deep-seated individual issues while also considering their impact on family dynamics.

Mindfulness-Based Stress Reduction (MBSR)

Integrating Satir's family therapy approach with MBSR creates a framework that addresses both family dynamics and individual physiology. This is particularly vital for caregivers; studies have shown that using Satir's tools (like the Self-Mandala) significantly reduces burnout in family caregivers by restoring their internal resources (Caston, 2009). Furthermore, Satir's emphasis on "caring for the self" aligns with modern understandings of the fuzzy boundary between nutrition, psychopharmacology, and mental health, suggesting that true congruence involves caring for the biological vessel as well as the spirit (Young, 2002).

Example of a Therapy Session Integrating Satir's Approach with MBSR

Therapist: In today's session, we're going to focus on understanding how each of you deals with stress and how this affects your family interactions. We'll integrate Satir's communication methods with mindfulness techniques from MBSR to enhance your interactions and individual well-being.

Helen (Mother): I find myself constantly worried about the kids and the house. It's like I can never relax, and this tension spills over to how I interact with everyone.

- **MBSR Technique – Mindfulness Meditation**: The therapist guides Helen through a brief mindfulness meditation, focusing on breath and present-moment awareness.

Therapist: Helen, let's take a moment to focus on your breathing. As you breathe in and out, notice the thoughts that come up without judgment.

INTEGRATING SATIR'S COMMUNICATION TECHNIQUES

Mike (Father): I didn't realize how much this was affecting you. I think I've been so wrapped up in work that I've missed these signs.

- **Satir's Technique – Reflective Listening**: The therapist encourages Mike to use reflective listening, a technique from Satir's model, to communicate his understanding back to Helen.

Therapist: Mike, can you reflect back what you heard Helen saying? It helps validate her experience and shows your understanding.

Mike: Helen, it sounds like you're under a lot of pressure and that it's hard for you to find a moment of peace.

MINDFULNESS EXERCISES IN A FAMILY CONTEXT

Therapist: Now, let's try a mindfulness exercise together. This exercise will help each of you become more aware of your current emotional state and how it impacts your interactions.

- **Group Mindfulness Practice**: The family participates in a mindfulness exercise, focusing on their breath and observing their thoughts and feelings in the present moment.

Therapist: What did you notice about your thoughts and feelings during this exercise? How might this awareness impact your interactions with each other?

FAMILY COMMUNICATION AND MINDFULNESS INTEGRATION

Therapist: Based on our mindfulness practice and understanding of each other's stressors, let's discuss new ways of communicating. How can we be more present with each other and respond more mindfully, especially in stressful moments?

- **Developing New Communication Strategies**: The family discusses how they can incorporate mindfulness in their daily interactions, using Satir's methods to communicate these strategies effectively.

Therapist: As we conclude, I encourage you to continue practicing mindfulness daily. Notice how being present impacts your communication and interactions as a family.

This session demonstrates how integrating Satir's family therapy with MBSR can enhance family dynamics by improving communication and increasing individual mindfulness. The therapist skillfully combines MBSR techniques for stress management and present-moment awareness with Satir's methods for effective family communication, fostering a supportive and mindful family environment.

Art Therapy

Blending Satir's family therapy approach with Art Therapy offers a creative and expressive way to explore and improve family dynamics. Satir's emphasis on communication and systemic understanding in the family pairs well with the non-verbal, imaginative expression facilitated by Art Therapy. Contemporary practitioners have also integrated musical interventions into Satir's experiential therapy, using rhythm and harmony to move families from dissonance to congruence (Nemesh, 2016). This integrated approach can be particularly beneficial for families who struggle to articulate their feelings and experiences in words.

Example of a Therapy Session Integrating Satir's Approach with Art Therapy

Therapist: Today, we're going to use art as a way to express and explore our feelings within the family. This will help us understand each other's perspectives in a different, perhaps deeper way, complementing our usual verbal communication.

Jake (Teenage Son): I don't know how to say what I'm feeling most of the time. It just gets frustrating.

- **Art Therapy Exercise**: The therapist provides art materials and invites Jake to create something that represents his feelings about being part of the family.

Therapist: Jake, use these materials to express what you feel. There's no right or wrong way to do this. Just let your creativity show what words might not.

ENCOURAGING FAMILY MEMBERS TO SHARE THROUGH ART

- As Jake works on his art piece, the therapist encourages other family members to engage in similar expressive activities.

Therapist: Each of you, take some time to create your own artwork. Think about how you experience being part of this family.

DISCUSSING THE ARTWORK

- Once everyone finishes their artwork, the therapist facilitates a discussion.

Therapist: *Let's share our artwork. Jake, can you tell us about your piece?*

Jake: (*Showing a fragmented collage*) This is how I feel – scattered and disconnected.

INTEGRATING SATIR'S COMMUNICATION TECHNIQUES

- **Reflective Listening and Validation**: The therapist guides the family in using reflective listening to respond to Jake's sharing.

Therapist: Family, let's reflect back what Jake's art is saying to us. What do you see and feel from his collage?

Sandra (Mother): Seeing this, I feel sad. I didn't realize you felt so disjointed from us, Jake.

EXPLORING UNDERLYING DYNAMICS THROUGH ART

Therapist: Now, let's use Satir's family sculpting technique, but with a twist. Arrange these art materials to represent where each of you stands in the family.

- **Combining Art with Family Sculpting**: The family creates a collective art piece that represents their family system.

Tom (Father): (*Arranging a part of the sculpture*) I see now how our communication gaps have contributed to these feelings.

DISCUSSING NEW INSIGHTS AND COMMITTING TO CHANGE

Therapist: What have we learned from this exercise? How can we use these insights to improve our interactions and understanding of each other?

- **Art as a Communication Tool**: The family discusses how they can use art and other non-verbal forms of expression to complement their verbal communication, based on Satir's techniques.

Therapist: As homework, I'd like you to continue using art as a way to express your feelings about your day or week. We'll use these creations as starting points for our discussions in future sessions.

This session exemplifies the integration of Satir's family therapy with Art Therapy, offering a creative avenue for expression and understanding. The therapist skillfully combines art exercises with Satir's communication techniques, enabling the family to explore their dynamics in a new and meaningful way. This approach not only helps in expressing and validating unspoken emotions but also enhances family connections through shared creative experiences.

Behavioral Therapy

Blending Satir's family therapy, specifically her iceberg metaphor, with Behavioral Therapy provides a robust framework for addressing both the observable behaviors and the underlying emotions, perceptions, and expectations within a family. This integration allows for a comprehensive approach, addressing the visible behavioral patterns (focus of Behavioral Therapy) and the deeper emotional and cognitive processes (focus of Satir's iceberg metaphor) within the family.

Example of a Therapy Session Integrating Satir's Iceberg Metaphor with Behavioral Therapy

Therapist: In today's session, we will explore the behaviors that each of you displays in your family interactions and delve deeper into what lies beneath these behaviors using Satir's iceberg metaphor. We'll also look at how we can modify these behaviors using principles from Behavioral Therapy.

Karen (Mother): I get very anxious and tend to overreact to small issues. I know it's not helpful.

- **Behavioral Analysis**: The therapist works with Karen to identify triggers and consequences of her anxious behaviors.

Therapist: Karen, let's first understand what triggers this anxiety. What thoughts or feelings come up before you react?

USING SATIR'S ICEBERG METAPHOR

- **Iceberg Metaphor Exploration**: The therapist uses the iceberg metaphor to help Karen explore the deeper emotions, perceptions, and expectations driving her behaviors.

Therapist: Imagine an iceberg. What we see above water is your behavior – the anxiety and overreaction. But beneath the surface are your feelings, thoughts, and perhaps past experiences. Let's explore what's beneath your "iceberg."

FAMILY MEMBERS' REFLECTIONS

- **Family's Behavioral Responses**: The therapist asks other family members to reflect on how they react to Karen's behavior.

Tyler (Teenage Son): When mom gets anxious, I just go to my room. I don't want to make things worse.

MODIFYING BEHAVIORS

- **Behavioral Modification**: The therapist discusses how the family can respond differently to avoid reinforcing Karen's anxiety.

Therapist: What are some ways we can support each other without reinforcing the anxiety? Let's think about new behaviors.

VISUALIZATION AND ART EXERCISE

- **Art Therapy Technique**: The therapist invites the family to draw their individual "icebergs," representing their behaviors and the underlying emotions and thoughts.

Therapist: Let's use art to express our icebergs. Draw what you feel is beneath the surface of your behaviors.

DISCUSSION AND INTEGRATION

- **Analyzing Artwork**: After sharing their drawings, the family discusses what each iceberg reveals about their internal experiences.

Therapist: Now that we see what's beneath our behaviors, how can we use this understanding to interact differently? How can we change our behaviors in a way that acknowledges these deeper feelings and thoughts?

APPLYING NEW STRATEGIES

Therapist: For our next week, I'd like you to practice the new behaviors we've discussed. Remember, the goal is to acknowledge and respect what lies beneath our "icebergs" while also working on changing our behavioral responses.

This session highlights how integrating the Satir iceberg metaphor with Behavioral Therapy can enrich family therapy. The therapist uses the iceberg metaphor to delve into the underlying emotions and cognitions behind observable behaviors and employs Behavioral Therapy techniques to develop strategies for modifying these behaviors. This integrative approach not only helps in understanding the depth of family dynamics but also provides practical ways to improve them.

Motivational Interviewing (MI)

Blending Satir's family therapy with Motivational Interviewing (MI) creates a unique therapeutic approach that combines Satir's focus on communication, emotional expression, and systemic change with the principles of MI, which are centered on eliciting and strengthening personal motivation for change. This integration can be particularly effective in families where ambivalence or resistance to change is a key issue.

Example of a Therapy Session Integrating Satir's Approach with Motivational Interviewing

Therapist: Today, we'll be focusing on understanding each family member's perspective and motivation towards the changes we've been discussing in our sessions. We'll use Satir's methods to facilitate open communication and MI to explore and enhance your individual motivations for these changes.

Paul (Father): I know we need to change how we handle conflicts, but it's hard to break old habits.

- **MI Technique – Exploring Ambivalence**: The therapist uses MI techniques to explore Paul's ambivalence about changing his conflict-handling habits.

Therapist: Paul, it sounds like there's a part of you that recognizes the need for change, but another part that finds comfort in the familiar. Let's explore these conflicting feelings a bit more.

USING SATIR'S SELF-ESTEEM MAINTENANCE TOOLKIT

- **Satir's Self-Esteem Exercise**: The therapist encourages Paul to identify and communicate his strengths and how they can be utilized in making these changes.

Therapist: Paul, let's use Satir's Self-Esteem Maintenance Toolkit. Think about your strengths. How might these strengths help you in adopting new ways of handling conflict?

MI'S READINESS RULER

- **MI Technique – Readiness Ruler**: To gauge and enhance motivation, the therapist introduces the Readiness Ruler, a tool from MI.

Therapist: On a scale from 0 to 10, where 0 is not ready at all and 10 is completely ready, where would you place yourself in terms of making these changes in conflict management?

FAMILY MEMBERS' PERSPECTIVES

- **Family's Input Using Satir's Temperature Reading Exercise**: The therapist asks other family members to share their views on the changes using Satir's Temperature Reading exercise.

Therapist: Let's do a Temperature Reading. Share your appreciations, new information, puzzles, complaints with request for change, and hopes for the family.

DEVELOPING PERSONAL GOALS AND FAMILY COMMITMENTS

- **Combining MI with Satir's Methods**: The family works together to set individual goals and family commitments, integrating insights from MI and Satir's techniques.

Therapist: With our understandings from both MI and Satir's work, let's each set a personal goal related to changing our conflict management. How can we support each other in these goals?

VISUALIZATION EXERCISE

- **Visualization Technique**: The therapist guides the family in a visualization exercise to imagine a future where these changes have been successfully implemented.

Therapist: Close your eyes and visualize how our family interactions have transformed with these changes. What does it look like? How does it feel?

WRAPPING UP THE SESSION

Therapist: In our next session, we'll continue to build on your individual motivations and family commitments, using both MI and Satir's approaches to guide us. Remember, change is a journey we take one step at a time.

This session demonstrates how integrating Satir's family therapy with Motivational Interviewing can effectively address family dynamics, especially in the context of resistance or ambivalence to change. The therapist uses MI to explore and enhance each member's motivation for change while employing Satir's methods to improve communication and emotional understanding. This approach not only helps the family understand each member's readiness for change but also fosters a supportive environment for these changes to occur.

Play Therapy

Blending Satir's family therapy approach with Play Therapy offers a unique and effective method for engaging families. This has been successfully expanded into Adventure-Based Counseling (ABC) for at-risk youth, where Satir's growth model is applied in outdoor, experiential settings to build trust and congruence (Klein, 2008). While Satir's model emphasizes communication, Play and Adventure therapies allow for the exploration of these themes in a non-threatening, imaginative way.

Example of a Therapy Session Integrating Satir's Approach with Play Therapy

Therapist: In today's session, we're going to use play as a way to understand and express our feelings within the family. This will help everyone, especially the younger members, to share their thoughts and feelings in a comfortable and creative way.

Lily (Youngest Daughter, Age 7): I don't like it when mommy and daddy fight. It makes me scared.

- **Play Therapy Activity**: The therapist provides toys and asks Lily to choose figures that represent each family member and act out a recent family situation.

Therapist: Lily, let's use these toys to show what happens in the family when you feel scared. You can use them to tell us the story.

ENCOURAGING FAMILY PARTICIPATION

- **Family Involvement**: The therapist invites the rest of the family to engage in the play activity, encouraging them to contribute to Lily's story or create their own.

Therapist: Let's all join in. This is a way for us to understand and share our feelings through play. You might choose a toy that represents how you feel in the family.

REFLECTING ON THE PLAY ACTIVITY

- **Discussion of Play Narratives**: After the play activity, the therapist leads a discussion about what was expressed.

Therapist: What did we notice during this play? How do these stories help us understand what each of us is feeling?

Tom (Father): I saw that when I raise my voice, Lily's toy character hides. That really made me think about how my actions affect her.

INTEGRATING SATIR'S COMMUNICATION TOOLS

- **Satir's Iceberg Metaphor**: The therapist uses the iceberg metaphor to help the family understand the deeper emotions and needs revealed through the play.

Therapist: Each character in our play has feelings, thoughts, and needs, much like an iceberg. Let's talk about what might be beneath the surface for each of us.

DEVELOPING NEW FAMILY DYNAMICS

Therapist: Based on what we learned from our play, let's think about how we can support each other in the family. How can we use what we played out to improve our communication and understanding?

- **Combining Techniques**: The family collaborates to develop new strategies for communication and support, drawing on insights from the play and applying Satir's communication techniques.

Therapist: For the coming week, let's try to remember what we learned today during our play. Think about how we can use these insights in our daily interactions.

This session illustrates how integrating Play Therapy with Satir's family therapy can be particularly effective for families with young children. The therapist uses play as a medium for expression and understanding, making it easier for younger members to participate and communicate. This approach, combined with Satir's methods, helps the family explore and address their dynamics in a safe, engaging, and insightful manner.

References

Banmen, A., Banmen, J. (1991). *Meditations of Virginia Satir: Peace Within, Peace Between, Peace Among*. Palo Alto, CA: Science and Behavior Books, Inc.

Banmen, J. (2002). The Satir model: Yesterday and today. *Contemporary Family Therapy: An International Journal, 24*(1), 7–22.

Banmen, J. (Ed). (2006). *Applications of the Satir Growth Model.* Seattle, WA: Avanta, the Virginia Satir Network.

Bentheim, S. (2006). Couple congruence and spirituality: Expanding Satir's model through seven couple narratives. *Dissertation Abstracts International Section A: Humanities and Social Sciences, 66*, 10A.

Boyatzis, R.E., Goleman, D., Rhee, K. (2013). Emotional and social intelligence competencies: Cross-cultural implications. *Cross Cultural Management: An International Journal, 20*(1), 20–30.

Brubacher, L. (2006). Integrating emotion-focused therapy with the Satir model. *Journal of Marital and Family Therapy, 32*(2), 141–153.

Burke, W.W., and Litwin, G.H. (1992). A causal model of organizational performance and change. *Journal of Management, 18*(3), 523–545.

Caston, C. (2009). Using the Satir family tools to reduce burnout in family caregivers. *The Satir Journal, 3*(2), 39–72.

Cheung, M. (1997). Social construction theory and the Satir model: toward a synthesis. *The American Journal of Family Therapy, 25*(4), 331–343.

Feng, L., Wang, W., Wu, M., Ma, H. (2021). Effect of WeChat-Based Health Education Combined with Satir Model on Self-Management Behaviors and Social Adaptation in Colorectal Cancer Patients during the Perioperative Period. *Journal of Healthcare Engineering*, 2701039. https://doi.org/10.1155/2021/2701039

Haber, R. (2002). Virginia Satir: An integrated humanist approach. *Contemporary Family Therapy: An International Journal, 24*(1), 23–37.

Haitoglou, D. (2017). The Satir Systemic Coaching Model. *The Satir International Journal, 5*(1), 4–18.

Haitoglou, D. (2022). *Enrich: A Practical Guide to Systemic Enrichment for Love, Abundance, Fulfilment, and Happiness*. Independently published.

Klein, K. (2008). Adventure-based therapy with at-risk youth using the Satir model. *The Satir Journal, 2*(3), 76–93.

Littlewood, P.J. (2009). The Satir model and emotionally focused therapy: A response to Lorrie Brubacher. *The Satir Journal, 3*(1), 26–37.

Loeschen, S. (2005). *Enriching Your Relationships Between Yourself and Others: Based on the Teachings of Virginia Satir*. Burien, WA: AVANTA.

Loeschen, S., Jendrusakova, K. (2015). Enriching your relationship program through the lens of empirical support. *Satir International Journal, 3*(1), 5–18.

Mazur, A., Booth, A. (1998). Testosterone and dominance in men. *Behavioral and Brain Sciences, 21*(3), 353–363.

McCarthy, M.M. (1995). Estrogen modulation of oxytocin and its relation to behavior. *Adv Exp Med Biol, 395*, 235–245.

Nemesh, B. (2016). Musical interventions in Satir's experiential family therapy: from dissonance to harmony. *Satir International Journal, 4*(1), 73–75.

Sapolsky, R.M. (2004). *Why Zebras Don't Get Ulcers*. New York: Holt Paperbacks.

Satir, V. (1983). *Conjoint Family Therapy*. Palo Alto, CA: Science and Behavior Books, Inc.

Strider, E. (2013). Re-sculpting an organization: A different kind of family. *Satir International Journal, 1*, 96–102.

The Virginia Satir Institute. (n.d.). The Virginia Satir Institute website. Available at: www.virginiasatir.co.uk (accessed 5 February 2026).

Wang, X., Zhao, Y., Zeng, G., Xiao, P., Wang. Z. (2022). Study on the classification problem of the coping stances in the Satir model based on machine learning. *Journal of Experimental and Theoretical Artificial Intelligence, 35*(1), 129–149. https://doi.org/10.1080/0952813X.2021.1960628

Young, S.N. (2002). Clinical nutrition: 3. The fuzzy boundary between nutrition and psychopharmacology. *CMAJ, 166*(2), 205–209.

6
Case Studies and Reflections

This chapter will feature an array of in-depth case studies from diverse settings. Each case study will include a detailed narrative, beginning with the family's background, the specific issues they face, and a step-by-step account of how Satir's methods were applied. The focus will be on the therapist's strategic adjustments to accommodate unique family dynamics, cultural backgrounds, and individual challenges. The outcomes of each case will be analyzed, highlighting both expected and unexpected results, providing real-world insights into the efficacy of Satir's methods.

Navigating Grief

Background: The Martinez family is struggling after the loss of the father. The mother, Elena, is trying to keep the family together while dealing with her own grief. Her two children, Maria (16) and Carlos (12), are each coping differently, leading to tension and emotional disconnection.

Therapist:	Today, *let's create a space where each of you can share your feelings about the loss of your father. Remember, there's no right or wrong way to feel.*
Elena:	I just try to stay strong for the kids, but it's hard.
Therapist:	Elena, it sounds like you're carrying a lot of weight. What do you need right now for your own grief?

DOI: 10.4324/9781003716419-6

Carlos: (*Quietly*) I miss dad. I don't know how to talk about it.

Therapist (using Satir's validation technique): Carlos, it's completely okay to feel that way. Your dad meant a lot to you.

Maria: I'm angry. Why did this happen to us?

Therapist (using Satir's normalization technique): Maria, anger is a natural part of grief. It's okay to feel angry and to express it.

Family Sculpting Activity

Therapist: Let's try an activity called family sculpting. This will help us see and feel how the loss has affected our family system.

(*The family physically arranges themselves to represent their emotional state and relationships.*)

Therapist: Notice the distance and the positions you've chosen. What does this tell us about our family right now?

Developing New Communication Patterns

Therapist: Let's work on how we can support each other during this time. Elena, what do you need from Maria and Carlos?

- Elena expresses her need for open conversations about their feelings.
- The family practices new ways of communicating their needs and supporting each other.

Homework Assignment

Therapist: For the next week, I want each of you to share one memory of your father every day. It can be a small thing. Let's keep his memory alive in our conversations.

Outcome: The family begins to understand and respect each other's unique grieving process. They develop healthier ways to communicate and support one another, slowly rebuilding their emotional connection. This mirrors the specific application of Satir's model to grief work, where sharing vulnerability transforms the pain of loss into connection (Belvins, 2008).

Addressing Intergenerational Conflict

Background: The Nguyen family, including parents and their adult daughter, Linda, are experiencing tension due to differing cultural and generational views. The parents hold traditional values, while Linda seeks more independence and modern lifestyle choices.

Therapist:	Let's explore what each of you values most in your family relationship.
Mother:	We raised Linda with our traditions, but she's drifting away.
Therapist:	It sounds like you're worried about losing a part of your family heritage. What does tradition mean to you?
Father:	Respect and following the way we were brought up.
Linda:	I respect our traditions, but I also want to make my own choices.
Therapist (using Satir's congruence model):	Linda, it's important to voice your needs. Let's find a way to honor both your individuality and your family's values.

Role-Playing for Empathy

Therapist: Let's try a role reversal. Linda, you'll be your mother, and vice versa. Express what you think the other feels.

- This exercise helps each family member understand the other's perspective.

Developing Mutual Understanding

Therapist: Now that we've seen each other's viewpoints, how can we bridge this gap?

- The family discusses ways to balance tradition with individual freedom.

Homework for Cultural Appreciation

Therapist: This week, I'd like each of you to share something meaningful about your culture with each other, and discuss how it can be part of your lives today.

Outcome: The family learns to communicate their needs and fears more openly, leading to a greater understanding of both cultural values and personal independence. They start finding ways to integrate tradition with modernity in their daily lives. This case exemplifies the delicate balance required when applying Satir's model in Asian contexts, where the goal is often to integrate individual growth within the collective worldview rather than disrupting it (Young, 2007; Cheung, 2006).

Strengthening Parent-Child Relationships

Background: The Robinson family is experiencing tension between the parents and their teenage son, Alex, who feels misunderstood and controlled.

Therapist: Today, let's focus on understanding each other's perspectives. Who wants to start?

Father: I just want what's best for Alex, but he thinks we're too controlling.

Therapist: It sounds like you're coming from a place of care. Alex, how does this make you feel?

Alex: I feel suffocated. They don't get me.

Therapist (using Satir's mirroring technique): Alex, it seems like you're looking for more independence. Let's explore that.

Mother: We're just worried about his choices.

Therapist: Let's each express our fears and hopes. Alex, we'll start with you.
Alex: I hope for more freedom to make my own decisions.
Father: My fear is that he'll make a wrong turn.
Therapist: Now, let's look at ways to balance these hopes and fears.

Building Trust and Communication

Therapist: Let's try an exercise. Alex, tell your parents one decision you made recently that you're proud of.
Alex: I studied extra hours for my math test and got a B.
Therapist: Parents, let's acknowledge Alex's effort and discuss how you can support his decision-making.

Homework for Building Understanding

Therapist: This week, each of you will share one thing daily that you appreciate about each other. It's a step towards understanding and respect.

Outcome: The Robinson family begins to develop a healthier communication pattern, balancing parental concern with Alex's need for independence. Recent studies emphasize that such congruent communication is vital for adolescent mental health, particularly in navigating post-pandemic stressors (Allen et al., 2022).

Reconciling After a Marital Conflict

Background: The Edwards, a couple in their mid-30s, are seeking therapy after a major argument that almost led to separation.

Therapist: Let's start by sharing your feelings about the conflict. Who would like to begin?
Mrs. Edwards: I feel like John doesn't listen to me anymore.
Mr. Edwards: And I feel like Sarah is always criticizing me.
Therapist (using Satir's validation technique): It sounds like you both feel misunderstood. Let's explore these feelings.

Therapist: John, can you repeat back what Sarah just said in your own words?

Mr. Edwards: You feel like I don't listen to you.

Therapist: Sarah, how does it feel hearing John acknowledge your feelings?

Mrs. Edwards: It feels good to be heard, but there's more to it.

Therapist (using Satir's congruence model): Let's go deeper into these feelings. What's at the heart of this for you, Sarah?

Role-Playing for Empathy and Understanding

Therapist: Now, let's switch roles. John, you'll be Sarah, and vice versa. Express what you believe the other is feeling.

Mr. Edwards (as Mrs. Edwards): I feel lonely and ignored.

Mrs. Edwards (as Mr. Edwards): I feel constantly judged and not good enough.

Therapist: This role reversal helps us empathize with each other's experience. What did you learn from this?

Developing a Plan for Improved Communication

Therapist: Let's identify one change each of you can make to improve communication.

Outcome: Both agree to set aside time for daily check-ins without distractions.

Homework for Relationship Growth

Therapist: This week, practice expressing appreciation for one thing the other person does each day. It's a step towards rebuilding your connection.

Outcome: The Edwards start to understand each other's perspectives better and commit to daily practices that enhance their communication and connection. This aligns with research on "couple congruence," which suggests that spiritual and emotional attunement is the foundation of marital resilience (Bentheim, 2008).

Rebuilding Communication in a Fragmented Family

Background: The Johnsons, a family of four with teenage children, were struggling with deep-seated conflicts and communication issues. Every member felt isolated, leading to frequent misunderstandings and emotional distress within the family.

Application of Satir's Methods

- **Initial Assessment**: The therapist started by observing the family's interaction patterns, identifying passive, aggressive, and passive-aggressive communication styles.
- **Creating a Safe Space**: The therapist established a non-judgmental environment, encouraging each member to openly express their feelings without fear of blame or criticism.
- **Identifying Communication Stances**: Each family member was guided to recognize their typical communication stances – blaming, placating, being irrelevant, or being super-reasonable – and how these were impacting their interactions.
- **Role-Playing and Family Sculpting**: Through these activities, the family members were able to step into each other's shoes, gaining insight into each other's perspectives and emotional needs.
- **Developing Congruent Communication**: The therapist worked with the family to practice more open, honest, and congruent communication, focusing on expressing their true feelings and needs.
- **Continuous Feedback and Adaptation**: The therapist provided ongoing feedback and made adjustments to the therapeutic approach based on the family's evolving dynamics.

Outcome: Over multiple sessions, the Johnson family developed a deeper understanding of each other. They learned to communicate more effectively, which led to fewer conflicts and a stronger emotional bond. The children felt more heard and understood, and the parents learned to express their concerns in a non-confrontational manner.

Addressing Individual Identity in a Collective Culture

Background: Meera, a 25-year-old woman from a South Asian background, was navigating the challenges of balancing her individual aspirations with her family's traditional expectations. Experiencing a clash between her personal goals and cultural roles, Meera faced significant stress and identity conflict.

Application of Satir's Methods

- **Exploring Personal Identity**: The therapist encouraged Meera to engage in self-reflection activities, helping her articulate her personal values, aspirations, and identity separate from her family's expectations.
- **Family Reconstruction Sessions**: Meera and her family participated in sessions aimed at understanding the family's cultural history and its impact on individual members. This approach helped the family see the influence of generational patterns on Meera's current situation.
- **Empowerment and Growth**: Utilizing Satir's self-esteem and growth model, the therapist worked on building Meera's self-worth and confidence. Techniques such as role-playing and visualization were used to strengthen her assertiveness skills.
- **Facilitating Family Dialogue**: The therapist guided the family in open discussions to address the tension between collective norms and individual desires, focusing on empathy and mutual respect.
- **Integrating New Behaviors**: Meera and her family were encouraged to practice new ways of communication and interaction, respecting both Meera's individual choices and the family's cultural values.

Outcome: Over time, Meera developed greater confidence in expressing her desires and negotiating her role within her family. Her family began to understand the importance of balancing individuality with cultural traditions, leading to a more supportive and harmonious family environment. This case illustrates the model's effectiveness in Korean and other Asian worldviews, where the "self" is often defined relationally (Young, 2007).

Enhancing Family Communication

Background: The Thompson family, with two parents and two teenagers, struggles with frequent conflicts and a lack of understanding. Each family member feels isolated and unheard.

Satir's Method Application

- **Initial Assessment**: The therapist begins by observing the family's interaction patterns and identifying their primary communication styles.
- **Creating a Safe Space**: A non-judgmental environment where each member feels safe to express their thoughts and feelings is established.
- **Identifying Communication Stances**: Using Satir's growth model, the therapist helps the family identify their predominant stances (blaming, placating, being irrelevant, and being super-reasonable) and the impact of these on their interactions.
- **Role-Playing Exercises**: Each member is guided to express a recent conflict using different communication stances, helping them understand the effects of their communication styles.
- **Family Sculpting**: This technique is used to physically represent the family dynamics and roles, providing a visual and experiential understanding of how each member fits into the family system.
- **Building Congruent Communication**: The therapist works with the family to develop more open, honest, and congruent ways of communicating.
- **Homework Assignments**: Each member is given tasks to practice these new communication skills at home.

Outcome: Improved communication, leading to a reduction in conflicts and a deeper understanding among family members. Each member feels more valued and connected within the family.

Addressing Jealousy and Favoritism

Context: In a large family with complex dynamics, issues like jealousy and favoritism have created significant discord. The family consists of parents, several children of varying ages, and extended family members who live together or are closely involved. The therapist, using Satir's approach, navigates these challenges.

Stage 1: Establishing Communication and Rapport

Therapist: Welcome, everyone. Today, we're here to create a space where each of you can share your feelings and thoughts openly. Let's start by hearing what brought each of you here today.

Stage 2: Identifying Patterns and Roles

Therapist: As we share, let's pay attention to any patterns that emerge in how we communicate and relate to each other. Are there certain roles that you find yourselves playing in the family?

Exploring the Issues of Jealousy and Favoritism

Therapist: I understand that feelings of jealousy and instances of favoritism have been concerns in the family. Let's explore these feelings. Remember, this is a safe space to express yourselves honestly.

Child 1: I always feel like Mom and Dad prefer my younger brother. It's like whatever he does is perfect.

Parent: We didn't realize you felt that way. It's not our intention to make you feel less valued.

Stage 3: Encouraging Open and Honest Dialogue

Therapist: It's important that everyone feels heard and understood. Let's use 'I' statements to express how we feel without blaming others.

Child 2: I feel overlooked when I see my sister getting more attention for her achievements.

Stage 4: Reconstructing Family Dynamics

Therapist: Let's consider how we might shift these dynamics. What are some ways we can ensure that everyone feels equally valued and seen?

Stage 5: Promoting Empathy and Understanding

Therapist: Empathy is key in understanding each other's perspectives. Let's try an exercise where each of you shares how you think another family member might be feeling.

Extended Family Member: I think the parents might feel overwhelmed trying to balance attention among all the kids.

Stage 6: Healing and Rebuilding

Therapist: Now that we've shared our feelings and perspectives, let's talk about healing. How can we rebuild our relationships based on mutual respect and understanding?

Family: (*Discussing practical steps like family meetings, individual time with parents, acknowledging each other's successes, and fair distribution of responsibilities.*)

Therapist: Let's delve deeper into the feelings of jealousy and favoritism. It's not uncommon in large families for these dynamics to develop. Understanding their root can help us address them more effectively.

Uncovering Historical Patterns

Therapist: Often, these patterns have historical roots. Can the parents share how favoritism and attention were handled in your families growing up?

Father: In my family, we were pretty competitive for our parents' attention. I guess some of that has carried over into how we raise our kids.

Mother I was an only child, so this dynamic is new to me. Maybe I overcompensate with some of the kids without realizing it.

Acknowledging Individual Feelings

Therapist: It's important for each of you to acknowledge how these dynamics make you feel. This isn't about assigning blame, but about understanding each other's experiences.

Child 3: I feel like I have to be perfect to get noticed. It's exhausting.

Satir's Communication Stances

Therapist: Let's look at how communication stances play a role here. Are some of you placating, blaming, or being overly reasonable to cope with these feelings?

Child 4: I guess I placate a lot. I don't want to cause more trouble.

Sculpting Exercise

Therapist: We're going to do a sculpting exercise. Let's physically arrange ourselves in a way that represents our perceived roles and feelings in the family.

During the Exercise: The family positions themselves, revealing visually the distances and closeness they feel towards each other.

Reflecting on the Sculpt

Therapist: What does this sculpt tell us about our family dynamics? How does seeing it visually impact your understanding of each other?

Child 5: Seeing how apart I am from everyone else makes me realize how isolated I've felt.

Developing New Patterns

Therapist: Now that we have this awareness, let's brainstorm ways we can change these patterns. How can we physically rearrange ourselves to represent a more connected and balanced family?

The Family: (*Repositions themselves into a more cohesive and connected arrangement.*)

Creating Actionable Steps

Therapist: This new arrangement is symbolic of the changes we want to make. Let's discuss concrete steps we can take in our daily lives to reflect this new, more connected family system.

Parents: We can make sure to spend individual time with each child every week.

Children: We can also make an effort to acknowledge and celebrate each other's achievements.

Reinforcing Positive Change

Therapist: These are excellent steps. Remember, change is a process. It's about making small adjustments and being aware of how our actions and words affect each other. Let's meet regularly to discuss how these changes are going and what else we can do to support each other.

In this session, the therapist uses various techniques from Satir's approach, including historical exploration, acknowledgment of individual feelings, communication stances, and sculpting exercises. This helps the family to not only understand the roots and impacts of their dynamics but also to actively work towards creating a more balanced, connected, and supportive family environment.

Family Exploration (Group Session)

Therapist: Today, we're planning to do a Family Reconstruction exercise. This can be a powerful way to understand our family dynamics and their impact on us. Sarah, would you be willing to participate today?

Client (Sarah): I'm not sure what this will change. My family is what it is.

[Therapist's Note: Sarah shows resistance and skepticism. Approach with empathy and without pushing too hard. Validate her feelings and gently encourage exploration.]

Therapist: (*Acknowledging her reluctance*) It's completely normal to feel uncertain about what this exercise can bring. The goal isn't to change your family but to understand how your experiences with them have shaped you. You're in control here and we can go at a pace that feels comfortable for you

Sarah: Okay, I guess we can try, but I don't see the point.

[Therapist's Note: Sarah's agreement to participate, even if hesitant, is a positive step. Start with general, less emotionally charged questions to ease her into the process.]

Therapist: (*Starting with broad questions*) Let's begin with you describing your family members in general terms. Who are they and what are they like?

Sarah: Well, my dad's always been distant, my mom is overbearing, and I never really got along with my brother.

[Therapist's Note: Note the descriptive language Sarah uses. It provides insight into her perceptions and feelings about her family.]

Therapist: Thank you for sharing that. If you're okay with it let's select some group members to stand in for your family. We'll explore these dynamics a bit more but remember you're in control

(*Sarah hesitantly agrees. Volunteers are chosen to stand in for the father, mother, and brother.*)

Therapist: (*guiding the sculpting process gently*) Sarah, please position each person to represent how you typically see your family interactions.

(*Sarah positions the volunteers. Her father figure is placed distantly, the mother figure is upfront, and the brother is off to the side.*)

Therapist: (*Observing her body language*) Can you tell us what this arrangement represents for you?

Sarah: It's how we always are. Dad's absent, mom's in everyone's business, and my brother and I just coexist.

[Therapist's Note: Sarah's descriptions are somewhat detached. Encourage a bit more exploration while respecting her comfort level.]

Therapist: (*Exploring with sensitivity*) How do these dynamics make you feel?

Sarah: (*Shrugging*) It's just how things are. I don't expect them to change.

[Therapist's Note: Acknowledge her acceptance of the situation. Gently challenge her to explore her feelings about these dynamics.]

Therapist: (*Encouraging reflection*) It's okay to accept things as they are. But understanding how they affect us can be helpful. For instance how does your dad's distance or your mom's involvement impact you in your current life?

Sarah: (*Thoughtful but still guarded*) I guess I don't really rely on others much. Maybe that's why.

[Therapist's Note: Sarah is beginning to make connections between her family experience and her current behavior. Reinforce this insight gently and explore further.]

Therapist: (*Offering gentle reinforcement*) That's an insightful connection. Understanding these patterns can help us see why we interact with others the way we do. Reflecting on this are there ways you'd like to be different in your relationships or interactions?

Sarah: Maybe… I could try to be a bit more open. I don't know.

[Therapist's Note: Plan to continue working with Sarah on understanding her family's influence and how it impacts her current relationships. Respect her pace and continue to provide a safe space for exploration.]

Therapist: (*Concluding with support and validation*) It's okay to be unsure. These are significant insights and exploring them takes time. We'll continue to work on this together at a pace that feels right for you. Every bit of understanding you gain is a step toward more fulfilling relationships and a clearer sense of self

(*Maintaining a supportive approach.*) It's important to recognize that exploring these family dynamics isn't about assigning blame. It's about understanding patterns that might be influencing your life now. How do you think recognizing these patterns could be helpful for you?

Sarah: Maybe it could help me understand why I am the way I am. I've always been pretty independent, maybe too much so.

[Therapist's Note: Sarah is beginning to see the potential value in understanding her family dynamics. Continue to draw connections between these insights and her current behaviors, doing so in a way that fosters self-discovery and empowerment.]

Therapist: (*Gently guiding exploration*) That independence is a strength Sarah. And understanding its roots can give you more choice in how you use it. For example think about a recent situation where you felt your independence was both a benefit and a challenge. How did that play out?

Sarah: (*Reflecting*) At work, I handle things on my own a lot. It's good because I get things done, but sometimes I feel isolated.

[Therapist's Note: Use these reflections to help Sarah balance her strengths with potential areas for growth, such as seeking collaboration or support when needed.]

Therapist: (*Suggesting balance*) Your ability to handle things independently is indeed a strength. And there's also strength in seeking collaboration and support. How might you find a balance between these in your work life?

Sarah: I suppose I could try to delegate more or ask for input sometimes. I don't always have to do everything myself.

[Therapist's Note: Acknowledge this willingness to consider change. Discuss practical steps she can take to implement this new approach.]

Therapist: (*Encouraging practical steps*): That sounds like a constructive approach. Starting with small changes can lead to a more balanced way of working. Now let's consider your personal relationships. How might this understanding of your family dynamics and your independent nature influence your interactions with friends or partners?

Sarah: *I guess I could try to be more open or rely on them a bit more. I've always kept people at a distance.*

[Therapist's Note: Recognize and validate the difficulty in changing long-standing patterns. Encourage gradual steps towards more open and interdependent relationships.]

Therapist: (*Offering support for gradual change*) It's okay to start small. Building trust and openness takes time. Remember acknowledging these patterns is the first step towards change. We can work together on strategies to gradually open up in your relationships at a pace that feels comfortable for you

Sarah: Thanks. I'm not sure how it'll go, but I'm open to trying.

[Therapist's Note: Plan to continue supporting Sarah in understanding her family dynamics and their impact on her current behavior. Focus on empowering her to make conscious choices in her interactions and relationships, respecting her pace and process.]

Therapist: (*Concluding with encouragement*) Exploring these areas can be challenging Sarah but it's also a path to greater self-awareness and fulfillment. We'll take it one step at a time. Your openness to trying is a big step in itself and I'm here to support you through this journey

(*Focusing on incremental change.*) You mentioned being open to trying new ways of interacting. Let's explore some small steps you can take. How about starting with your communication style? Are there moments where you feel you could express yourself differently?

Sarah: Sometimes, I think I could be more open about how I feel, but I usually end up keeping it to myself.

[Therapist's Note: Recognize her awareness of her communication patterns. Encourage small, manageable changes in expressing her emotions.]

Therapist: (*Suggesting specific actions*) Expressing emotions can be a big step. What if you started by identifying moments when you feel like sharing even if you decide not to? Just noticing these moments can be progress

Sarah: (*Considering the idea*) I could try that. Maybe being aware is a start.

[Therapist's Note: Validate this approach. Building awareness is the first step towards change.]

Therapist: (*Building awareness*) Awareness is indeed the first step. As you become more aware you might find opportunities where it feels safe to share a little more. Remember there's no rush. This is about finding what works for you

Sarah: Okay, I'll keep that in mind.

[Therapist's Note: Plan to review these moments of awareness in future sessions, using them as a foundation for further exploration and growth.]

Therapist: (*Addressing resistance to change*) Sarah it's also important to acknowledge that change can be uncomfortable especially when we're used to certain patterns. How do you usually handle discomfort or resistance when trying something new?

Sarah: I usually back off when things get uncomfortable. It's easier to stick with what I know.

[Therapist's Note: Discuss the concept of "leaning into discomfort" as a growth opportunity. Provide strategies for managing discomfort in a healthy way.]

Therapist: (*Offering coping strategies*) It's natural to retreat to comfort zones. But sometimes leaning into that discomfort can lead to growth. Next time you feel resistant try to pause and explore what's behind that feeling. It could be fear uncertainty or something else. Understanding this can help you navigate through it

Sarah: That's a different way to look at it. I can try to be more mindful of why I feel resistant.

[Therapist's Final Note: Encourage Sarah to explore the underlying reasons for her resistance in future sessions. Support her in developing a more mindful approach to her emotions and reactions.]

Therapist: (*Concluding with encouragement*) Exploring these patterns and learning to work through discomfort is a significant part of personal growth. We'll continue this journey together Sarah at a pace that's right for you. Every small step you take is valuable

Family Dynamics

Therapist: Today, we're going to engage in a Family Dynamics session. This will help us understand how your family dynamics have shaped your current behaviors and feelings. Are you ready to begin?

James (Client): Yes, I'm ready. I've been curious about how my family background affects me now.

[Therapist's Note: Client appears open but slightly apprehensive. Important to ensure a sense of safety and support throughout the session.]

Therapist: Let's start by mapping out your family. Tell me about your family members and your role in the family

James: Well, my dad was always the strict one, very authoritative. Mom was more nurturing but often passive. I guess I tried to keep the peace, avoid conflicts.

[Therapist's Note: Client's role as a peacemaker may contribute to conflict-avoidance in adulthood. Possible suppression of own needs and desires.]

Therapist: How did these dynamics make you feel as a child?

James: I often felt like I couldn't express my true feelings. I had to be the good son, always agreeable.

[Therapist's Note: Acknowledge the client's feelings of suppression. Explore how this might relate to current issues of self-expression and assertiveness.]

Therapist: Let's explore that further. Imagine you could speak to your father now. What would you want to say to him?

James: (*Hesitant at first*) I'd tell him that his strictness made me feel trapped. I wish I could have been more open about my feelings.

[Therapist's Note: Client is accessing deeper emotions. Facilitate this expression while ensuring emotional safety.]

Therapist: (*Encouragingly*) That's a powerful expression James. How about your mother? What would you say to her?

James: I wish she had been more assertive, maybe stood up for her own opinions more. It might have shown me it's okay to have my own voice.

[Therapist's Note: Client recognizes the lack of assertive modeling from parents. This insight is key to understanding his current relational patterns.]

Therapist: It sounds like these experiences deeply impacted you. How do you see these dynamics playing out in your current life?

James: I guess I still avoid conflicts. I don't assert myself much, especially at work or in my relationships.

[Therapist's Note: Client is making connections between past family roles and current behavior. Important to guide him towards redefining these roles in a healthier way.]

Therapist: Understanding this link is a big step. Now let's think about how you can start to change these patterns. What's one way you could start asserting yourself more?

James: (*Pauses to think*) Maybe I could start by expressing my opinions in small ways, like choosing where to eat out instead of always going along with others.

[Therapist's Note: Client is identifying practical steps for change. Reinforce these small actions and build upon them in future sessions.]

Therapist: (*Positively*) That's a great start James. Small steps lead to big changes. Remember this is a journey of redefining yourself separate from your family's defined roles. We'll continue to explore and support this in our sessions

[Therapist's Final Note: Client is beginning to understand and challenge family-imposed roles. Future sessions will focus on reinforcing new patterns of behavior and further exploring family dynamics.]

~

Therapist: (*Maintaining a supportive and non-judgmental tone*) James, now let's explore how your family's communication style has influenced your current relationships. How do you communicate your needs to others?

James: I often find it hard to express what I really need. I guess I'm afraid of being a burden.

[Therapist's Note: Client's difficulty in expressing needs likely stems from the family dynamic of suppressing emotions. Encourage exploration of healthier communication strategies.]

Therapist: (*Gently prompting*) That fear is understandable considering your family background. How might you start to overcome this in your current relationships?

James: (*Reflective*) Perhaps I could start by sharing small things, to test the waters and build confidence.

[Therapist's Note: Client is recognizing the need for incremental change. Validate this approach and discuss practical steps.]

Therapist: (*Nodding encouragingly*) That's a good approach. Small steps can lead to significant changes. Let's also consider how you can create a supportive environment around you. Who in your life do you feel safe sharing your feelings with?

James: My friend Mark is a good listener. I think I could start by opening up to him more.

[Therapist's Note: Identify and reinforce existing support systems. Encourage the client to utilize these relationships to practice new communication skills.]

Therapist: (*With a reassuring smile*) Mark sounds like a valuable support. Utilizing these existing relationships can be very helpful. Now reflecting on your family's influence how do you think you can begin to redefine your role within your family?

James: That's tough. Maybe I can start by setting some boundaries, like saying no when I'm uncomfortable.

[Therapist's Note: Client is considering boundary setting. Discuss ways to effectively set and maintain boundaries while respecting family dynamics.]

Therapist: (*Offering practical advice*) Setting boundaries is a crucial step. It's about respecting your own needs as well as those of your family members. We can work on strategies to communicate these boundaries assertively but compassionately

James: I like the idea of being both assertive and compassionate. I've never thought about it that way.

[Therapist's Note: Highlighting assertiveness and compassion as complementary, not contradictory, can empower the client to adopt a balanced communication style.]

Therapist: (*Concluding the session*) As we continue we'll explore these concepts further and practice new ways of interacting based on your newfound understanding. Remember this process is about growth and learning to express your true self both within and outside your family

James: I'm starting to see things differently. It feels like a new beginning.

[Therapist's Final Note: Client is gaining new perspectives and is open to change. Future sessions will focus on reinforcing assertive communication, boundary setting, and further exploring the impact of family dynamics on current relationships.]

~

Therapist: (*Creating an empathetic and reflective atmosphere*) James, let's delve a bit deeper into your role as the peacemaker in your family. How do you think this role has affected your ability to stand up for yourself?

James: I've always put others' needs before mine. It's hard for me to assert what I want without feeling selfish.

[Therapist's Note: Client's peacemaker role has led to a pattern of self-neglect. Important to challenge this perception and encourage self-care.]

Therapist: (*Encouraging self-compassion*) Caring for yourself isn't selfish James. It's necessary for your well-being. Can you think of situations where you could have prioritized your needs more?

James: (*Pondering*) There have been many times at work where I agreed to tasks I didn't want, just to keep the peace.

[Therapist's Note: Client recognizes the pattern of self-neglect in professional settings. Explore ways to assert needs in the workplace.]

Therapist: (*Offering a new perspective*) In those moments it's important to remember that your needs are as valid as anyone else's. Let's brainstorm ways you can express your preferences at work without compromising your role as a team player

James: Maybe I can start by voicing my opinions in team meetings, even if it's just small contributions at first.

[Therapist's Note: Encourage small, achievable steps towards assertiveness. Validate efforts and progress.]

Therapist: (*Smiling affirmatively*): That's a great start. It's about finding your voice in a way that feels authentic to you. Now thinking about your personal relationships how can you apply these insights there?

James: I need to be more honest with my partner about my feelings. I tend to just go along with things to avoid arguments.

[Therapist's Note: Client is identifying similar patterns in personal relationships. Discuss communication techniques to express feelings authentically.]

Therapist: (*Suggesting communication strategies*) Open and honest communication is key in any relationship. It might help to express your feelings using 'I' statements which focus on your experiences rather than placing blame

James: I've heard of that but never really tried it. It could help make conversations less confrontational.

[Therapist's Note: Introduce and practice 'I' statements in session to build client's confidence in using them outside therapy.]

Therapist: (*Concluding with an action plan*) In our next sessions we'll practice these communication techniques and continue exploring how you can assert your needs while maintaining harmony. Remember every step you take towards expressing your true self is a step towards a more fulfilling life

James: I feel more hopeful about making these changes. It's like I'm learning to balance being kind to others and to myself.

[Therapist's Final Note: Client is showing readiness for change and a growing understanding of the need for self-care. Future sessions will focus on practical application of communication skills and reinforcing self-compassion and assertiveness.]

~

Therapist: (*Facilitating deeper self-exploration*) James, reflecting on your family's communication styles, how do you feel they influenced your understanding of emotions and how to express them?

James: Emotions weren't really discussed in our family. It was like they were there, but we never openly acknowledged them.

[Therapist's Note: The family's avoidance of emotional expression likely contributes to James's difficulty in recognizing and articulating his emotions. Encourage emotional literacy.]

Therapist: (*Gently probing*): How comfortable are you with expressing emotions now especially those considered vulnerable like sadness or fear?

James: (*With hesitation*) I find it really hard. I usually keep those feelings to myself.

[Therapist's Note: Work on creating a safe space in therapy for James to express and explore these vulnerable emotions. Introduce emotional expression as a skill to be developed.]

Therapist: (*Offering validation and support*) It's okay to feel uncomfortable with this James. Recognizing and expressing emotions is a skill that can be developed over time. Let's start by identifying emotions you feel regularly. We can then explore healthy ways to express them

James: That sounds helpful. I often feel stressed but don't really know how to deal with it.

[Therapist's Note: Use stress as a starting point for exploring emotional expression. Discuss coping strategies and emotional release techniques.]

Therapist: (*Suggesting coping strategies*) When you feel stressed acknowledging the emotion is the first step. Then you can try techniques like deep breathing writing down your feelings or talking it out with someone you trust

James: I haven't tried writing down my feelings before. That might be a good way to start.

[Therapist's Note: Encourage journaling as a tool for emotional exploration. Plan to review and discuss journal entries in future sessions.]

Therapist: (*Encouraging continued growth*) Journaling can be a very effective way to process emotions. In our next sessions we can look at some of your entries and explore what they reveal about your emotional world. We'll also continue to work on expressing these emotions in safe and healthy ways

James: I'm willing to try that. I think understanding my emotions better could really change things for me.

[Therapist's Final Note: Client shows openness to new emotional expression techniques. Future sessions will focus on building emotional literacy and expression skills, particularly in the context of stress and vulnerability.]

~

Therapist: (*Shifting focus to family influence on relationships*): James, considering how your family's communication style has influenced you, how do you think it impacts your current relationships, especially in terms of emotional intimacy?

James: I guess I struggle with opening up. I keep things to myself, like I learned to do at home.

[Therapist's Note: The client's family dynamic of emotional suppression impacts his ability to form emotionally intimate relationships. Address this by exploring ways to foster openness and vulnerability.]

Therapist: (*Encouraging exploration*) Learning to be open and vulnerable can be challenging especially if it wasn't modeled in your family. Let's think about small steps you could take to gradually open up more in your relationships

James: (*Thoughtfully*) Maybe I could start by sharing more about my day with my partner, including how I really feel about things.

[Therapist's Note: Validate this approach. Discuss the importance of creating a safe and non-judgmental space for these conversations.]

Therapist: (*Offering guidance*) That sounds like a positive step. Creating a safe space for such conversations is key. How do you think your partner would respond to you sharing more?

James: I think she'd be supportive. She's often asked me to open up more.

[Therapist's Note: Encourage the client to take advantage of this supportive environment. Plan to follow up on these efforts in future sessions.]

Therapist: (*Building on client's support system*) It sounds like you have a supportive partner. Let's also consider other relationships like friendships or work colleagues. How might you foster deeper connections there?

James: I've kept colleagues at a distance. Maybe I could join them for lunch sometimes, or just engage in more casual conversations.

[Therapist's Note: Promote the idea of expanding comfort zones in social interactions. Reinforce the concept that emotional connections can be built gradually.]

Therapist: (*Suggesting gradual social engagement*) That's a good way to start building connections. Remember, emotional intimacy doesn't have to happen all at once it can develop over time through shared experiences and mutual understanding

James: That takes some pressure off. I always thought it had to be all or nothing.

[Therapist's Note: The client is beginning to understand the gradual nature of building emotional intimacy. Future sessions will focus on continuing to challenge his comfort zones and reinforcing the value of emotional expression in building relationships.]

Therapist: (*Concluding the session with a forward-looking statement*) James you're making important strides in understanding how your family background influences your current life. As we continue we'll work on applying these insights more broadly helping you build richer more emotionally connected relationships

James: I'm starting to see how all these pieces fit together. It's challenging, but I'm feeling hopeful about making these changes.

Therapist: (*Exploring further application of insights in the next session*) James, in addition to improving communication in your relationships, let's also consider how your family dynamics influence your self-esteem and self-image. How do you see yourself as a result of these early experiences?

James: I've always felt like I had to earn approval. Maybe that's why I'm so hard on myself.

[Therapist's Note: Client's need for approval and harsh self-judgment are likely rooted in family dynamics. Important to challenge these perceptions and promote self-acceptance.]

Therapist: (*Encouraging self-reflection*) That need for approval can be quite burdensome. Let's work on ways you can start to validate and approve of yourself. What are some qualities you appreciate about yourself?

James: (*Pausing to think*) I guess I'm a good listener and I'm reliable. But I don't often think about my positive traits.

[Therapist's Note: Encourage regular acknowledgment of personal strengths. This practice can help shift the client's focus from external validation to internal self-appreciation.]

Therapist: (*Affirming the client's strengths*) Those are significant qualities James. Recognizing and appreciating your strengths is a key step in building self-esteem. Let's also consider how you can challenge the critical voice that seeks external approval. What might you say to that part of yourself?

James: Maybe I can remind myself that I'm worthy regardless of what others think. That I don't always have to be perfect.

[Therapist's Note: Validate the client's approach to challenging critical self-talk. Discuss strategies for replacing critical thoughts with affirming ones.]

Therapist: (*Suggesting cognitive reframing*) That's a powerful realization. When you notice the critical voice consciously replace it with affirming thoughts. It's a practice that can gradually shift your internal dialogue

James: I'll try that. It seems like a simple shift, but I can see how it might make a big difference.

[Therapist's Final Note: The client is beginning to recognize and challenge ingrained patterns of self-criticism. Future sessions will focus on reinforcing positive self-talk and exploring the impact of these changes on his overall well-being.]

Therapist: (*Concluding with a supportive statement*) James today's session has brought some important insights to light. Remember changing long-standing patterns takes time and patience. We'll continue to build on these strategies and explore new ways to foster a positive self-image and robust self-esteem

James: Thank you. Today has opened up a lot for me to think about. I feel like I'm on the right track.

~

Therapist: (*Introducing new concepts for personal growth*) James, let's also explore how your family dynamics may have influenced your approach to personal goals and aspirations. How do you make decisions about your future, and what role do your family's expectations play in this?

James: I've always tried to live up to what I thought my family expected of me. It's like I'm following a path they set out, not one I chose for myself.

[Therapist's Note: Client's decision-making is heavily influenced by perceived family expectations. Focus on empowering him to explore and define his own aspirations.]

Therapist: (*Fostering independence in decision-making*) It's important to consider what you truly want for yourself. What are some dreams or goals you've put aside?

James: (*Reflecting deeply*) I've always been interested in photography, but I never pursued it seriously. I guess I thought it wasn't a practical career choice.

[Therapist's Note: Encourage exploration of personal interests as a means of self-discovery and fulfillment. Discuss balancing practical considerations with personal passions.]

Therapist: (*Suggesting exploration of interests*) Photography could be a wonderful way to express yourself. How about starting it as a hobby? It doesn't have to be a career move but rather a personal pursuit for fulfillment

James: That might be a good way to start. It's been a long time since I did something just because I enjoyed it.

[Therapist's Final Note: Client shows openness to exploring personal interests. Future sessions will explore how engaging in personal passions can impact his sense of self and overall well-being.]

Therapist: (*Concluding with an encouraging plan*) Engaging in activities that bring you joy can be incredibly liberating and fulfilling. It allows you to connect with parts of yourself that you may have neglected. In our next sessions we can look at how pursuing photography or other interests might enrich your life. We'll also continue to work on defining your path based on your values and aspirations not just the expectations of others

James: I'm excited about that. It feels like I'm starting to take control of my life.

Therapist: (*Building on the theme of personal agency*) James, gaining control over your life is about making choices that align with your true self. Let's explore areas where you might feel you lack control. Are there aspects of your life where you feel you're just going through the motions?

James: Definitely. At work, I often just do what's expected without really thinking if it's what I want.

[Therapist's Note: Client experiences a sense of autopilot in professional life, indicating a lack of personal engagement. Explore ways to introduce more conscious decision-making in this area.]

Therapist: (*Encouraging proactive engagement*) It's important to bring more of yourself into your work. How can you make your job more aligned with your interests or values?

James: (*Contemplative*) I haven't really thought about it that way. Maybe I can find ways to be more creative in my role, or suggest projects that are more in line with my interests.

[Therapist's Note: Encourage small, innovative changes in the client's work approach to foster a sense of personal fulfillment and agency.]

Therapist: (*Suggesting practical steps*) That sounds like a positive approach. Finding small ways to infuse your personal strengths and interests into your work can make a significant difference. Remember, change doesn't have to be drastic even small shifts can lead to greater job satisfaction

James: I'll think about what those small changes could be. It feels good to consider having more of a say in my work.

[Therapist's Final Note: Continue to support the client in identifying and implementing small changes in his professional life. Monitor how these changes impact his sense of agency and fulfillment.]

~

Therapist: (*Addressing broader life choices*) Besides work, let's think about your lifestyle and relationships. Are there choices you're making by default rather than intention? How can we apply this newfound sense of agency there?

James: I've been in a routine for so long, maybe it's time to evaluate my hobbies, my social circle, even where I live.

[Therapist's Note: Client is showing readiness to reassess various aspects of his life. Facilitate this process by encouraging reflection and exploration of personal values and desires.]

Therapist: (*Guiding towards self-reflection*) That's an excellent idea. Reflecting on what truly brings you joy and fulfillment in these areas can guide you towards more authentic choices. Let's use our next sessions to explore these aspects in more detail aligning your lifestyle and relationships with your true self

James: Looking at everything through this new lens is exciting. I feel like I'm waking up to my own life.

Parts Party in a 1:1 session

Therapist: Today, we're going to try the Parts Party exercise. It's a way to explore different parts of yourself, to understand how they influence your thoughts and feelings. Are you ready to start?

Anna (Client): Yes, I'm ready. I feel a bit nervous but curious.

Therapist: That's perfectly normal. Let's begin with the part you've identified as the "Protector." Please move to the "Protector" chair. Tell me, what does the Protector part of you say?

Anna (as Protector): I need to keep Anna safe. I make her stay away from risky things. It's better to be safe than sorry.

Therapist: Thank you, Protector. Now, let's switch to the "Adventurer." What does this part of you feel about what the Protector just said?

Anna (as Adventurer): I feel trapped! I want to try new things, meet new people. I don't want to be held back all the time.

Therapist: I hear that longing for freedom. Let's turn toward the part that feels hesitant about this – Inner Critic, what's coming up for you?

Anna (as Inner Critic): Honestly, I just want to protect Anna. If she takes risks, she might fail, and I don't want her to experience that pain. I push her because I'm trying to keep her safe.

Therapist: That makes so much sense. It sounds like you care deeply for Anna.

Therapist (to Anna's Self-Energy): Would you like to speak to this part from a place of Self?

(*Anna takes a breath, placing a hand on her heart.*)

Anna (as Self-Energy): I see you, Critic. I hear that you're afraid for me. You don't want me to get hurt.

(*For the first time, the Critic pauses.*)

Inner Critic: Yes… I've seen her struggle before. I don't want her to feel that again.

Anna (as Self-Energy): I understand. And I also know that failing is part of growing. What if I checked in with you along the way, so you don't feel the need to push so hard?

(The Inner Critic nods slightly, as if loosening its grip.)

Therapist: How does it feel to hear these words from your Self-Energy?

(*Anna closes her eyes for a moment, then opens them with a softer expression.*)

Anna: It's… comforting. My Critic isn't against me – it's just scared for me.

Therapist: Yes. And now, as Self, you can support this part instead of being at odds with it. Let's continue this dialogue. Can the Adventurer and the Protector find a common ground? Adventurer, what do you need?

Anna (as Adventurer): I need freedom, but I also understand the need for safety. Maybe we can take calculated risks?

Anna (as Protector): That could work. I want her to be safe, but I see the importance of exploring and growing.

Therapist: I hear that both of you have important roles. Instead of negotiating, let's listen to what each of you truly need. Protector, what concerns do you have?

Anna (as Protector): I worry that if she takes too many risks, she might get hurt. My job is to keep her safe.

Therapist: That makes so much sense. You've been protecting Anna for a long time. Adventurer, how do you feel hearing that?

Anna (as Adventurer): I get it. I don't want to be reckless, but I feel stuck when I don't get to explore.

Therapist: It sounds like both of you ultimately want Anna's well-being. What if you worked together instead of feeling like you're in opposition?

Anna (as Protector): I can support her exploring new things as long as she takes precautions.

Therapist: That's a great step. Anna, how does it feel to hear this conversation between your parts?

Anna: It feels like they're not just fighting me – they actually want what's best.

Therapist: Exactly. Now, let's bring in the Inner Critic. Critic, what are your concerns?

Anna (as Inner Critic): I just worry she'll make mistakes and get hurt. I push her because I don't want her to fail.

Therapist: That makes sense. It sounds like you have a deep desire to help her succeed. Compassionate Self, how do you feel hearing this?

Anna (as Compassionate Self): I understand the concern, but constant criticism makes things harder for Anna. I want to remind her of her strengths and support her growth.

Therapist: Critic, what do you need to feel less pressure?

Anna (as Inner Critic): I need to know she won't ignore mistakes but learn from them.

Therapist: That's a valuable role. Critic, could you support Anna with constructive feedback rather than harsh criticism?

Anna (as Inner Critic): I think I could try.

Therapist: Anna, how do you feel hearing this shift?

Anna: It's reassuring. It feels like I don't have to fight with myself so much.

Therapist: That's a big realization. This isn't about pushing parts aside – it's about understanding them so they work together. Now, let's look at a real-life scenario. Think of a time when you felt stuck in a decision.

Anna: Last week, I was offered a project at work but turned it down because I was scared.

Therapist: Let's revisit that moment. Adventurer, what do you wish had happened?

Anna (as Adventurer): I wanted to take it! It was exciting and a chance to grow.

Therapist: Protector, what were your concerns?

Anna (as Protector): I worried it would be too stressful and overwhelming. I was trying to protect her.

Therapist: Can you both work together in this situation? What would that look like?

Anna: (*Integrating parts*) Maybe the Adventurer can approach it with excitement, while the Protector makes sure I set limits and take breaks.

Therapist: That sounds like a balanced approach. Critic, how can you contribute?

Anna (as Inner Critic): I can provide helpful feedback rather than being overly negative.

Therapist:	Compassionate Self, what's your role?
Anna (as Compassionate Self):	To remind Anna that success isn't everything – learning and growth matter too.
Therapist:	Wonderful. How does it feel seeing your parts cooperate?
Anna:	Empowering. It's like I have a whole support team inside me.
Therapist:	Exactly. This is how your parts can work together to support your goals. Moving forward, how will you remind yourself to check in with your parts?
Anna:	I'll pause before making decisions and listen to what each part has to say.
Therapist:	That's a great practice. Remember, your parts aren't obstacles – they're allies. The more you listen to them, the more they'll work with you rather than against you. Let's continue exploring this in our next session.

As Anna deepens her understanding of her internal parts, she experiences a greater sense of inner balance and cooperation. Rather than struggling against conflicting voices within, she learns to engage with them, fostering an internal dialogue rooted in curiosity and compassion. This self-leadership not only enhances her personal growth but also transforms her interactions with others. By recognizing the complex interplay of her own internal system, she becomes more attuned to the dynamics present in her relationships and family system.

Building on this foundation of internal integration, we now turn our focus to the broader context of family dynamics, exploring how individual parts interact within relational systems. The ways in which family members express, suppress, or support each other's parts can profoundly shape the overall health of the family unit. The following case study illustrates how these dynamics unfold and how therapeutic approaches can foster deeper understanding, connection, and healing within family relationships.

Family Reconstruction (Group Session)

Therapist: Today, we're going to do a Family Reconstruction with James. This process will help us understand the dynamics in his family and how they've shaped his current behavior and feelings. We'll need some volunteers to play roles from James's family. James, please tell us who we need for the reconstruction.

James: We need someone to play my dad, my mom, and my younger sister.

[Therapist's Note: Ensure that volunteers understand the importance of their roles and the sensitivity of the process.]

Therapist: (*Selecting volunteers*) Can we have volunteers for these roles? Remember your role is to represent James's perception of these family members

(*Three group members volunteer and are assigned roles: Dad, Mom, and Sister.*)

Therapist: (*Guiding the family sculpt*) James, I'd like you to position each person in a way that represents how you see your family dynamics. Think about physical distance, posture, and expression.

(*James positions the volunteers. Dad is standing, authoritative; Mom is seated, looking passive; Sister is somewhat distanced from the others.*)

[Therapist's Note: Observe the physical representation for insights into family roles and emotional distances.]

Therapist (to James): Describe what you see in this sculpt and how it feels

James: It feels like my dad's dominating, my mom's not really present, and I'm always trying to bridge the gap.

[Therapist's Note: James's description aligns with his earlier depiction of family roles. Facilitate exploration of the emotional impact of these dynamics.]

Therapist (to role players): Can each of you in your role express what you might be feeling in this family scenario?

(Volunteers express emotions as per their roles: Dad is stern, Mom is subdued, Sister feels overlooked.)

Therapist (to James): Hearing this, how does it resonate with your experience?

James: It's pretty accurate. It's like seeing my family from the outside.

[Therapist's Note: Use this external perspective to help James gain new insights into his family dynamics and their impact on him.]

Therapist: (*Encouraging new perspectives*) Let's try something different. James rearrange the sculpt to represent how you wished your family could have interacted

(*James rearranges the sculpt. This time, the family members are closer and facing each other.*)

Therapist (to James): Tell us about this new arrangement.

James: Here, everyone's connected and communicating. It's what I always wanted.

[Therapist's Note: Highlight the contrast between the actual and ideal family dynamics. Discuss how this understanding can inform James's current relationships and self-perception.]

Therapist: (*Concluding the exercise*) Thank you everyone. James let's reflect on this experience and how it might inform your current relationships and choices. How can you bring some of this desired connection into your life now?

James: I need to start communicating more openly, like in this ideal sculpt. Maybe I can be the one to initiate change.

[Therapist's Final Note: Use the insights from this reconstruction to help James develop strategies for open communication and emotional connection in his current relationships. Plan to follow up on the implementation of these strategies in future sessions.]

Therapist (instructing James): James take a moment to think about each family member's role and how they relate to each other. When you're ready position each stand-in to represent these relationships

(James stands contemplatively before the group members who have volunteered as stand-ins.)

Positioning the Father (Stand-in for Dad)

James: My dad was always the authority figure, very commanding.

(*James directs the stand-in for his dad to stand upright, central, and slightly apart from the others, looking down as if overseeing them. His posture is rigid, exuding control.*)

[Therapist's Note: Observe James's body language and emotional response as he positions each stand-in. It may reveal underlying feelings towards each family member.]

Positioning the Mother (Stand-in for Mom)

James: Mom was there but often in the background.

(*James places the stand-in for his mom to one side, seated, with a posture that seems withdrawn and passive. Her gaze is directed away from the father figure, suggesting disengagement.*)

Positioning the Sister (Stand-in for Sister)

James: My sister often felt left out, I think.

(*James positions the stand-in for his sister a bit away from the parents, with a posture that suggests uncertainty and a longing to be closer.*)

[Therapist's Note: The physical distances and postures in the sculpt reflect emotional distances and roles within the family. This setup can reveal unspoken emotions and dynamics.]

Therapist (to James): Can you describe what you're seeing and feeling with this arrangement?

James: (*Observing the sculpt*) It's like seeing my family's emotional layout. Dad's dominating presence, Mom's disconnection, and my sister's feeling of being an outsider.

[Therapist's Note: Validate James's feelings and perceptions. The sculpt is a representation of his internalized family image.]

Therapist: (*Exploring emotions*) How does seeing this layout make you feel?

James: It's a bit overwhelming. I always knew these dynamics were there, but seeing them like this makes it more real.

[Therapist's Final Note: Use this realization to delve deeper into how these dynamics affect James's current life. The next step will be to explore modifications to this sculpt to reflect how James wishes his family could have interacted, facilitating a discussion on changes he can make in his own life patterns.]

Therapist: (*Facilitating deeper exploration*) James now that you've set up the sculpt reflecting your family dynamics let's explore each relationship more deeply. Walk up to the stand-in for your dad and tell him what you wished you could have said as a child

(*James approaches the stand-in for his dad, taking a moment before speaking.*)

James (to stand-in for Dad): I wish you had been less authoritative and more approachable. I wanted to talk to you about so many things, but I was afraid.

[Therapist's Note: Observe James's emotional response during this interaction. It may reveal unresolved feelings and needs.]

Therapist (to James): How does it feel saying that now?

James: It's liberating but also sad. I realize how much I held back.

[Therapist's Note: Acknowledge and validate these feelings. This expression is a significant step towards healing.]

Therapist: (*Guiding the interaction with the Mother stand-in*) Let's turn to your mom now. Share with her what you needed from her

(*James faces the stand-in for his mom, his expression softening.*)

James (to stand-in for Mom): Mom, I wish you had been more present and assertive. I needed to see that it was okay to speak up and express my feelings.

[Therapist's Note: This interaction may highlight James's need for emotional validation and modeling of assertive behavior.]

Therapist: (*Encouraging compassion*) It's important to recognize that your parents had their limitations. Understanding this can help in finding compassion for them and for yourself. Now let's address your sister. What would you like to say to her?

(*James turns to the stand-in for his sister, his demeanor indicating a sense of responsibility.*)

James (to stand-in for Sister): I'm sorry if I ever made you feel overlooked. I was trying to keep the peace, but I wish I had been there for you more.

[Therapist's Note: Explore feelings of guilt or responsibility that James may have towards his sister. Discuss how he can address these feelings in his current life.]

Therapist: (*Guiding towards resolution*) Reflecting on these conversations how do you think you can apply these insights in your current relationships and interactions?

James: I need to be more open and assertive. And I want to make sure I'm there for the people I care about, not just caught up in keeping the peace.

[Therapist's Note: James is connecting past dynamics with current behavior patterns. Encourage him to develop new, healthier patterns of interaction.]

Therapist: (*Concluding with a forward-looking approach*) This understanding is a powerful tool for change James. In our next sessions we'll work on developing these new patterns focusing on open communication assertiveness and fulfilling your emotional needs. Remember you have the power to create new dynamics in your life informed by but not confined to your past

James: This has been eye-opening. I feel ready to start making these changes.

[Therapist's Final Note: Plan to continue supporting James in translating these insights into actionable changes, focusing on enhancing his communication skills and emotional intelligence in relationships.]

Therapist: (*Transitioning to the next phase*) James now that we've explored your feelings towards each family member let's re-create the family sculpt but this time arrange it to reflect how you wish your family had interacted. This can help us understand what you yearn for in relationships

(*James thoughtfully rearranges the stand-ins. He positions the father figure to be less imposing, the mother more engaged, and the sister closer to the parents.*)

Therapist: (*Observing the new sculpt*) Tell us about this arrangement. How is it different from the first one?

James: In this setup, everyone is more connected. My dad is less intimidating, my mom is actively involved, and my sister doesn't feel excluded.

[Therapist's Note: The new sculpt reflects James's desire for a more balanced and cohesive family dynamic. Discuss how these desired dynamics can inform his current and future relationships.]

Therapist: (*Exploring the ideal dynamic*) How does seeing this ideal version make you feel?

James: It's bittersweet. I wish it had been like this, but it also gives me hope for the kind of relationships I can build now.

[Therapist's Note: Validate the mixed emotions. Highlight the potential for creating fulfilling relationships based on this new understanding.]

Therapist: (*Connecting insights to current life*) Let's use these insights to guide your interactions moving forward. For example how can you bring this sense of connection and balance into your current relationships?

James: (*Considering new possibilities*) I can try to be more open and present, like this version of my mom. And maybe not be as intimidating in my opinions, kind of like how I repositioned my dad.

[Therapist's Note: Encourage the application of these insights in a practical, day-to-day context. This will help James in forming healthier relationship patterns.]

Therapist: (*Suggesting practical applications*) That sounds like a good approach. Also consider how you can support others in feeling included and heard as you wanted for your sister. In what ways can you apply this in your current family or social circle?

James: I can make more of an effort to reach out and listen, to really understand what others are going through. I don't want anyone to feel left out, like my sister did.

[Therapist's Final Note: Plan to focus on developing these empathetic and inclusive communication skills in future sessions. Support James in translating his family reconstruction insights into meaningful changes in his interpersonal interactions.]

Therapist: (*Wrapping up the session*): James today's session has been very insightful. We've uncovered significant aspects of your family dynamics and how they've influenced you. Moving forward we'll continue to work on translating these insights into positive changes in your communication and relationships. You have the tools and understanding to create the kind of connections you've always desired

James: Thank you. This has been challenging, but I feel like I'm moving in the right direction.

Therapist: (*Building on positive changes*) James, as we continue to work with the insights from today's session, let's think about how you can nurture these changes in your daily life. What are some daily practices that could reinforce the healthier communication styles you desire?

James: I think being more mindful of how I interact with people could help. Maybe I could reflect each evening on my conversations and interactions, considering how I could improve them.

[Therapist's Note: Encourage self-reflection as a tool for growth. Reinforce the idea that change is a continuous process requiring regular practice and awareness.]

Therapist: (*Suggesting a reflective practice*) That's a great idea. Reflecting on your interactions can provide valuable insights and help you make continuous improvements. Also consider how you can proactively create opportunities for open and balanced communication in your interactions

James: Maybe I can initiate more conversations where I actively listen and share, creating a space for mutual understanding.

[Therapist's Note: Promote proactive engagement in relationships. This will help James practice and solidify the new communication skills he's learning.]

Therapist: (*Encouraging proactive relationship building*) Initiating these conversations can be very powerful. It helps build trust and understanding. In addition how can you apply your insights into maintaining healthy boundaries like those you wished your family had?

James: (*Thoughtfully*) I need to be clear about my limits and communicate them respectfully. I've started doing this at work, and it's been helpful.

[Therapist's Note: Validate progress and encourage the continuation of boundary setting in various aspects of life.]

Therapist: (*Affirming progress*): That's excellent progress James. Setting and maintaining boundaries is key to healthy relationships. Remember it's okay to adjust these boundaries as needed. Now thinking about your family how can you start to introduce some of these healthier dynamics into your interactions with them?

James: I can start by being more open about my feelings. It might be challenging, but maybe it can change our patterns over time.

[Therapist's Note: Discuss strategies for introducing new communication patterns within the family. Prepare James for potential resistance and encourage persistence.]

Therapist: (*Offering support for family interactions*) Introducing new patterns can indeed be challenging but also very rewarding.

Be patient and persistent. We can discuss specific strategies for these interactions in our next session. It's about taking one step at a time towards the family dynamics you desire

James: I understand it won't be easy, but I'm ready to try. Today's session has given me a lot to work with.

[Therapist's Final Note: Plan to continue supporting James in applying these new communication strategies in his family interactions, while reinforcing his personal growth and self-awareness.]

Therapist: (*Concluding with a forward-looking statement*) You've shown great courage and openness today James. We'll build on this foundation in our coming sessions focusing on practical applications and continuous growth. You're on a path to creating more fulfilling and authentic relationships

The Iceberg Metaphor in Family Reconstruction

Therapist: (*Introducing the iceberg metaphor*) Sarah, I'd like to introduce a concept called the iceberg metaphor, which Virginia Satir developed. It helps us understand that what we see in our behaviors is just the tip of the iceberg. Below the surface, there are feelings, perceptions, expectations, and more. Let's use this model to explore what might be beneath your family's and your own behaviors. How does that sound?

Sarah: (*Curiously*) Sounds interesting. I'm not sure what we'll find, but okay.

[Therapist's Note: Use the iceberg metaphor to help Sarah explore underlying emotions and needs that might not be immediately apparent. This can provide a deeper understanding of family dynamics and her responses.]

Therapist: (*Guiding the exploration*) Let's start with your dad's distant behavior which is the "tip of the iceberg"' What feelings or needs might be beneath that behavior?

Sarah: (*Thinking*) Maybe he was stressed or didn't know how to show emotions. I never really thought about what was behind his behavior.

[Therapist's Note: Encourage empathy and a shift in perspective. Understanding underlying emotions can lead to a new understanding of family members' behaviors.]

Therapist: (*Exploring deeper*) That's a good insight. How about your mom's overbearing behavior? What might be underneath that?

Sarah: Perhaps she was anxious or needed to feel in control. It always seemed like she was trying to hold everything together.

[Therapist's Note: Relate these insights back to Sarah's current patterns. Discuss how recognizing these underlying aspects can influence her current relationships and self-perception.]

Therapist: (*Connecting insights*) Understanding these underlying aspects can change how we see others' actions. How might this new perspective affect your view of your own behaviors and needs?

Sarah: I guess I've been independent because I felt I had to be. Maybe underneath, I wanted more connection but didn't know how to ask for it.

[Therapist's Note: Guide Sarah in exploring her underlying feelings and needs. This can be a starting point for developing new, healthier ways of interacting.]

Therapist: (*Suggesting new approaches*) That's a significant realization. How can you start to address this need for connection in a way that feels safe for you?

Sarah: (*Contemplatively*) I could try reaching out more, maybe start small with friends or colleagues.

[Therapist's Final Note: Support Sarah in taking small steps towards fulfilling her underlying needs. Continue to use the iceberg metaphor to explore and understand behaviors, both in her family context and in her personal life.]

Therapist: (*Concluding with encouragement*) That's a great approach Sarah. Using the iceberg metaphor we can continue to uncover and understand the deeper aspects of your experiences. This understanding can guide you in making more informed and authentic choices in your life

(*Expanding on the iceberg metaphor application.*) Now that we've started to explore the underlying aspects of your family's behaviors, let's apply the iceberg metaphor to a specific situation in your life where you felt particularly challenged. Can you think of a recent example?

Sarah: I had a disagreement with a colleague last week. I got defensive quickly and shut down the conversation.

[Therapist's Note: Use the iceberg metaphor to dissect this situation, revealing underlying feelings and perceptions that influenced Sarah's reaction.]

Therapist: (*Guiding the dissection*) Let's break down that interaction using the iceberg metaphor. The tip of the iceberg is your defensiveness. What feelings might be lying beneath that reaction?

Sarah: (*Reflecting*) I was feeling threatened, I guess. Like my ideas were being attacked.

[Therapist's Note: Validate her feelings and encourage exploration of deeper layers, including perceptions and unmet needs.]

Therapist: (*Probing deeper*) Feeling threatened can definitely lead to defensiveness. Let's go deeper. What perceptions or beliefs about yourself or the situation might have contributed to that feeling of being threatened?

Sarah: Maybe I believed that any criticism of my ideas was a criticism of me as a person. I felt I had to defend my worth.

[Therapist's Note: Highlight the distinction between self-worth and external criticism. Encourage Sarah to challenge perceptions that equate her value with her ideas or performance.]

Therapist: (*Suggesting perspective shift*) It's important to separate your worth from your ideas or performance. Your value as a person isn't diminished by a disagreement. How might recognizing this change your response in future similar situations?

Sarah: (*considering a new approach*) I might not take things so personally. I could try to see criticism as just about the idea, not about me.

[Therapist's Note: Reinforce this new perspective and discuss strategies for maintaining it in challenging interactions.]

Therapist: (*Encouraging application*) That's a healthier way to view it. Practicing this perspective can reduce feelings of threat and defensiveness. Also think about what needs were unmet in that situation. How could those needs be addressed more constructively?

Sarah: I need to feel heard and respected. Maybe I can communicate that more clearly instead of just shutting down.

[Therapist's Final Note: Plan to explore communication strategies that allow Sarah to express her needs effectively. Continue to use the iceberg metaphor to help her understand and manage her reactions in various interactions.]

Therapist: (*Concluding with a forward plan*) Expressing your needs is key to healthy interactions. We'll work on developing these communication skills in our upcoming sessions. The iceberg metaphor can be a useful tool in many situations helping you understand and manage your reactions more effectively. Let's continue to explore and apply this model to support your growth.

Applying the Self-Esteem Toolkit in Triads

Integrating Satir's Self-Esteem Maintenance Toolkit – which includes the Wishing Wand, Detective Hat, Yes-No Medallion, Courage Stick, Wisdom Box, Golden Key, and the Heart – with the concept of Triads offers a dynamic approach to group therapy or coaching. In this setup, three individuals work together, using the elements of the toolkit to explore and enhance their self-esteem and interpersonal dynamics.

Wishing Wand (Exploring Aspirations):

- **In Triads**: Each member takes turns sharing their aspirations using the Wishing Wand, symbolizing their hopes and dreams. The other two provide feedback and encouragement.
- **Example**: *"I wish to become more confident in my abilities. Holding this wand, I feel more connected to this goal."*

Detective Hat (Investigating Personal Beliefs):

- **In Triads**: Members wear the Detective Hat to explore and question their beliefs about themselves, with others acting as supportive investigators.
- **Example**: "*Wearing this hat, I want to understand why I feel anxious in social settings.*"

Yes-No Medallion (Setting Boundaries):

- **In Triads**: The medallion is used to practice setting and respecting boundaries. Each member states a boundary they wish to set, using the medallion as a symbol of their decision.
- **Example**: "*Holding this medallion, I say 'no' to overworking and neglecting my health.*"

Courage Stick (Encouraging Bravery):

- **In Triads**: Members use the Courage Stick to share something they find challenging, with the group offering support and strategies to face these challenges.

- **Example**: "*With this stick, I find the courage to speak up about my ideas in meetings.*"

Wisdom Box (Sharing Insights):

- **In Triads**: Each person shares a piece of wisdom or a learning experience, placing symbolic items or notes in the Wisdom Box.
- **Example**: "*Into this box, I place a reminder of the importance of patience from my own journey.*"

Golden Key (Unlocking Inner Thoughts):

- **In Triads**: The key is used to "unlock" deeper thoughts or feelings, encouraging open and honest sharing.
- **Example**: "*This key helps me unlock my thoughts about changing careers, which I haven't shared before.*"

Heart (Fostering Empathy and Connection):

- **In Triads**: The Heart symbolizes empathy and understanding. Members hold the heart when expressing emotions, ensuring a supportive and empathetic response from others.
- **Example**: "*Holding the heart, I feel safe to share my feelings of loneliness.*"

Benefits of the Toolkit in Triads

- **Enhanced Self-Awareness**: Triads provide a safe space for self-exploration with supportive feedback.
- **Improved Communication**: The toolkit facilitates open and honest communication within the group.
- **Peer Support**: Triad members learn from each other's experiences and perspectives.
- **Empathy Development**: The format encourages understanding and empathy among members.
- **Practice of Skills**: Members get to practice setting boundaries, expressing needs, and offering support.

Using Satir's Self-Esteem Maintenance Toolkit within Triads is a highly effective approach in therapy, coaching, or personal development groups. It leverages the power of group dynamics and symbolic tools to facilitate personal growth, self-awareness, and mutual support, enhancing both individual and collective self-esteem.

The Iceberg Metaphor and Five Freedoms

Combining Satir's iceberg metaphor with her concept of the Five Freedoms creates a powerful framework for self-awareness and personal growth. This integration allows individuals to understand and express their internal experiences (captured in the iceberg metaphor) while exercising their fundamental freedoms (as outlined in the Five Freedoms). Here's how these two concepts can be synergistically used.

The Iceberg Metaphor

The iceberg metaphor illustrates that a person's behavior (visible above the waterline) is supported by underlying feelings, perceptions, expectations, and desires (hidden beneath the surface).

The Five Freedoms

1. To see and hear what is here, instead of what should be, was, or will be.
2. To say what one feels and thinks, instead of what one should.
3. To feel what one feels, instead of what one ought.
4. To ask for what one wants, instead of always waiting for permission.
5. To take risks on one's own behalf, instead of choosing to be only "secure" and not rocking the boat.

Integration in Practice

Behavior and Freedom to See and Hear:

- **Application**: Recognizing and acknowledging the reality of one's behavior and situation, rather than being constrained by expectations or denial.
- **Example**: *"I acknowledge that I avoid confrontations. I see this behavior as a response to my fear of conflict, not just as being 'non-confrontational.'"*

Feelings and Freedom to Say:

- **Application**: Expressing genuine emotions and thoughts that lie beneath one's behavior.
- **Example**: "*I feel anxious in group settings. Instead of masking it, I'll express my discomfort and ask for understanding.*"

Perceptions and Freedom to Feel:

- **Application**: Allowing oneself to fully experience and acknowledge underlying perceptions and emotions.
- **Example**: "*I perceive that I'm not valued in my relationships. It's okay for me to feel hurt about this and explore these feelings.*"

Expectations and Freedom to Ask:

- **Application**: Recognizing personal expectations and feeling empowered to ask for what is genuinely needed or desired.
- **Example**: "*I expect mutual respect in my relationships. I will ask for it clearly, rather than silently hoping for it.*"

Desires and Freedom to Take Risks:

- **Application**: Understanding one's deeper desires and being willing to take risks to fulfill them.
- **Example**: "*I desire a career change. I'll take the risk to pursue this, even though it's outside my comfort zone.*"

Integrating the Iceberg Metaphor with the Five Freedoms provides a comprehensive approach to understanding oneself and making empowered choices. It encourages individuals to explore and express their deeper internal experiences while asserting their right to see, hear, feel, ask, and take risks. This approach is particularly useful in therapy, personal development, and any context where deeper self-awareness and assertiveness are essential for growth.

Family Sculpting and Five Freedoms

Integrating Satir's "Family Sculpting" technique with her concept of the "Five Freedoms" creates a dynamic approach to exploring and understanding family dynamics and individual behaviors within a familial context. This combination can be particularly effective in family therapy sessions, providing a powerful tool for members to express and understand their roles, feelings, and interactions.

Integration in Family Sculpting

Using Sculpting to See and Hear the Family Dynamics:

- **Application**: Members create a sculpture that visually represents how they truly see and hear each other in the family, not how they think they should.
- **Example**: A child positions themselves far from a parent, visually expressing feelings of emotional distance.

Sculpting to Say and Express Feelings and Thoughts:

- **Application**: Each member verbally explains their reasoning for the positions and distances in the sculpture, honestly expressing their thoughts and feelings.
- **Example**: "*I placed myself away from the rest because I feel overlooked in our family.*"

Reflecting Genuine Feelings in the Sculpt:

- **Application**: The sculpture becomes a medium for members to express their actual emotions about their family roles and relationships.
- **Example**: A parent showing their position as burdened or overwhelmed, indicating stress or exhaustion.

Asking for Change through Sculpting:

- **Application**: Members can suggest alterations to the sculpture to represent changes they desire in the family dynamics.

- **Example**: A sibling might move closer to another, indicating a desire for a stronger relationship.

Taking Risks in Redefining Family Roles:

- **Application**: The sculpture allows members to experiment with and propose changes in family roles, challenging the status quo.
- **Example**: A typically passive member positions themselves at the center, indicating a desire to be more engaged or heard.

By combining Family Sculpting with the Five Freedoms, family therapy can become a more powerful, revealing, and transformative process. This approach not only visualizes the often unseen emotional and relational patterns in a family but also empowers its members to acknowledge, express, and explore possibilities for change. It's a pathway towards a more open, communicative, and understanding family dynamic, aligned with each member's genuine needs and aspirations.

Navigating Resistant Family Dynamics

In my practice, one particularly challenging case was the Smith family. The parents, Linda and Tom, were on the brink of separation, and their teenage children, Sarah and Alex, seemed disconnected and resistant. This family's journey through the therapy was a profound learning experience, both for them and for me.

Initial Resistance: Setting the Scene

From the first session, the resistance was palpable. Linda and Tom barely spoke to each other, while Sarah and Alex sat sullenly, absorbed in their phones.

Me: I sense there's a lot of tension here. It's okay. This is a safe space to express whatever you're feeling.

Silence greeted my words. I knew then that traditional conversation wouldn't suffice.

Adapting Satir's Family Sculpting: A Creative Approach

Drawing from Satir's family sculpting, I introduced a unique exercise. I provided them with clay and asked each to create a sculpture representing their view of the family.

Me: Let's try to express our feelings through this clay. Think of it as creating a metaphor for our family.

Initially met with skepticism, they slowly began to mold the clay, and gradually, their expressions softened, a sign that the walls were coming down.

Linda: (*Crafting a fragmented sculpture*) It feels like we're pieces of the same puzzle, just not fitting together.

Tom (*Building a wall-like structure*): I guess this wall represents the barriers between us. I'm not even sure how they got so high.

Sarah and Alex, initially reluctant, started to engage, their sculptures revealing feelings of chaos and being overlooked.

Insights and Reflections

The sculptures became the gateway to understanding the unspoken emotions and perceptions within the family.

Me: These sculptures are powerful representations. Let's talk about what they mean to each of you.

Sarah: (*Pointing to her chaotic sculpture*) It's always loud arguments or cold silence at home. It's like living in a storm.

Alex: I made this small figure because that's how I feel. Small and ignored.

This exercise brought a breakthrough in communication. For the first time, Linda and Tom heard their children's perspectives, and they began to open up about their own feelings.

Moving Forward: Integrating Insights into Family Dynamics

Using the insights gained from the sculpting, we started working on breaking down the "walls" Tom mentioned and finding ways to "fit the puzzle pieces together," as Linda described.

Me: How can we start bringing down these walls? What's one thing each of you can do to start fitting these pieces together?

Gradually, the family began to develop strategies to improve their communication and rebuild their relationships.

The Smith family's case reaffirmed the transformative power of creative expression in therapy, especially when dealing with resistance. By adapting Satir's family sculpting into a more accessible form, the family could externalize their feelings, leading to breakthroughs that traditional conversation could not facilitate. It was a testament to the resilience of families and the potential for healing even in the most challenging dynamics.

The Silent Executive Team

I was approached by a high-profile corporate executive team grappling with a unique challenge. Despite their individual competencies, the team was marred by superficial communication, preventing them from harnessing their collective potential. My task was to break through this veneer of corporate politeness and unravel the underlying issues.

Initial Observations: A Team Lost in Decorum

In our first session, I observed a pattern. Discussions were polite to the point of being non-productive. It was as if each member was playing a part, masking their true thoughts and feelings behind a façade of professionalism.

Me: I notice a pattern of guarded communication. What are your thoughts on how this is affecting the team's effectiveness?

Responses were predictably diplomatic, further emphasizing the need for a breakthrough.

Adapting Satir's Communication Stances: Role-Play with a Twist

To address this, I adapted Satir's communication stances into a role-play exercise. Each member was assigned a stance to adopt during a simulated board meeting – but with an exaggerated twist.

Me: Let's reenact a recent contentious meeting. However, this time, exaggerate the communication stance you usually take.

The Role-Play: Verbatim from the Session

CEO: (*Exaggerating the Blamer stance*) This project's failure is unacceptable! Whose fault is it?

CFO: (*Exaggerating the Placater stance*) We'll do whatever it takes to fix this, even if it means extra hours at no charge!

The exercise brought to light the absurdity of their communication extremes. Laughter broke out, easing the tension and opening the door to more genuine dialogue.

Reflecting on the Exercise

Post role-play, the team reflected on how these exaggerated stances mirrored, in a heightened way, their usual communication patterns.

Me: What did you notice about your communication during this exercise?

COO: It made me realize how often I avoid direct confrontation. I could see how that might lead to unresolved issues.

Developing New Communication Strategies

Using insights from the role-play, we worked on developing new communication strategies that encouraged openness and honesty while maintaining respect.

Me: How can we apply the Congruent stance, communicating honestly and assertively, without falling into these extremes?

The team brainstormed and committed to strategies that fostered more transparent and effective communication.

Implementing Change: Verbatim from a Follow-Up Meeting

In a follow-up meeting, the changes were evident.

Marketing Director: I have concerns about our campaign timeline. Let's discuss realistic expectations.

Sales Director: I appreciate your honesty. Let's work together to find a feasible solution.

The shift from guarded to constructive communication marked a significant turnaround for the team.

Conclusion: Breaking Barriers to Authentic Communication

This case with the executive team highlighted the transformative impact of adapting Satir's communication stances into a corporate environment. By creating a space for exaggerated expression, the team was able to see the counterproductive nature of their usual communication styles and work towards more authentic and effective interactions. It was a powerful reminder of the importance of genuine communication in any high-functioning team.

The role-play exercise had set the stage for a profound shift in communication within the executive team. As they gathered for a subsequent session, there was a noticeable change in the air – a sense of readiness to peel back the layers of guarded dialogue.

Enhancing the Dialogue: Detailed Verbatim from the Session

As we reconvened, I sensed a newfound willingness among the team members to engage more openly.

Me: Reflecting on our last session, what stood out to you about your communication styles?

The responses were more introspective this time.

CFO: (*Thoughtfully*) I realized I often placate to avoid conflict. It's easier than addressing issues head-on, but it's not productive in the long run.

This admission opened the floor to others.

HR Director: I think we've all been avoiding real issues to some extent. We're so focused on maintaining harmony that we miss the opportunity to genuinely connect and solve problems.

A Moment of Honesty: Delving Deeper into Communication Patterns

I encouraged the team to delve deeper into these patterns, asking them to share specific instances where these tendencies hindered effective communication.

Marketing Director: During budget discussions, I often hold back my true opinion, fearing backlash. But that just leads to frustration when things don't work out.

Me: Let's explore that. How can you communicate your concerns in a way that's both honest and constructive?

Developing a New Framework: Building on the Insights

The team began to work collectively on developing a new framework for communication, one that encouraged honesty tempered with respect.

Me: Imagine a scenario where you can express your concerns openly without fear of repercussion. How would that look?

The team members, now more engaged, began to role-play this new approach.

Verbatim from the New Communication Role-Play

Sales Director: I have reservations about our current sales strategy. Can we discuss alternative approaches?

Product Manager: I appreciate your honesty. Let's open this up to the team and brainstorm together.

This role-play was markedly different from the previous one. The exaggerated stances were replaced by genuine, respectful dialogue.

Reflection and Commitment: Cementing the Change

As the session drew to a close, each team member reflected on their commitment to sustaining this new communication style.

Me: What will you take from today's session into your daily interactions within the team?

CEO: (*Resolutely*) I commit to fostering an environment where everyone feels safe to express their ideas and concerns.

As the team delved into the narrative exploration and strategy sessions, their conversations began to shed light on the profound impact of the past scandal and their path to recovery.

Deepening the Narrative Exploration

Me: As we reframe this story, consider how this experience has shaped you as a team. What strengths have emerged from this adversity?

The team members, initially hesitant, slowly began to open up, their narratives weaving a tapestry of resilience.

Team Member 3: I've learned to question things more, not just follow orders blindly. It's about being more responsible for my part.

Team Member 4: This experience forced us to confront our flaws, to be honest about where we failed. It's a tough lesson, but it's made us more vigilant.

Building Strategies for Trust and Openness

Moving from reflection to action, the team started discussing concrete steps to rebuild their dynamics.

Me: What specific actions can we take to ensure these lessons translate into positive changes in your team culture?

Their responses reflected a commitment to creating a new, healthier work environment.

Team Leader: We need to establish a culture where speaking up is encouraged, where we don't just sweep concerns under the rug.

Team Member 5: Maybe we can start peer review groups, where we openly discuss and review our work processes. It's about keeping each other accountable.

Verbatim from the Implementation Phase

In the sessions that followed, the team began implementing their new strategies. The atmosphere in these meetings was markedly different – more open, more collaborative.

Team Member 6: In today's peer review session, I felt we were all genuinely engaged in finding solutions, not just pointing fingers.

Team Leader: (*Reflecting on the changes*) I see a shift in how we communicate. There's more honesty, less fear. We're not just trying to avoid another scandal; we're working to be a better team.

Conclusion: A New Chapter of Team Dynamics

This case exemplified the transformative power of facing and reframing past trauma. Through narrative therapy and strategic planning, the team moved from a state of paralysis to one of proactive engagement and resilience. Their journey from the depths of a scandal to the heights of renewed trust and collaboration was a powerful testament to the healing and unifying potential of open, honest communication and collective problem-solving.

Bridging Cross-Cultural Misunderstanding

In a globalized corporate environment, cross-cultural misunderstandings can often lead to tension and inefficiency. I was approached by a team grappling with such issues, where cultural differences had led to stereotyping and miscommunication. The journey of this team highlights the importance of understanding and respecting cultural diversity in the workplace.

Initial Meeting: Unveiling the Cultural Challenges

The first session with the team revealed a mosaic of cultures, each with its own unique set of values and communication styles.

Me: I notice a variety of cultural backgrounds in this team. How do you think this diversity is influencing your team dynamics?

Responses varied, but the underlying theme was a lack of understanding and appreciation of these cultural differences.

Introducing Cultural Mapping: A Satir-Inspired Approach

To address these issues, I introduced a cultural mapping exercise, inspired by Satir's models, where team members mapped out their cultural backgrounds, values, and communication styles.

Me: Let's each create a map that represents our cultural background and how it shapes our approach to work and communication.

The Cultural Mapping Session: Verbatim

As team members shared their maps, revelations unfolded.

Team Member from Germany: In my culture, being direct is valued. It's about efficiency and clarity.

Team Member from Japan: That's interesting. In Japan, we often communicate more indirectly to maintain harmony.

The exercise sparked curiosity and a willingness to learn about each other's cultural norms.

Exploring Cultural Influences: A Deeper Dive

I encouraged the team to delve deeper into how these cultural influences played out in their day-to-day interactions.

Me: How can these insights help us understand and adapt to each other's communication styles?

The discussion that followed was rich with insights.

Verbatim from the Discussion

Team Member from India: I realized that what I perceive as reluctance to participate in meetings might actually be a cultural preference for listening and observing first.

Team Member from the USA: And I see now how my straightforwardness might come off as abrasive to some team members. I need to be more mindful of that.

Developing a Framework for Cross-Cultural Communication

Building on these insights, we worked on developing a framework for effective cross-cultural communication, integrating elements of Satir's congruent communication model.

Me: Let's identify strategies that honor our diverse communication styles while promoting clear and respectful dialogue.

The team collaboratively developed a set of communication guidelines that acknowledged and respected their cultural differences.

Implementing the Change: Verbatim from a Follow-Up Session

In a follow-up session, the changes were noticeable.

Team Leader: We've started implementing "cultural moments" in our meetings, where team members can share aspects of their culture. It's been eye-opening and has brought us closer.

The team's approach had shifted from avoidance of cultural differences to embracing and celebrating them.

Embracing Cultural Diversity for a Cohesive Team

This case with the culturally diverse team underscored the importance of understanding and respecting cultural differences in a corporate environment. By using cultural mapping and adapting Satir's communication models, the team learned to navigate their cultural complexities, turning potential misunderstandings into opportunities for growth and unity. It was a powerful example of how embracing diversity can lead to a more cohesive and effective team.

As the culturally diverse team continued to work on their communication and understanding, each session brought new layers of complexity and richness to their interactions.

Deepening Cultural Understanding: Detailed Verbatim from Continued Sessions

The team's commitment to embracing cultural diversity evolved into more than just an exercise; it became a crucial part of their team identity.

Me: Let's explore specific instances where cultural differences have impacted your teamwork. How did you navigate those situations?

The team members shared experiences that highlighted both challenges and learning opportunities.

Team Member from Brazil: In a recent project, I felt my ideas were overlooked. In Brazil, we're used to a more collaborative approach, but I didn't feel comfortable asserting myself.

Team Member from the UK: I didn't realize that. In our culture, we often equate assertiveness with confidence. Let's work on a more inclusive approach to idea-sharing.

Implementing Inclusive Strategies

Based on these discussions, the team implemented inclusive strategies that acknowledged and utilized their diverse cultural strengths.

Me: What can we do to ensure that everyone feels heard and valued, regardless of their cultural communication style?

The team brainstormed and agreed on a set of inclusive practices.

Verbatim from Strategy Implementation

During a subsequent project meeting, the impact of these strategies was evident.

Team Leader: Let's go around the table and give everyone a chance to share their thoughts on this project, respecting each person's communication style.

This approach led to a more balanced and comprehensive discussion, with valuable contributions from all team members.

Celebrating Cultural Diversity: A New Team Tradition

The team began to celebrate their cultural diversity more openly, creating a tradition of sharing cultural stories and practices.

Team Member from China: I'd like to share a traditional Chinese problem-solving approach that might be beneficial for our project.

Team Member from Canada: That's a great idea. Let's incorporate different cultural strategies into our brainstorming sessions.

Reflecting on the Journey

In our final session, the team reflected on their journey of integrating cultural diversity into their work.

Me: How has this focus on cultural understanding and inclusion impacted your team dynamics?

Team Leader: (*With a sense of accomplishment*) It's transformed our team. We're not just co-workers; we're cultural ambassadors, learning from each other and strengthening our collaboration.

Conclusion: A Model for Global Teamwork

The journey of this culturally diverse team became a model for how embracing and integrating cultural differences can enhance teamwork and productivity. Their experience illustrated that in today's globalized work environment, cultural diversity is not just a challenge to be managed but a resource to be celebrated and harnessed. It demonstrated the incredible potential of teams that leverage the richness of their cultural diversity to foster a more inclusive, innovative, and effective work environment.

Inner Resistance

In this session, the therapist uses Satir's techniques to help Alex move beyond his automatic response. By encouraging congruence and connecting current defenses to family rules, the therapist facilitates what Gross (1994) describes as the "process of change" – moving from the status quo through the chaos of vulnerability toward a new integration.

Exploring the Surface Response

Therapist: Alex, I've noticed that when I ask about how you're feeling, your response is often "I'm fine." Can we explore what "fine" means for you?

Alex: It just means everything is okay. There's not much to say.

Encouraging Congruence

Therapist: In my experience, 'fine' can sometimes be a word we use when we're not sure how to express what's really going on. It's okay to take a moment to check in with yourself. What are you feeling right now, in this moment?

Alex: (*Pauses*) I don't know... I guess I'm just used to saying "fine." It's easier.

Validating and Reflecting

Therapist: It sounds like saying "fine" has become a habit, perhaps a way to avoid delving into deeper feelings. It's common to use certain words as a shield. What might you be shielding yourself from?

Alex: Maybe… I guess I don't want to seem like I'm complaining or burdening anyone.

Exploring Underlying Feelings

Therapist: So, it's about not wanting to impose on others. That's understandable. But this is a safe space for you to share whatever you're going through. If 'fine' were a color or an image, what would it be?

Alex: Maybe a flat line? Nothing too high or low, just… steady.

Deepening the Exploration

Therapist: That's a powerful image, Alex. A flat line – steady, but perhaps lacking the ups and downs that make up our experiences. Can you think of a time recently when your feelings weren't just "fine" or "steady?"

Alex: Well, last week at work, I was really overwhelmed, but I didn't tell anyone.

Facilitating Self-Discovery

Therapist: That sounds like it was a challenging experience. How did it feel to keep that to yourself?

Alex: Frustrating, I guess. And lonely.

Connecting to the Family System

Therapist: Frustration and loneliness – those are significant feelings. Let's connect this back to your family. Growing up, how were emotions handled in your home?

Alex: We didn't really talk about emotions much. It was about just getting on with things.

Encouraging New Perspectives

Therapist: It seems like there might be a pattern from your past influencing how you express yourself now. What would it be like to allow yourself not to be "fine" sometimes?

Alex: It'd be scary, but maybe a bit freeing, too. I wouldn't have to pretend all the time.

In this session, the therapist uses Satir's techniques to help Alex move beyond his automatic response of "I'm fine." By encouraging congruence, exploring underlying feelings, and connecting these to his family background, the therapist helps Alex begin to recognize and express a more authentic range of emotions. This is a step towards breaking habitual communication patterns and fostering deeper self-understanding.

Legacy and Future Directions

Virginia Satir's legacy extends far beyond the therapy room. Her systemic insights have proven adaptable to the most pressing challenges of the 21st century, demonstrating the universality of her "humanizing" approach. Satir's vision of "peace within, peace between, peace among" has been applied to alleviating prejudice and hate, offering a psychological framework for conflict resolution on a global scale (Novak, 2006; Freeman, 2006). Contemporary practitioners recognize that her model addresses not just family systems, but the "world family," asking pertinent questions about our collective direction in times of crisis (Dodson, 2016).

Her model has found profound resonance across cultures, particularly in Asia and Europe. In Singapore, practitioners have adapted her methods to empower women experiencing spousal violence, providing a path to self-worth within rigid social structures (Chia Sok Hia, 2007). Similarly, in Taiwan and China, the model has been successfully applied to student mental health and counseling, bridging Western psychological concepts with Eastern values of harmony (Pan, 2000; Wu, 2016; Yang and Vivian, 2010). In Europe, community-based interventions in Spain have utilized her "Human Value" concepts to foster socio-educative work in municipalities (Solé, Poyatos, Viñas, and Sharp, 2016), while long-term training programs in the Czech Republic have demonstrated the cross-cultural transferability of her systemic therapy training (Beránková and Petrovská, 2016). The model's versatility is evident in its application to diverse professional and clinical groups. It has been used to enhance the "life force" and resilience of college students navigating academic pressure (Wang, 2016) and to support social workers facing high-stress environments and burnout, providing them with the internal resources necessary to sustain their caregiving roles (Vivian, 2009).

Furthermore, the model has proven effective for deep trauma work, such as with female adult survivors of childhood sexual abuse, where reclaiming the "self" from the "victim" identity is paramount (Morrison and Ferris, 2002). Contemporary thinkers have even bridged Satir's systemic concepts with ecological awareness, utilizing her workshops to process the grief and anxiety surrounding climate change, based on the work of Joanna Macy (Christie-Seely, 2017). Finally, modern research continues to validate her intuitive concepts with empirical rigor. Studies using congruence scales and qualitative analysis confirm the efficacy of her training models (Mun-Jeong and Bong-Whan, 2010; Sekera, 2017) and the tangible benefits of her "energy" work in therapeutic settings (Leslie, 2016). By bridging theory and lived experience, this chapter demonstrates how Satir's legacy continues to guide practitioners in facilitating transformational growth and sustainable relational change.

References

Allen, E.E., Anaya, I.M., Dearing, T.A., D'Aniello, C., Roberts, F.E., Smith, M. (2022). Satir family therapy and adolescent mental health implications of COVID-19. *The American Journal of Family Therapy*, *51*(5), 659–672.

Belvins, S. (2008). A personal journey through the grief and healing process with Virginia Satir, Dr. E. Kubler-Ross, and J. William Worden. *The Satir Journal*, *2*(2), 89–105.

Bentheim, S. (2008). Couple congruence and spirituality: Part II. *The Satir Journal*, *2*(1), 37–54.

Beránková, A., Petrovská, J. (2016). 15 years of accredited Satir Transformational Systemic Therapy training in the Czech Republic. *Satir International Journal*, *4*(1), 52–55.

Cheung, G.Y.K. (2006). From the Satir model to the I Tao: Reconstructing family rules in a Hong Kong cultural context. *The Satir Journal*, *1*(1), 7–63.

Chia Sok Hia, S. (2007). Self empowerment for women experiencing spousal violence: A study of the residential program of the Good Shepherd Centre of Singapore. *The Satir Journal*, *1*(2), 5–39.

Christie-Seely, J. (2017). Workshop on climate change based on the work of Macy, and informed by the Satir Model. *Satir International Journal*, *5*(1), 19–35.

Dodson, L. (2016). What is the world trying to do now? *Satir International Journal*, *4*(1), 44–49.
Freeman, M. (2006). Peace within, peace between, peace among. In R.M. MacNair (Ed.), *Working for Peace: A Handbook for Practical Psychology and Other Tools* (pp. 63–72). Atascadero, CA, US: Impact Publishers.
Gross, S.J. (1994). The process of change: Variations on a theme by Virginia Satir. *Journal of Humanistic Psychology*, *34*(3), 87–110.
Leslie, M. (2016). Widening our lens, deepening our practice: an exploration of energy within the teachings of Virginia Satir. *Satir International Journal*, *4*(1), 5–20.
Morrison, A., Ferris, J. (2002). The Satir model with female adult survivors of childhood sexual abuse. *Contemporary Family Therapy: An International Journal*, *24*(1), 161–180.
Mun-Jeong, K., Bong-Whan, K. (2010). Development and validity of the congruence scale based on Satir's growth model. *The Satir Journal*, *4*(1), 53–83.
Novak, S. (2006). Alleviating prejudice and hate: The strategies of Virginia Satir. *The Satir Journal*, *1*(1), 65–80.
Pan, P.J.D. (2000). The effectiveness of structured and semistructured Satir model groups on family relationships with college students in Taiwan. *Journal for Specialists in Group Work*, *25*(3), 305–318.
Sekera, O. (2017). Outcome of psychotherapeutic training MOVISA (Model of Virginia Satir). *Satir International Journal*, *5*(1), 67–75.
Solé, J., Poyatos, P., Viñas, A., Sharp, I. (2016). Human value: the socioeducative work in the municipality of Castell-Platia d'Aro. *Satir International Journal*, *4*(1), 76–86.
Vivian, L.W.Q. (2009). Enhancing personal growth for social workers using the Satir model. *The Satir Journal*, *3*(2), 5–21.
Wang, Y. (2016). Practical research on Improving the life force of college students by using Satir's Model. *Journal of Marxism Studies*, *2*, 135–140.
Wu, S. (2016). Application of the Satir Model to college student education in China. *Satir International Journal*, *4*(1), 97–102.
Yang, L., Vivian, L. (2010). Applying the Satir model of counseling in mainland China: Illustrated with case studies. *The Satir Journal*, *4*(1), 24–52.
Young, A.K. (2007). An analysis of the Satir transformational systemic therapy in the Korean worldview. *The Satir Journal*, *1*(2), 54–72.

Appendix: Satir's Quotes

"I am me, and I am okay."

"We must not allow other people's limited perceptions to define us."

"Life is not what it's supposed to be. It's what it is. The way you cope with it is what makes the difference."

"Feelings of worth can flourish only in an atmosphere where individual differences are appreciated, mistakes are tolerated, communication is open, and rules are flexible."

"I want to love you without clutching, appreciate you without judging, join you without invading, invite you without demanding, leave you without guilt, criticize you without blaming, and help you without insulting. If I can have the same from you, then we can truly meet and enrich each other."

"We get together on the basis of our similarities; we grow on the basis of our differences."

"Problems are not the problem; coping is the problem."

"The greatest gift I can conceive of having from anyone is to be seen by them, heard by them, to be understood and touched by them."

"You must learn to be still in the midst of activity and to be vibrantly alive in repose."

"Most people think the problem is to find the right answer; I think the real problem is to find the real question."

"Our greatest joy and our greatest pain come in our relationships with others."

"What lingers from the parent's individual past, unresolved or incomplete, often becomes part of her or his irrational parenting."

"Human beings are not things needing to be motivated and controlled; they are four-dimensional – body, mind, heart, and spirit."

"Making the best of things is a damn poor way of dealing with them. My life has been a series of escapes from that quicksand."

"Each person you meet is an aspect of yourself, clamoring for love."

"We need to learn to tolerate our own feelings and attitudes and not automatically act them out."

"Over the years, your bodies become walking autobiographies, telling friends and strangers alike of the minor and major stresses of your lives."

"Communication is to relationships what breath is to life."

"The problem is not that there are problems. The problem is expecting otherwise and thinking that having problems is a problem."

"It is important to remember that we all have magic inside us."

"In my work, I have chosen to regard the family as a microcosm of the world. By knowing how to heal the family, I know how to heal the world."

"The recommended daily requirement for hugs is: four per day for survival, eight per day for maintenance, and twelve per day for growth."

"Instead of raising children who turn out okay despite their childhood, let's raise children who turn out extraordinary because of their childhood."

"Trust is to human relationships what faith is to gospel living. It is the beginning place, the foundation upon which more can be built. Where trust is, love can flourish."

"The key to understanding others is to first understand yourself."

"Under every behavior there is a feeling. And under each feeling is a need. And when we meet that need rather than focus on the behavior, we begin to deal with the cause, not the symptom."

"As I began to love myself, I freed myself of anything that is no good for my health – food, people, things, situations, and everything that drew me down and away from myself. At first, I called this attitude a healthy egoism. Today I know it is 'Love of Oneself.'"

Bibliography

Virginia Satir's transformative tools and methodologies have been extensively documented and analyzed in various sources, offering insights into mastering transformations. These sources encompass a range of materials including books, academic journals, and workshop materials. Key texts often delve into her unique approach to family therapy and personal development, highlighting her strategies for fostering self-esteem and improving communication within relationships. Additionally, scholarly articles analyze the efficacy and impact of Satir's methods, often comparing them with other therapeutic models. Workshops and training programs, often led by practitioners trained in Satir's methods, provide practical, hands-on experience in applying these tools in both personal and professional contexts. These diverse sources collectively offer a comprehensive understanding of Satir's enduring influence in the field of psychotherapy and personal growth.

Allen, E.E., Anaya, I.M., Dearing, T.A., D'Aniello, C., Roberts, F.E., Smith, M. (2022). Satir family therapy and adolescent mental health implications of COVID-19, *The American Journal of Family Therapy*, *51*(5), 659–672. https://doi.org/10.1080/01926187.2022.2031342

Andreas, S. (1999). *Virginia Satir: Patterns of Her Magic.* Moab, UT: Real People Press.

Andreas, S. (2008). The true genius of Virginia Satir. Retrieved from http://steveandreas.com/Articles/virginia_genius.html

Andreas, S. (2012). The true genius of Virginia Satir. *The Satir Journal*, *5*(1), 9–20.

Bandler, R., Grinder, J., Satir, V. (1976). *Changing with Families: A Book About Future Education for Being Human*. (Vol. 1). Palo Alto, CA: Science and Behavior Books, Inc.
Banmen, A., Banmen, J. (1991). *Meditations of Virginia Satir: Peace Within, Peace Between, Peace Among*. Palo Alto, CA: Science and Behavior Books, Inc.
Banmen, J. (1986). Virginia Satir's family therapy model. *Individual Psychology: Journal of Adlerian Theory, Research and Practice*, *42*(4), 480–492.
Banmen, J. (2002). Introduction: Virginia Satir today. *Contemporary Family Therapy: An International Journal*, *24*(1), 3–5. DOI: 10.1023/A:1014302720012
Banmen, J. (2002). The Satir model: Yesterday and today. *Contemporary Family Therapy: An International Journal*, *24*(1), 7–22. DOI: 10.1023/A:1014365304082
Banmen, J. (Ed). (2006). *Applications of the Satir Growth Model*. Seattle, WA: Avanta, the Virginia Satir Network.
Banmen, J. (2007). If depression is the solution, what are the problems? *The Satir Journal*, *1*(2), 40–53.
Banmen, J. (Ed.). (2008). *In Her Own Words: Virginia Satir Selected Papers 1963–1983*. Phoenix, AZ: Zeig, Tucker and Theisen, Incorporated.
Banmen, J. (Ed). (2008). *Satir Transformational Systemic Therapy*. Palo Alto, CA: Science and Behavior Books, Inc.
Banmen, J. (2008). Suicide prevention using the Satir model. *The Satir Journal*, *2*(1), 6–36.
Banmen, J. (2009). Satir model developmental phases. *The Satir Journal*, *3*(1), 14–19.
Banmen, J. (2009). Virginia Satir: A short story. *The Satir Journal*, *3*(1), 62–68.
Banmen, J. (2010). Forgiveness as therapy in the Satir model. *The Satir Journal*, *4*(1), 6–23.
Banmen, J. (Ed). (2006). *Applications of the Satir Growth Model*. Seattle, WA: Avanta, the Virginia Satir Network.
Banmen, J., Maki-Banmen, K. (2014). What has become of Virginia Satir's Therapy Model Since she left us in 1988? *Journal of Family Psychotherapy*, 25, 117–131. DOI: 10.1080/08975353.2014.909706
Baron, S. (2009). Metaphor and the Satir therapist. *The Satir Journal*, *3*(1), 49–60.
Beaudry, G. (2002). The family reconstruction process and its evolution to date: Virginia Satir's transformational process. *Contemporary Family Therapy: An International Journal*, *24*(1), 79–94. DOI: 10.1023/A:1014373605900
Belvins, S. (2008). A personal journey through the grief and healing process with Virginia Satir, Dr. E. Kubler-Ross, and J. William Worden. *The Satir Journal*, *2*(2), 89–105.
Bentheim, S. (2006). Couple congruence and spirituality: Expanding Satir's model through seven couple narratives. *Dissertation Abstracts International Section A: Humanities and Social Sciences*, 66, 10A.
Bentheim, S. (2007). Couple congruence and spirituality: Part I. *The Satir Journal*, *1*(3), 27–63.
Bentheim, S. (2008). Couple congruence and spirituality: Part II. *The Satir Journal*, *2*(1), 37–54.
Bentheim, S. (2009). Integrating Wilber: A therapist's reflections on the Integral theories of Ken Wilber. *The Satir Journal*, *3*(2), 101–112.
Bentheim, S. (Ed.). (2009). The seed model – part II. *The Satir Journal*, *3*(3), 5–18.
Bentheim, S. (2013). Evolving to become more fully human- Early contributors to the Satir model. *Satir International Journal*, 1, 40–52.
Bentheim, S.S., Carlock, J., Mandzuk, A. (2009). The seed model – part I. *The Satir Journal*, *3*(2), 115–125.
Beránková, A., Petrovská, J. (2016). 15 years of accredited Satir Transformational Systemic Therapy training in the Czech Republic. *Satir International Journal*, *4*(1), 52–55.
Berg, I.A. (1965). Comments on current books and the passing scene. *Journal of Counseling Psychology*, *12*(1), 107–110.

Bermudez, D. (2008). Adapting Virginia Satir techniques of Hispanic families. *The Family Journal 16*(1), 51–57. DOI: 10.1177/1066480707309543

Bitter, J.R. (1987). Communication and meaning: Satir in Adlerian context. In R. Sherman and D. Dinkmeyer (Eds.), *Systems of Family Therapy: An Adlerian Integration* (pp. 109–130). New York: Taylor and Francis Group.

Bitter, J.R. (1988). Family mapping and family constellation: Satir in Adlerian context. *Individual Psychology: Journal of Adlerian Theory, Research, and Practice*, 44, 106–111.

Bitter, J.R. (2014). *The Theory and Practice of Family Therapy and Counseling*. Belmont, CA: Cengage Learning.

Bodin, A.M. (1988). Virginia Satir: A memoriam. *Journal of Family Psychology*, *2*(2), 117–118. DOI: 10.1037/h0084987

Boyatzis, R.E., Goleman, D., Rhee, K. (2013). Emotional and social intelligence competencies: Cross-cultural implications. *Cross Cultural Management: An International Journal*, *20*(1), 20–30.

Braverman, S. (1986). Heinz Kohut and Virginia Satir: Strange bedfellows? *Contemporary Family Therapy*, *8*(2), 101–121. DOI: 10.1007/BF00891872

Brothers, B.J. (1990). Intimacy and autonomy: Connecting. *Journal of Couples Therapy*, *1*(3/4), 1–8.

Brothers, B.J. (1990). Self esteem and congruent communication: Virginia Satir's road to integration. *Advanced Development*, 2, 23–34.

Brothers, B.J. (1991). Ask not for whom the siren wails. *Journal of Couples Therapy*, *2*(3), 11–16.

Brothers, B.J. (1991). Healthy coupling…what makes it? *Journal of Couples Therapy*, *1*(1), 7–19.

Brothers, B.J. (Ed). (1996). *Couples and the Tao of Congruence*. New York: Haworth Press.

Brothers, B.J. (1998). The Satir model: Excerpts from circle of influence. *Journal of Couples Therapy*, 7(2/3), 1120. DOI:10.1300/J036v07n02_02

Brothers, B.J. (2000). Virginia Satir and wholeness. *Journal of Couples Therapy*, 9(1/2), 1–4.

Brothers, B.J. (Ed.). (2000). *The Person of the Therapist*. Philadelphia, PA: Haworth Press.

Brothers, B.J., (Ed.). (2013). *Virginia Satir: Foundational Ideas*. New York: Routledge.

Brothers, B.J. (2019). *Well-Being Writ Large: The Essential Work of Virginia Satir*. Hillsborough, OR: Beyond Words.

Brubacher, L. (2006). Integrating emotion-focused therapy with the Satir model. *Journal of Marital and Family Therapy*, *32*(2), 141–153.

Buckbee, S. (2009). Love before the ashes: A story from the Holocaust. *The Satir Journal*, *3*(1), 69–74.

Buckbee, S., Dupont, M. (2016). The Mandala, a model for teaching and therapy. *Satir International Journal*, *4*(1), 56–58.

Burke, W.W., Litwin, G.H. (1992). A causal model of organizational performance and change. *Journal of Management*, *18*(3), 523–545.

Carlock, C.J. (Ed.). (1999). *Building Healthy Self-Esteem* (3rd ed.). New York: Routledge.

Carlock, C.J. (2000). The therapist's many faces. *Journal of Couples Therapy*, *9*(3/4), 69–83.

Carlock, C.J. (2006). Wheel of resources: Preventative services of hurricane Katrina workers. *The Satir Journal*, *1*(1), 81–95.

Carlock, C.J. (2008). Building healthy self-esteem in gays and lesbians: A Satir approach. *The Satir Journal*, *2*(3), 20–75.

Carlock, C.J. (2008). Reflections: The oral history of Virginia Satir – an interview with Dr. Bunny Duhl. *The Satir Journal*, *2*(2), 7–44.

Carlock, J. (2009). Reflections: The oral history of Virginia Satir: An interview with Jane Gerber, M.S.W. *The Satir Journal*, *3*(3), 25–68.

Carlock, J. (2013). Preparing emergency first responders using a "wheel of resources". *Satir International Journal*, 1, 1–9.

Carlock, J. (2015). The solo parts party. *Satir International Journal*, 3, 36–57.
Carlock, J. (2017). An interview with Dr. John Banmen on the Satir Model C. Jesse Carlock, Ph.D., Wright State University. *Satir International Journal*, *5*(1), 36–52.
Carré, J.M., Archer, J. (2018). Testosterone and human behavior: The role of individual and contextual variables. *Social and Personality Psychology Compass*, *12*(9).
Carter, C.S. (1998). Neuroendocrine perspectives on social attachment and love. *Psychoneuroendocrinology*, *23*(8), 779–818.
Caston, C. (2009). Using the Satir family tools to reduce burnout in family caregivers. *The Satir Journal*, *3*(2), 39–72.
Chang, P. (1996). The application of the Satir model of family therapy to the families in Hong Kong: A personal reflection. *Contemporary Family Therapy: An International Journal*, *18*(4), 489–505. DOI: 10.1007/BF02195712
Chen, P., Tsai, S., Lai, N. (2001). The construction of a process-change model of unmet expectations based on the Satir model. *Asian Journal of Counselling*, *8*(1), 5–34.
Cheung, G.Y.K. (2006). From the Satir model to the I Tao: Reconstructing family rules in a Hong Kong cultural context. *The Satir Journal*, *1*(1), 7–63.
Cheung, G.Y.K., Chan, C. (2002). The Satir model and cultural sensitivity: A Hong Kong reflection. *Contemporary Family Therapy: An International Journal*, *24*(1), 199–215. DOI: 10.1023/A:1014338025464
Cheung, M. (1997). Social construction theory and the Satir model: toward a synthesis. *The American Journal of Family Therapy*, *25*(4), 331–343. DOI: 10.1080/01926189708251077
Chia Sok Hia, S. (2007). Self empowerment for women experiencing spousal violence: A study of the residential program of the Good Shepherd Centre of Singapore. *The Satir Journal*, *1*(2), 5–39.
Childers, J.H. (1989). Virginia Satir's family of origin map: Discussion of goals, construction process, and application in clinical work. *TACD Journal*, *17*(12), 91–99.
Christie-Seely, J. (2017). Workshop on climate change based on the work of Macy, and informed by the Satir Model. *Satir International Journal*, *5*(1), 19–35.
Chung, C., Leung, P. (2016) The effectiveness of a Satir-based personal growth workshop among Chinese people (preliminary report). *Satir International Journal*, *4*(1), 59–60.
Cowley, A.S., Adams, R.S. (2000). On Satir's use of self. *Journal of Couples Therapy*, *9* (3/4), 51–68.
De Little, M. (2012). Transformation in the sand tray: Examples of the Satir model in sand try therapy. *The Satir Journal*, *5*(1), 49–64.
Dodson, L. (2016). What is the world trying to do now? *Satir International Journal*, *4*(1), 44–49.
Duhl, B. (2007). Virginia Satir: In memoriam. *Journal of Marital and Family Therapy*, *15*(2), 109–110. DOI: 10.1111/j.1752-0606.1989.tb00786.x
Durlak, J.A., Weissberg, R.P., Dymnicki, A.B., Taylor, R.D., Schellinger, K.B. (2011). The impact of enhancing students' social and emotional learning: A meta-analysis of school-based universal interventions. *Child Development*, 82(1), 405–432.
Eisenegger, C., Haushofer, J., Fehr, E. (2011). The role of testosterone in social interaction. *Trends in Cognitive Sciences*, *15*(6), 263–271.
Englander-Golden, P., Elconin, J., Satir, V. (1986). Assertive/leveling communication and empathy in adolescent drug abuse prevention. *Journal of Primary Prevention*, *6*(4), 231–243. DOI: 10.1007/BF01330264
Englander-Golden, P., Golden, D. (2018). *BEING Within-Between-Among-Beyond*. New York: Page Publishing Inc.
Englander-Golden, P., Satir, V. (1991). *Say it Straight: From Compulsions to Choices*. Palo Alto, CA: Science and Behavior Books, Inc.

Erker, J. (2017). A summary of a qualitative study of Satir Family Therapy: theoretical and practical development over the past 30 years. *Satir International Journal, 5*(1), 76–81.

Feng, L., Wang, W., Wu, M., & Ma, H. (2021). Effect of WeChat-Based Health Education Combined with Satir Model on Self-Management Behaviors and Social Adaptation in Colorectal Cancer Patients during the Perioperative Period. *Journal of Healthcare Engineering*, 2701039. https://doi.org/10.1155/2021/2701039

Fix, L., Sutton, J. (2015). A recursive frame analysis of Virginia Satir's "Of rock and flowers" session. *Satir International Journal*, 3, 19–35.

Ford, S. (2007). Satir in the sand tray: Facilitating peace within. *The Satir Journal, 1*(3), 1–26.

France, H., Rodriguez, C. (2013). "Good" vs. "Right": Awareness of self in counselor training. *Satir International Journal*, 1, 10–17.

Freeman, M. (1999). Gender matters in the Satir growth model. *American Journal of Family Therapy, 27*(4), 345–363. DOI: 10.1080/019261899261907

Freeman, M. (2000). Incorporating gender issues in practice with the Satir growth model. *Families in Society, 81*(3), 256–268.

Freeman, M. (2006). Peace within, peace between, peace among. In R.M. MacNair's (Ed.) *Working for peace: A handbook for practical psychology and other tools* (pp. 63–72). Atascadero, CA, US: Impact Publishers.

Gabriel, C. (2014). I am. *Satir International Journal*, 2, 29–31.

Golden, D., Englander-Golden, P. (2014). Say it straight – From breakdowns to breakthroughs. *Satir International Journal, 2*(1), 9–28.

Goldenberg, I., Goldenberg, H. (2013). *Family Therapy: An Overview*. Boston, MA: Cengage Learning.

Gomori, M. (2015). *Satir Family Therapy in Action*. Gabriola Island, British Columbia: The Haven Institute Press.

Gomori, M., Adaskin, E. (2008). *Personal Alchemy: The Art of Satir Family Reconstruction*. Hong Kong: The Hong Kong Satir Center for Human Development.

Gottlieb, F. (1985). Review of Family Kaleidoscope and *Satir step by step: A guide to creating change in families. American Journal of Orthopsychiatry, 55*(4), 623–626.

Gross, S.J. (1994). The process of change: Variations on a theme by Virginia Satir. *Journal of Humanistic Psychology, 34*(3), 87–110. DOI: 10.1177/00221678940343007

Gross, S.J. (2007). Satir's internal process, self-esteem and non-defensive responses to threat. *The Satir Journal, 1*(3), 73–86.

Haber, R. (2002). Virginia Satir: An integrated humanist approach. *Contemporary Family Therapy: An International Journal, 24*(1), 23–37. DOI: 10.1023/A:1014317420921

Haber, R. (2011). Virginia Satir's family camp experiment: An intentional growth community still in process. *Contemporary Family Therapy: An International Journal, 33*(1), 71–84. DOI: 10.1007/s10591-010-9140-4

Haitoglou, Darya., (2016). Stance-Dance: Integrative movement theory. *Satir International Journal, 4*(1), 61–67.

Haitoglou, Darya., (2017). The Satir Systemic Coaching Model. *The Satir International Journal, 5*(1), 4–18.

Hunter, R.J. (1977). Book Reviews. *Pastoral Psychology, 25*(4), 305–310.

Innes, M. (2002). Satir's therapeutically oriented educational process: A critical appreciation. *Contemporary Family Therapy: An International Journal, 24*(1), 35–56. DOI: 10.1023/A:1014369504991

Innes, M. (2009). How do you view your clients in couple therapy? *The Satir Journal, 3*(1), 20–25.

Jackson, D., Riskin, J., Satir, V. (1961). A method of analysis of a family interview. *Achieves of General Psychiatry*, 5, 321–339. DOI: 10.1001/archpsyc.1961.01710160001001

Kane, C.M. (1994). Family making: A Satir approach to treating the H. family. *The Family Journal*, *2*(3), 256–258. DOI: 10.1177/1066480794023013

Klein, K. (2008). Adventure-based therapy with at-risk youth using the Satir model. *The Satir Journal*, *2*(3), 76–93.

Konecki, J. (2006). An analysis of published literature on the Satir model. *The Satir Journal*, *1*(1), 96–109.

Kosch, S.G. (1990). Together or apart: Focusing on level of cohesion in couples counseling. *Journal of Couples Therapy* *1*(1), 29–43.

Lang, K. (2016). Living a spirit filled life: being in the "I AM" for everything. *Satir International Journal*, *4*(1), 68–72.

Lee, B.K. (2001). *The Religious Significance of the Satir Model: Philosophical, Ritual and Empirical Perspective*. Doctoral dissertation. University of Ottawa, Ontario.

Lee, B.K. (2002). Congruence in Satir's model: Its spiritual and religious significance. *Contemporary Family Therapy: An International Journal*, *24*(1), 57–81. DOI: 10.1023/A:1014321621829

Lee, B.K. (2002). Development of a congruence scale based on the Satir model. *Contemporary Family Therapy: An International Journal*, *24*(1), 217–239. DOI: 10.1023/A:1014390009534

Lee, K. (2016). From "Saving Satir" to "Evolving Satir." *Social Work*. *61*(4) 372–374. DOI: http://dx.doi.org/10.1093/sw/sww056

Leslie, M. (2016). Widening our lens, deepening our practice: An exploration of energy within the teachings of Virginia Satir. *Satir International Journal*, *4*(1), 5–20.

Leung, P., Lau, W., Chung, C. (2018). Development and validation of perceived self transformation scale for the Satir model. *Contemporary Family Therapy: An International Journal*, 1–12. DOI: 10.1007/s10591-018-9477-7

Li, Y., Weiqun, V. (2013). Applying the Satir model of counselling in mainland China. *Satir International Journal*, 1, 18–39.

Littlewood, P.J. (2009). The Satir model and emotionally focused therapy: A response to Lorrie Brubacher. *The Satir Journal*, *3*(1), 26–37.

Loeschen, S. (1998). *Systematic Training in the Skills of Virginia Satir*. Pacific Grove, CA: Brooks/Cole.

Loeschen, S. (2005). *Enriching Your Relationships Between Yourself and Others: Based on the Teachings of Virginia Satir*. Burien, WA: AVANTA.

Loeschen, S. (2005). *The Satir Process – Practical Skills for Therapists*. Fountain Valley, CA: Halcyon Publishing Design.

Loeschen, S., Jendrusakova, K. (2015). Enriching your relationship program through the lens of empirical support. *Satir International Journal*, *3*(1), 5–18.

Lum, W. (2008). Therapists' experience using Satir's personal iceberg metaphor. *The Satir Journal*, *2*(2), 45–88.

Lum, W. (2016). Zero Infinity: multidimensional healing of experiences. *Satir International Journal*, *4*(1), 21–34.

Lum, W., Smith, J., Ferris, J. (2002). Youth suicide intervention using the Satir model. *Contemporary Family Therapy: An International Journal*, *24*(1), 139–159. DOI: 10.1023/A:1014381807717

Maki-Banmen, K. (2012). Review of Personal alchemy: The art of Satir family reconstruction by Maria Gomori with Eleanor Adaskin. *The Satir Journal*, *5*(1), 71–74.

Martinez, J., Hollingsworth, B., Shephard, R., Stanley, C., Lee, L. (2011). Satir human validation process model. In L. Metcalf (Ed.), *Marriage and Family Therapy: A Practice Oriented Approach* (pp. 175–199). New York: Springer Publishing Co.

Mazur, A., Booth, A. (1998). Testosterone and dominance in men. *Behav Brain Sci.*, Jun; 21(3): 353–363; discussion 363–397. PMID: 10097017.

McCarthy, MM. (1995). Estrogen modulation of oxytocin and its relation to behavior. *Adv Exp Med Biol.*, 395: 235–245. PMID: 8713972.

McGing, K. (1990). Introduction to the Virginia Satir memorial lecture. *Contemporary Family Therapy: An International Journal, 12*(4), 267–270.

McLendon, J.A., Bitter, J.R. (2011). A path to wholeness: Couple therapy with the Satir model. In D.K. Carson and C.K. Montserrat (Eds.), *Case Studies in Couple Therapy: Theory Based Approaches* (pp. 177–190). New York: Routledge/Taylor and Francis Group.

Middelburg, C., Gross, S. Families' affective rules and their relationship to the families' adjustment. *The American Journal of Family Therapy*, *7*(2), 37–45. DOI: 10.1080/01926187908250314

Morrison, A., Ferris, J. (2002). The Satir model with female adult survivors of childhood sexual abuse. *Contemporary Family Therapy: An International Journal, 24*(1), 161–180. DOI: 10.1023/A:1014333924555

Mun-Jeong, K., Bong-Whan, K. (2010). Development and validity of the congruence scale based on Satir's growth model. *The Satir Journal, 4*(1), 53–83.

Nemesh, Beth. (2016). Musical interventions in Satir's experiential family therapy: from dissonance to harmony Beth Nemesh, *Satir International Journal, 4*(1), 73–75.

Nerin, W.F. (1991). Family reconstruction: The masterpiece of Virginia Satir. *Journal of Couples Therapy, 2*(1–2), 103–118. DOI: 10.1300/J036v02n01_08

Nesbit, C. (2009). Being in charge of self: A series of meditations by Virginia Satir. *The Satir Journal, 3*(2), 126–129.

Nesbit, C. (2009). Ingredients of our internal process: A series of meditations from Virginia Satir. *The Satir Journal, 3*(3), 71–75.

Nesbit, C. (2010). A series of meditations from Virginia Satir: Self-esteem maintenance kit. *The Satir Journal, 4*(1), 157–162.

Nesbit, C. (2012). Love and light. *The Satir Journal, 5*(1), 75–77.

Nicholas, W.C. (2007). In memoriam. *Contemporary Family Therapy, 29*(1–2), 3–8.

Novak, S. (2006). Alleviating prejudice and hate: The strategies of Virginia Satir. *The Satir Journal, 1*(1), 65–80.

Novak, S. (2012). An example of the use of self in Satir-based family therapy. *The Satir Journal, 5*(1), 21–34.

Oz, S. (1988). A modified "Parts Party" for couples work. *Contemporary Family Therapy, 10*(3), 183–193. DOI: 10.1007/BF00895620

Pan, P.J.D. (2000). The effectiveness of structured and semistructured Satir model groups on family relationships with college students in Taiwan. *Journal for Specialists in Group Work, 25*(3), 305–318. DOI:10.1080/01933920008411469

Pei, Y. (2008). From caterpillar to butterfly: Action research study of a Satir-based women's program in Taiwan. *The Satir Journal, 2*(1), 55–107.

Phinney, J.S. (2006). *Acculturation and Ethnic Identity in Adolescence*. Handbook of Adolescent Psychology.

Piddocke, S. (2010). The self: Reflections on its nature and structure according to the Satir model. *The Satir Journal, 4*(1), 109–154.

Robinson, K.J. (2018). Satir human validation process model. In L. Metcalf (Ed.), *Marriage and Family Therapy: A Practice-Oriented Approach* (pp. 165–181). New York: Springer.

Sapolsky, R.M. (2004). *Why Zebras Don't Get Ulcers*. New York: Holt Paperbacks.

Satir, V. (1967). Family systems and the approach to family therapy. *Journal of Fort Logan Mental Health Center, 4*(2), pp. 81–93.

Satir, V. (1975). Family life education: A perspective on the educator. *Small Group Behavior, 6*(1), 3–10. DOI: 10.1177/104649647500600101

Satir, V. (1983). *Conjoint Family Therapy*. Palo Alto, CA: Science and Behavior Books, Inc.

Satir, V. (1988). *The New Peoplemaking*. Palo Alto, CA: Science and Behavior Books, Inc.

Satir, V. (1995). *Meditations and Inspirations*. J. Banmen and J. Gerber (Eds.). Berkeley, CA: Celestial Arts.

Satir, V. (1995). *Self-Esteem*. Berkeley, CA: Celestial Arts.

Satir, V. (1997). Congruent communication builds bridges. In B.J. Brothers (Ed.), *Couples: Building Bridges* (pp. 1–10). New York: Routledge.

Satir, V. (1997). Ways of viewing the world: ways of putting things together to form the big picture: A view of resistance as a blessing. *Journal of Couples Therapy*, *7*(1), 1–7.

Satir, V. (2000). Hope, wholeness, and helping the flat to grow round. *Journal of Couples Therapy*, *9* (1/2), 5–9.

Satir, V. (2009). *Your Many Faces: The First Step to Being Loved* (3rd ed.). Berkeley, CA: Celestial Arts.

Satir, V. (2011). *Making Contact*. Madison, WI: Virginia Satir Global Network.

Satir, V., Baldwin, M. (1984). *Satir Step-by-Step: A Guide to Creating Change in Families*. Palo Alto, CA: Science and Behavior Books, Inc.

Satir, V., Banmen, J., Gerber, J., Gomori, M. (1991). *The Satir Model: Family Therapy and Beyond*. Palo Alto, CA: Science and Behavior Books, Inc.

Satir, V., Bitter, J.R., Krestensen, K.K. (1988). Family Reconstruction: The family within – a group experience. *Journal for Specialists in Group Work*, *13*(4), 200–208. DOI: 10.1080/01933928808411877

Schonert-Reichl, K.A., Oberle, E., Lawlor, M.S., Abbott, D., Thomson, K., Oberlander, T.F., Diamond, A. (2015). Enhancing cognitive and social–emotional development through a simple-to-administer mindfulness-based school program for elementary school children: A randomized controlled trial. *Developmental Psychology*, 51(1), 52–66.

Schultz, W. (2007) Multiple dopamine functions at different time courses. *Annu Rev Neurosci.*, 30, 259–288. DOI: 10.1146/annurev.neuro.28.061604.135722. PMID: 17600522.

Schwartz, R.C. (2001). *Introduction to Internal Family Systems*. New York: Guilford Press.

Sekera, O. (2017). Outcome of psychotherapeutic training MOVISA (Model of Virginia Satir). *Satir International Journal*, *5*(1), 67–75.

Seo, S.H., Kim, S.J. (2016). The effects of a parental education program based on Satir transformational systemic therapy model for preschoolers' *mothers. Journal of Korean Academy of Psychiatric and Mental Health Nursing*, 24, 330–341.

Shao, S. (2021). Intervention effect of dance therapy based on the Satir model on the metal health of adolescents during the COVID-19 epidemic. *PsyD*, *33*(3), 411–417. https://doi.org/10.24869/psyd.2021.411

Shud, M., Dodson, L., Gomori, M. (2001). *Virginia Satir: Her Life and Circle of Influence*. Toronto, ON: Hushion House.

Smith, J.W. (2010). Dead kids talking: Youth suicide prevention using the Satir Transformational Systemic Therapy. *The Satir Journal*, *4*(1), 84–108.

Solé, J., Poyatos, P., Viñas, A., Sharp, I. (2016). Human value: the socioeducative work in the municipality of Castell-Platia d'Aro, *Satir International Journal*, *4*(1), 76–86.

Springer, P.R., Wheeler, M.A. (2012). Relational self-esteem plot: A Satir intervention in family therapy. *The Satir Journal*, *5*(1), 35–48.

Srikosai, S. (2008). Effects of individual psychotherapy using the Satir model on an alcoholdependent and depressed patient. *The Satir Journal*, *2*(3), 5–19.

Starr, S. (1991). An interview with Virginia Satir. *Journal of Couples Therapy*, *2*(3), 5–10.

Strang, H., Sherman, L.W., Mayo-Wilson, E., Woods, D.J., Ariel, B. (2013). Restorative justice conferencing (RJC) using face-to-face meetings of offenders and victims: Effects on offender recidivism and victim satisfaction. *Journal of Experimental Criminology*, 9(4), 325–334.

Strider, E. (2007). Reconstructing a company. *The Satir Journal*, 1(3), 100–110.

Strider, E. (2013). Re-sculpting an organization: A different kind of family. *Satir International Journal*, 1, 96–102.

Taylor, G. (2002). Family reconstruction. *Contemporary Family Therapy: An International Journal*, *24*(1), 129–138. DOI: 10.1023/A:1014329823646

Tougas, J. (2006). *Yes, Santa Claus... There is a Virginia; Based on the Teachings of Virginia Satir*. Winnipeg, Manitoba: Noel Productions.

van der Kolk, B.A. (2014). *The Body Keeps the Score: Brain, Mind, and Body in the Healing of Trauma*. New York: Viking.

Vivian, L.W.Q. (2009). Enhancing personal growth for social workers using the Satir model. *The Satir Journal*, *3*(2), 5–21.

Voit, R. (2009). Review of "In her own words: Virginia Satir: Selected papers." *American Journal of Clinical Hypnosis*, 51(4), 406–407.

Wang, E.N., Peng, X. (2017). Intervention effect of group counseling on meaning of life: A therapy based on sand play and the Satir model. *Chinese Journal of Clinical Psychology*, 25, 315–318.

Wang, X., Zhao, Y., Zeng, G., Xiao, P., Wang. Z. (2022). Study on the classification problem of the coping stances in the Satir model based on machine learning. *Journal of Experimental and Theoretical Artificial Intelligence*, *35*(1), 129–149. https://doi.org/10.1080/0952813X.2021.1960628

Wang, Y. (2016). Practical research on Improving the life force of college students by using Satir's Model. *Journal of Marxism Studies*, 2, 135–140.

West, C.P., Dyrbye, L.N., Erwin, P.J., Shanafelt, T.D. (2016). Interventions to prevent and reduce physician burnout: A systematic review and meta-analysis. *The Lancet*, 388(10057), 2272–2281.

Wetchler, M., Piercy, F. (1996). Experiential family therapies. In Piercy, F., Sprenkle, D., Wetchler, M., et al. (Eds.), *Family Therapy Sourcebook* (2nd ed.). New York: Guilford Press.

Woods, M., Martin, D. (1984). The work of Virginia Satir: Understanding her theory and technique. *The American Journal of Family Therapy*, *12*(4), 3–11. DOI: 10.1080/01926188408250192

Wretman, C.J. (2015). Saving Satir: Contemporary perspectives on the change process model. *Social Work*, *61*(1), 61–68. DOI: 10.1093/sw/swv056

Wu, S. (2016). Application of the Satir Model to college student education in China. *Satir International Journal*, *4*(1), 97–102.

Yang, L., Vivian, L. (2010). Applying the Satir model of counseling in mainland China: Illustrated with case studies. *The Satir Journal*, *4*(1), 24–52.

Yehuda, R. (2015). Transgenerational transmission of trauma effects: Putative biological mechanisms. *Progress in Brain Research*, 221, 51–66.

Yldrm, N. (2017). Virginia Satir's family education and therapy model. *International Journal of Social Science Studies*, 5, 72–79.

Young, A.K. (2007). An analysis of the Satir transformational systemic therapy in the Korean worldview. *The Satir Journal*, *1*(2), 54–72.

Young, S.N. (2002). Clinical nutrition: 3. The fuzzy boundary between nutrition and psychopharmacology. *CMAJ*, Jan 22; 166(2), 205–209. PMID: 11826946; PMCID: PMC99276.

INDEX

Please note that page references to Figures will be in **bold**.

For Product Safety Concerns and Information please contact our EU representative GPSR@taylorandfrancis.com Taylor & Francis Verlag GmbH, Kaufingerstraße 24, 80331 München, Germany